D0618447

QL 83 .N35 2004 v.1

Benson, Sonia.

Endangered species

DISCARD

	DATE	

Nicolet Area Technical College
Richard J. Brown Library

BAKER & TAYLOR

Endangered Species

2nd EDITION

Endangered Species

2nd EDITION

VOLUME 1
Mammals

Sonia Benson,
Rob Nagel

Nicolet College
Richard J. Brown Library
P.O. Box 518
Rhinelander, WI 54501

U·X·L®

THOMSON
GALE

Detroit • New York • San Diego • San Francisco • Cleveland • New Haven, Conn. • Waterville, Maine • London • Munich

Endangered Species, 2nd Edition

Sonia Benson and Rob Nagel

Project Editors
Julie L. Carnagie, Allison McNeill

Editorial
Diane Sawinski, Sarah Hermsen

Permissions
Margaret Chamberlain

Imaging and Multimedia
Robyn Young

Product Design
Michelle DiMercurio, Kate Scheible

Composition
Evi Seoud

Manufacturing
Rita Wimberley

©2004 by U•X•L. U•X•L is an imprint of The Gale Group, Inc., a division of Thomson Learning, Inc.

U•X•L® is a registered trademark used herein under license. Thomson Learning™ is a trademark used herein under license.

For more information, contact:
The Gale Group, Inc.
27500 Drake Rd.
Farmington Hills, MI 48331-3535
Or you can visit our Internet site at
http://www.gale.com

ALL RIGHTS RESERVED
No part of this work covered by the copyright hereon may be reproduced or used in any form or by any means—graphic, electronic, or mechanical, including photocopying, recording, tap-ing, Web distribution, or information storage retrieval systems—without the written permission of the publisher.

For permission to use material from this product, submit your request via Web at http://www.gale-edit.com/per-missions, or you may download our Permissions Request form and submit your request by fax or mail to:

Permissions Department
The Gale Group, Inc.
27500 Drake Rd.
Farmington Hills, MI 48331-3535

Permissions Hotline:
248-699-8006 or 800-877-4253, ext. 8006
Fax: 248-699-8074 or 800-762-4058

Volume 1 cover photograph reproduced by permission of Photo Researchers, Inc. Volume 2 cover photograph reproduced by permission of the Cincinnati Zoo. Volume 3 cover photograph reproduced by permission of Photo Researchers, Inc.

While every effort has been made to ensure the reliability of the information presented in this publication, The Gale Group, Inc. does not guarantee the accu-racy of the data contained herein. The Gale Group, Inc. accepts no payment for listing; and inclusion in the publication of any organization, agency, institution, publication, service, or individual does not imply endorsement by the editors or publisher. Errors brought to the atten-tion of the publisher and verified to the satisfaction of the publisher will be cor-rected in future editions.

LIBRARY OF CONGRESS CATALOGING-IN-PUBLICATION DATA

Benson, Sonia.
  Endangered species / Sonia Benson ; Julie L. Carnagie, project editor. — 2nd ed.
    p. cm.
  Rev. ed. of: Endangered species / Rob Nagel. ©1999.
  Summary: Entries on more than 200 extinct, endangered, vulnerable, and threatened animals and plants describe the individual species, its habitat and current distribution, and efforts to protect and preserve it.
Includes bibliographical references.
    ISBN 0-7876-7618-7 (set : hardcover) — ISBN 0-7876-7619-5 (vol. 1) — ISBN 0-7876-7620-9 (vol. 2) — ISBN 0-7876-7621-7 (vol. 3)
    1. Endangered species—Juvenile literature. [1. Endangered species—Encyclopedias.] I. Carnagie, Julie. II. Nagel, Rob. Endangered species. III. Title.
QL83.N35 2003
333.95′42—dc22   2003016691

Contents

VOLUME 1: Mammals

VOLUME 2: Arachnids, Birds, Crustaceans, Insects, and Mollusks

VOLUME 3: Amphibians, Fish, Plants, and Reptiles

Reader's Guide

Endangered Species, 2nd Edition, presents information on endangered and threatened mammals, birds, reptiles, amphibians, fish, mollusks, insects, arachnids, crustaceans, and plants. Its 240 entries were chosen to give a glimpse of the broad range of species currently facing endangerment. While well-publicized examples such as the American bison, northern spotted owl, and gray wolf are examined, so, too, are less conspicuous—yet no less threatened—species such as the Australian ant, Cape vulture, freshwater sawfish, and Peebles Navajo cactus.

The entries are spread across three volumes and are divided into sections by classes. Within each class, species are arranged alphabetically by common name.

Each entry begins with the species's common and scientific names. A fact box containing classification information—phylum (or division), class, order, and family—for that species follows. The box also lists the current status of the species in the wild according to the International Union for Conservation of Nature and Natural Resources (IUCN) and the U.S. Fish and Wildlife Service (which administers the Endangered Species Act). Finally, the box lists the country or countries where the species currently ranges.

Locator maps outlining the range of a particular species are included in each entry to help users find unfamiliar countries or locations. In most entries, a color photo provides a more concrete visualization of the species. Sidebar boxes containing interesting and related information are also included in some entries.

Each entry is broken into three sections:

- The information under the subhead **Description and Biology** provides a general description of the species. This includes physical dimensions, eating and reproductive habits, and social behavior.

- The information under the subhead **Habitat and Current Distribution** describes where the species is found today, its preferred habitat, and, if available, recent estimates of its population size.

- The information under the subhead **History and Conservation Measures** relates, if possible, the history of the species and the factors currently threatening it. Conservation efforts to save the species, if any are underway, are also described.

Beginning each volume of *Endangered Species,* 2nd Edition, is an overview of the history and current state of endangerment and its causes and a discussion of the International Union for Conservation of Nature and Natural Resources (IUCN–The World Conservation Union) that includes a brief history of the organization, its current focus, and a brief explanation of the status categories in which the IUCN places imperiled species. The final section focuses on the Endangered Species Act, briefly examining its passage, purpose, implementation, status categories, and current state.

Each volume ends with a Where to Learn More section composed of books, periodicals, Internet addresses, and environmental organizations. The book listing is annotated. The environmental organizations list—a selected catalog of organizations focusing on endangered species—contains mailing addresses, telephone numbers, Internet addresses (if available), and a brief description of each organization.

Finally, the volumes conclude with a cumulative index providing access to all the species discussed throughout *Endangered Species,* 2nd Edition.

The scope of this work is neither definitive nor exhaustive. No work on this subject can be. The information presented is as current as possible, but the state of endangered species, sadly, changes almost daily.

A note about the 2nd Edition

Since the publication of *Endangered Species* in 1999, the endangered or threatened status of many of the species included in these volumes has changed. Through the efforts of conservationists and legislators, some of these species have recovered or were upgraded to a less threatened status. The Przewalski's horse, for example, was considered extinct in the wild in 1996 by the IUCN, but a program to reintroduce horses bred in captivity into their historical habitat was unexpectedly successful. By 2000, 84 Przewalski's horses had been reintroduced and 114 foals (baby horses) had been born in the wild. In the early 2000s, a population of around 142 Przewalski's horses roamed freely, and the animals appear to be doing better each year they spend in the wild. Other species have declined to the very brink of extinction. Some—like the scimitar-horned oryx—have dramatically fallen on the IUCN Red List. The status of the scimitar-horned oryx fell from endangered to critically endangered in 1996 to extinct in the wild in 1999. It is likely that, with a captive-bred population now being prepared for reintroduction to the wild, the scimitar-horned oryx will be upgraded on the Red List in the near future. There are also new stories in many of the existing entries. Chimpanzees and gorillas, for one sad example among many, began making the news in 2003 when a scientific study found that their populations had been reduced by nearly one-half since the 1980s and that an Ebola virus is currently ravaging the populations.

Endangered Species cannot cover all threatened species worldwide, but 40 new species have been included in the 2nd Edition to ensure that the situations of species worldwide—as it stands five years after the first publication—are represented. Conservationists today are facing the same concerns as five years ago, many with more urgency and some new twists. The issues range from a worldwide decline in the amphibian and reptile populations to declining fish species that seem unable to recover from overfishing; from the effects of inbreeding in populations that have become very tiny to the lack of appropriate habitats in which to release the new captive-bred populations. Many of the new entries chronicle the enormous efforts of scientists to save species on the brink of extinction. For instance, the Chatham Islands robin population had dwindled to five birds in 1981, with only one female, "Old Blue," remaining. Through a breeding-in-captivity program, that species now has 259 members, but all of them are direct descendants of Old Blue and her mate, Old Yellow. And sometimes these efforts may not be enough: There were only three Po'oulis (honeycreepers) left in 2003, and because their ranges did not overlap, they had no chance of mating in the wild. Scientists were preparing to take these last remaining members of the species into custody as the only hope for saving the species.

Acknowledgments

Special thanks are due for the invaluable comments and suggestions provided by the *Endangered Species* advisors:

Valerie Doud, Science Teacher, Peru Junior High School, Peru, Indiana

Melba Holland, Earth Science/Science Department Head, Slaton Junior High School, Slaton, Texas

Bonnie L. Raasch, Media Specialist, C. B. Vernon Middle School, Marion, Iowa

The editors of *Endangered Species* also graciously thank Tom Romig and Julie Carnagie for their commitment to this project and for their patience and understanding during its completion. It is a continuing privilege and pleasure to work with the U•X•L family.

Comments and Suggestions

We welcome your comments on *Endangered Species* and suggestions for species to be included in future editions of *Endangered Species*. Please write: Editors, *Endangered Species*, U•X•L, 27500 Drake Rd., Farmington Hills, Michigan 48331–3535; call toll free: 1–800–877–4253; fax: 248–699–8097; or send e-mail via www.gale.com.

Endangerment and Its Causes: An Overview

Living organisms have been disappearing from the face of Earth since the beginning of life on the planet. Most of the species that have ever lived on Earth are now extinct. Extinction and endangerment can occur naturally as a normal process in the course of evolution. It can be the result of a catastrophic event, such as the collision of an asteroid with Earth. Scientists believe an asteroid struck the planet off Mexico's Yucatán Peninsula some 65,000,000 years ago, bringing about the extinction of almost 50 percent of the plant species and 75 percent of the animal species then living on Earth, including the dinosaurs. Widespread climate changes, disease, and competition among species can also result in natural extinction. To date, scientists believe there have been five great natural extinction episodes in Earth's history.

Since humans became the dominant species on the planet, however, the rate at which other species have become extinct has increased dramatically. Especially since the seventeenth century, technological advances and an ever-expanding human population have changed the natural world as never before. At present, scientists believe extinctions caused by humans are taking place at 100 to 1,000 times nature's normal rate between great extinction episodes. Species are disappearing faster than they can be created through evolution. In fact, some biologists estimate that in the early 2000s three or more plant and animal species become extinct each day.

Because scientists have described and named only a small percentage of Earth's species, it is impossible to measure the total number of species endangered or going extinct. Just 1,400,000 species—out of an estimated 10,000,000 to 100,000,000—have been described to date.

Scientists do know that humans are endangering species and the natural world primarily in three ways: habitat destruction, commercial exploitation of animals and plants, and the transplantation of species from one part of the world to another.

Habitat destruction

The destruction of habitats all over the world is the primary reason species are becoming extinct or endangered. Houses, highways, dams, industrial buildings, and ever-spreading farms now dominate landscapes formerly occupied by forests, prairies, deserts, scrublands, and wetlands. Since the beginning of European settlement in America, over 65,000,000 acres of wetlands have been drained. One million acres alone vanished between 1985 and 1995.

Habitat destruction can be obvious or it can be subtle, occurring over a long period of time without being noticed. Pollution, such as sewage from cities and chemical runoff from farms, can change the quality and quantity of water in streams and rivers. To species living in a delicately balanced habitat, this disturbance can be as fatal as the clear-cutting of a rain forest.

As remaining habitats are carved into smaller and smaller pockets or islands, remaining species are forced to exist in these crowded areas, which causes further habitat destruction. These species become less adaptable to environmental change; they become more vulnerable to extinction. Scientists believe that when a habitat is cut by 90 percent, one-half of its plants, animals, insects, and microscopic life-forms will become extinct.

Commercial exploitation

Animals have been hunted by humans not only for their meat but for parts of their bodies that are used to create medicines, love potions, and trinkets. Overhunting has caused the extinction of many species and brought a great many others to the brink of extinction. Examples include species of whales, slaughtered for their oil and baleen. The rhinoceroses of Africa are critically endangered, having been killed mainly for their horns. Sharks' fins, cruelly cut off of the live animal, are used in Asia as an aphrodisiac, and 75 shark species are now endangered.

International treaties outlaw the capture and trade of many endangered or threatened species. These laws, however, are difficult to enforce. The smuggling of endangered species is a huge business. In the early 2000s, the illegal trade in wildlife products was estimated at $15 billion a year worldwide—second only to the value of the international illegal drug trade.

Introduced species

Native species are those that have inhabited a given biological landscape for a long period of time. They have adapted to the environment, climate, and other species in that locale. Introduced or exotic species are those that have been brought into that landscape by humans, either accidentally or intentionally.

In some cases, these introduced species may not cause any harm. They may, over time, adapt to their new surroundings and fellow species, becoming "native." Most often, however, introduced species seriously disrupt ecological balances. They compete with native species for food and shelter. Often, they prey on the native species, who lack natural defenses against the intruders. In the last 500 years, introduced insects, cats, pigs, rats, and others have caused the endangerment or outright extinction of hundreds of native species.

Endangered Species Fact Boxes and Classification: An Explanation

Each entry in *Endangered Species,* 2nd Edition, begins with the common name of a species, followed by its scientific name. Underneath is a shaded fact box. This box contains the classification information for that species: phylum (or division), class, order, and family. It also lists the current status of that species in the wild according to the International Union for Conservation of Nature and Natural Resources (IUCN; see page xxiii) and the Endangered Species List compiled under the Endangered Species Act (ESA; see page xxvii). (Note: For a listing of species whose status has changed since the publication of the first edition, see page xxxi.) Finally, the box lists the country or countries where the species is currently found and provides a locator map for the range of the species.

Classification

Biological classification, or taxonomy, is the system of arranging plants and animals in groups according to their similarities. This system, which scientists around the world currently use, was developed by eighteenth-century Swedish botanist (a person specializing in the study of plants) Carolus Linnaeus. Linnaeus created a multilevel system or pyramid-like structure of nomenclature (naming) in which living organisms were grouped according to the number of physical traits they had in common. The ranking of the system, going from general to specific, is: kingdom, phylum (or division for plants), class, order, and family. The more specific the level (closer to the top of the pyramid), the more traits shared by the organisms placed in that level.

Scientists currently recognize five kingdoms of organisms: Animalia (animals, fish, humans); Plantae (plants, trees, grasses); Fungi (mushrooms, lichens); Protista (bacteria, certain algae, other one-celled organisms having nuclei); and

Monera (bacteria, blue-green algae, other one-celled organisms without nuclei).

Every living organism is placed into one of these kingdoms. Organisms within kingdoms are then divided into phylums (or divisions for plants) based on distinct and defining characteristics. An example would be the phylum Chordata, which contains all the members of the kingdom Animalia that have a backbone. Organisms in a specific phylum or division are then further divided into classes based on more distinct and defining characteristics. The dividing continues on through orders and then into families, where most organisms probably have the same behavioral patterns.

To further define an organism, Linnaeus also developed a two-part naming system—called binomial nomenclature—in which each living organism was given a two-part Latin name to distinguish it from other members in its family. The first name—italicized and capitalized—is the genus of the organism. The second name—italicized but not capitalized—is its species. This species name is an adjective, usually descriptive or geographic. Together, the genus and species form an organism's scientific name.

How similar organisms are separated by their scientific names can be seen in the example of the white oak and the red oak. All oak trees belong to the genus *Quercus*. The scientific name of white oak is *Quercus alba* (*alba* is Latin for "white"), while that of the red oak is *Quercus rubra* (*rubra* is Latin for "red").

Since each species or organism has only one name under binomial nomenclature, scientists worldwide who do not speak the same languages are able to communicate with each other about species.

International Union for Conservation of Nature and Natural Resources (IUCN–The World Conservation Union)

The IUCN is one of the world's oldest international conservation organizations. It was established in Fountainbleau, France, on October 5, 1947. It is a worldwide alliance of governments, government agencies, and nongovernmental organizations. Working with scientists and experts, the IUCN tries to encourage and assist nations and societies around the world to conserve nature and to use natural resources wisely. At present, IUCN members represent 74 governments, 105 government agencies, and more than 700 nongovernmental organizations.

The IUCN has six volunteer commissions. The largest and most active of these is the Species Survival Commission (SSC). The mission of the SSC is to conserve biological diversity by developing programs that help save, restore, and manage species and their habitats. One of the many activities of the SSC is the production of the *IUCN Red List of Threatened Animals* and the *IUCN Red List of Threatened Plants*.

These publications, which have provided the foundation for *Endangered Species,* present scientifically based information on the status of threatened species around the world. Species are classified according to their existence in the wild and the current threats to that existence. The categories differ slightly between animals and plants.

IUCN Red List categories

The *IUCN Red List of Threatened Animals* places threatened animals into one of nine categories:

- **Extinct:** A species that no longer exists anywhere around the world.

- **Extinct in the wild:** A species that no longer exists in the wild, but exists in captivity or in an area well outside its natural range.

- **Critically endangered:** A species that is facing an extremely high risk of extinction in the wild in the immediate future.

- **Endangered:** A species that is facing a high risk of extinction in the wild in the near future.

- **Vulnerable:** A species that is facing a high risk of extinction in the wild in the medium-term future.

- **Lower risk: Conservation dependent:** A species that is currently the focus of a conservation program. If the program is halted, the species would suffer and would qualify for one of the threatened categories above within a period of five years.

- **Lower risk: Near threatened:** A species that does not qualify for Conservation Dependent status, but is close to qualifying for Vulnerable status.

- **Lower risk: Least concern:** A species that qualifies for neither Conservation Dependent status or Near Threatened status.

- **Data deficient:** A species on which there is little information to assess its risk of extinction. Because of the possibility that future research will place the species in a threatened category, more information is required.

The *IUCN Red List of Threatened Plants* places threatened plants into one of six categories:

- **Extinct:** A species that no longer exists anywhere around the world.

- **Extinct/Endangered:** A species that is considered possibly to be extinct in the wild.

- **Endangered:** A species that is in immediate danger of extinction if the factors threatening it continue.

- **Vulnerable:** A species that will likely become endangered if the factors threatening it continue.

- **Rare:** A species with a small world population that is currently neither endangered nor threatened, but is at risk.

- **Indeterminate:** A species that is threatened, but on which there is not enough information to place it in the appropriate category of Extinct, Endangered, Vulnerable, or Rare.

The IUCN issues its Red List assessments of animal and plant endangerment periodically. The Red List of 2000 revised the previous 1996 list. The trends shown in the 2000 report were not encouraging. In 2002, the IUCN listed 11,167 threatened species worldwide. Of these, 3,521 were vertebrates, 1,932 were invertebrates, and 5,714 were plants. The majority of these species were listed as vulnerable. From 1996 to 2000, the number of endangered species rose. Notably, the number of critically endangered mammals rose from 169 to 180, and the number of critically endangered birds rose from 168 to 182. Among mammals, there were dramatic population declines in amphibians, reptiles, and primates, among other groups. At the same time there was an upward shift in levels of endangerment.

Endangered Species Act

The Endangered Species Act (ESA) was passed by the U.S. Congress in 1973 and was reauthorized in 1988. The purpose of the ESA is to recover species around the world that are in danger of human-caused extinction. There are three basic elements to the ESA program: the creation of a list of endangered animals and plants (the Endangered Species List), the formulation of recovery plans for each species on the list, and the designation of critical habitat for each species listed. Through this program, the act seeks to provide a means of conserving those species and their ecosystems.

The U.S. Fish and Wildlife Service (USFWS), a part of the Department of Interior, is the federal agency responsible for listing (or reclassifying or delisting) endangered and threatened species on the Endangered Species List. The National Marine Fisheries Service is responsible for many species that live in the oceans. The decision to list a species is based solely on scientific factors. Once a species is placed on the list, the USFWS is required to develop a plan for its recovery and to designate "critical habitat" for the species. Critical habitat is an area that has been deemed essential to the physical and biological needs of the species, either in their original range or an area similar to it. The designated critical habitat must provide appropriate space for population growth and normal behavior so that a species may recover. The critical habitat designation does not prohibit human activity or create a refuge for the species. Once it has been established, however, any federal agencies planning to build on that land (a highway, for example) must seek the permission of the USFWS. Any other activities requiring federal permits must go through the USFWS as well. Private landowners are not affected, except that the designation alerts the public to the importance of the area in the species' survival. The ESA explicitly states that the economic interests of the human community must be given ample consideration in designating critical habitats and requires the balancing of species protection with economic development.

When a species is placed on the Endangered Species List, it is positioned in one of two categories:

- **Endangered:** A species that is in danger of extinction throughout all or a significant part of its range.
- **Threatened:** A species that is likely to become endangered in the foreseeable future.

The ESA outlaws the buying, selling, transporting, importing, or exporting of any listed species. Most important, the act bans the taking of any listed species within the United States and its territorial seas. "Taking" is defined as harassing, harming, pursuing, hunting, shooting, wounding, cutting, trapping, killing, removing, capturing, or collecting. The taking of listed species is prohibited on both private and public lands.

Violators of the ESA are subject to heavy fines. Individuals can face up to $100,000 in fines and up to one year's imprisonment. Organizations found in violation of the act may be fined up to $200,000.

In 2003 there were 1,253 species on the Endangered Species List. This total included 517 animals and 746 plants.

In the 30 years since its passage, the ESA has been continually targeted by its many opponents. Some of those opponents believe the ESA prohibits human progress, placing the rights of other species ahead of the rights of humans. There are many interest groups who lobby against the ESA: building and real estate development associations oppose ESA because it could present some federal impediments to the large financial gains to be made in constructing new communities or facilities; loggers, farmers, fishers, hunters, fur traders, and others whose means of making a living are affected are also heavily represented in anti-ESA activism. Politicians, even those who nominally support the ESA, do not often find it politically advantageous to provide the necessary support and funding to rescue little-known animals or to oppose large and powerful companies.

On May 28, 2003, the USFWS announced a moratorium (suspension of activity) on designating critical habitat for endangered species—a required step under the ESA. The Department of the Interior said that its critical habitat program had run out of money. Of all the 1,253 endangered species to date, only 426 had critical habitats, and since 2000, those had shrunk in size considerably. Large conservation groups had repeatedly taken the government to court for its failure to designate critical habitat for a listed endangered species. The courts continuously upheld the requirement under the ESA for the USFWS to designate critical habitat for a species once it had been listed on the Endangered Species List.

Spokespeople from the Department of the Interior contend that the critical habitation designation system is unreasonably expensive and that it is not effective in saving endangered species. They also argue that the cost of these lawsuits over critical habitat designation is depleting the budget for protecting species. Many environmental groups, however, argue that critical habitat designation, flawed though the program may be, has been effective in the recovery of many species. Since habitat loss is considered to be the largest factor in the recovery of endangered species, the limited power of the program to protect habitats often represents the only hope for many species. Many endangered species, even if their populations could be increased, are simply running out of places where they can survive in the wild.

In the early 2000s, the issue of endangered species has increasingly become one of the arenas in which U.S. political divisions are playing out very dramatically. In the meantime, some of the species included in *Endangered Species,* 2nd Edition, are losing the last few acres or streams or caves or hillsides they require to survive; others stand only a few individual animals away from extinction.

Changes in Status from First Edition

Key: OFF = Delisted because of recovery; LR–CD = Lower Risk, Conservation Dependent; LR–NT = Lower Risk, Near Threatened; TH = Threatened; R = Rare; VU = Vulnerable; EN = Endangered; CE = Critically Endangered; EXEN = Extinct/Endangered (plants); EW = Extinct in the Wild

Species That Moved to a Less Threatened Status, 1998–2003

Mammals

Horse, Przewalski's: EW to OFF (IUCN)

Wolf, gray: LR–CD to OFF (IUCN); EN to TH (ESA)

Birds

Albatross, short tailed: EN to VU (IUCN)

Egret, Chinese egret: EN to VU (IUCN)

Falcon, American peregrine: EN to OFF (ESA)

Ground–dove, purple–winged: CE to EN (IUCN)

Kakapo: EW to CE (IUCN)

Kestrel, Mauritius: EN to VU (IUCN)

Lovebird, black-cheeked: EN to VU (IUCN)

Pelican Dalmatian: VU to LR–CD (IUCN)

Vireo, black-capped: EN to VU (IUCN)

Woodpecker, ivory-billed: EW to CE (IUCN)

Plants

Aloe, spiral Aloe: EN to OFF (IUCN)

Cactus, agave living–rock: EN to VU (IUCN)

Cactus, Peebles Navajo: VU to OFF (IUCN)

Cinquefoil, Robbins': EN to OFF (IUCN); EN to OFF (ESA)

Palm, Argun: EXEN to CE (IUCN)

Reptiles

Caiman, black: EN to LR–CD (IUCN)

Species That Moved to a More Threatened Status, 1998–2004

Mammals

Addax: EN to CE (IUCN)

Camel, bactrian: EN to CE (IUCN)

Jaguar: LR–NT to NT (IUCN)

Mandrill: LR–NT to VU (IUCN)

Monkey, woolly spider: EN to CE (IUCN)

Orangutan: VU to EN (IUCN)

Oryx, scimitar-horned: CE to EW (IUCN)

Tapir, Central American: VU to EN (IUCN)

Arachnids

No-eyed big-eyed cave wolf spider: No status to EN (ESA)

Birds

Booby, Abbott's: VU to CE (IUCN)

Crane, Siberian: EN to CE (IUCN)

Murrelet, Marbled : LR to VU (IUCN)

Parrot, Imperial Parrot: VU to EN (IUCN)

Penguin, yellow-eyed : VU to EN (IUCN)

Fish

Coelacanth: EN to CE (IUCN)

Plants

Cypress, Saharan: EN to CE(IUCN)

Fir, Baishan: EN to CE (IUCN)

Palm, Carossier: EN to CE (IUCN)

Rosewood, Brazilian: R to VU(IUCN)

Torreya, Florida: EN to CE(IUCN)

Reptiles

Leatherback Sea Turtle: EN to CE (IUCN)

Words to Know

A

Adaptation: A genetically determined characteristic, or inherited trait, that makes an organism better able to cope with its environment.

Alpine: Relating to mountainous regions.

Arid: Land that receives less than 10 inches (250 millimeters) of rainfall annually and has a high rate of evaporation.

B

Biodiversity: The entire variety of life on Earth.

Brackish: A mixture of freshwater and saltwater; briny water.

Browse: A method of grazing in which an animal eats the leaf and twig growth of shrubs, woody vines, trees, and cacti.

C

Canopy: The uppermost spreading branchy layer of a forest.

Carapace: A shell or bony covering on the back of animals such as turtles, lobsters, crabs, and armadillos.

Carnivore: An animal that eats mainly meat.

Carrion: Dead and decaying flesh.

Cetacean: An aquatic mammal that belongs to the order Cetacea, which includes whales, dolphins, and porpoises.

Chaparral: An ecological community of shrubby plants adapted to long, dry summers and natural forest fire cycles, generally found in southern California.

CITES: Abbreviation for Convention on International Trade in Endangered Species of Wild Fauna and Flora; an international agreement by 143 nations to prohibit trade of endangered wildlife.

Clear-cutting: The process of cutting down all the trees in a forest area.

Clutch: The number of eggs produced or incubated at one time.

Competitor: A species that may compete for the same resources as another species.

Conservation: The management and protection of the natural world.

Critical habitat: A designated area considered necessary for the protection and preservation of a species that has been listed under the Endangered Species Act in the United States. The area, either within or near the species' historical range, must provide an environment for normal behavior and reproduction so that the species may recover. The critical habitat designation does not prohibit human activity or create a refuge for the species. Once it has been established, though, any federal agencies planning to build or conduct activities within that area must seek the permission of the USFWS. The designation also serves to alert the public to the importance of the area in the species' survival.

D

Deciduous: Shedding seasonally; a tree whose leaves fall off annually or a forest made up of trees that shed their leaves annually, for example.

Deforestation: The loss of forests as they are rapidly cut down to produce timber or to make land available for agriculture.

Desertification: The gradual transformation of productive land into that with desertlike conditions.

Diurnal: Active during the day.

Domesticated: Animals trained to live with or be of use to humans.

E

Ecosystem: An ecological community, including plants, animals, and microorganisms, considered together with their environment.

Endangered: Species in danger of extinction in the foreseeable future.

Endangered Species Act (ESA): The legislation, passed by the U.S. Congress in 1973, which protects listed species.

Endangered Species List: The list of species protected under the Endangered Species Act.

Endemic species: A species native to, and found only in, a certain region.

Estivate: To hibernate (or sleep) through the summer.

Estuary: The place where freshwater enters the sea (e.g., at a river mouth).

Extinction: A species or subspecies is extinct when no living members exist.

Extirpated species: A species that no longer survives in the regions that were once part of its range.

F

Fauna: The animal life of a particular region, geological period, or environment.

Feral: An animal that has escaped from domestication and has become wild.

Fledge: When birds grow the feathers needed for flight.

Flora: The plants of a particular region, geological period, or environment.

G

Gene: The basic biological unit of heredity that determines individual traits. Part of the DNA molecule, the gene is transmitted from parents to children during reproduction, and contains information for making particular proteins, which then make particular cells.

Gestation: Pregnancy.

H

Habitat: The environment in which specified organisms live.

Herbivore: An animal that eats mainly plants.

Historic range: The areas in which a species is believed to have lived in the past.

I

Inbreeding: The mating or breeding of closely related individuals, usually within small communities. Inbreeding occurs when both parents have at least one common ancestor.

Introduced species: Flora or fauna not native to an area, but introduced from a different ecosystem.

IUCN: Abbreviation for International Union for the Conservation of Nature and Natural Resources; publishes *IUCN Red List of Threatened Animals* and *IUCN Red List of Threatened Plants*.

L

Larval: The immature stage of certain insects and animals, usually of a species that develops by complete metamorphosis.

Lichen: A plantlike composite consisting of a fungus and an alga.

M

Marsupial: Mammals, such as the kangaroo and the opossum, whose young continue to develop after birth in a pouch on the outside of the mother's body.

Metamorphosis: A change in the form and habits of an animal during natural development.

Migrating: The act of changing location periodically, usually moving seasonally from one region to another.

Molting: The process of shedding an outer covering, such as skin or feathers, for replacement by a new growth.

N

Native species: The flora or fauna indigenous or native to an ecosystem, as opposed to introduced species.

Nocturnal: Most active at night.

O

Old-growth forest: A mature forest dominated by long-lived species (at least 200 years old), but also including younger trees; its complex physical structure includes multiple layers in the canopy, many large trees, and many large dead standing trees and dead logs.

P

Perennial: A plant that lives, grows, flowers, and produces seeds for three or more continuous years.

Poaching: Illegally taking protected animals or plants.

Pollution: The contamination of air, water, or soil by the discharge of harmful substances.

Population: A group of organisms of one species occupying a defined area and usually isolated from similar groups of the same species.

Predator: An animal that preys on others.

Prehensile: Adapted for grasping or holding, especially by wrapping around something.

Pupal: An intermediate, inactive stage between the larva and adult stages in the life cycle of many insects.

Words to Know

R

Rain forest: A dense evergreen forest with an annual rainfall of at least 100 inches (254 cm); may be tropical (e.g., Amazon) or temperate (e.g., Pacific Northwest).

Range: The area naturally occupied by a species.

Recovery: The process of stopping or reversing the decline of an endangered or threatened species to ensure the species' long-term survival in the wild.

Reintroduction: The act of placing members of a species in their original habitat.

Reserve: An area of land set aside for the use or protection of a species or group of species.

Rhizomatous plant: A plant having an underground horizontal stem that puts out shoots above ground and roots below.

S

Savanna: A flat, treeless tropical or subtropical grassland.

Scrub: A tract of land covered with stunted or scraggly trees and shrubs.

Slash-and-burn agriculture: The process whereby a forest is cut down and all trees and vegetation are burned to create cleared land.

Species: A group of individuals related by descent and able to breed among themselves but not with other organisms.

Steppe: Vast, semiarid grass-covered plains found in southeast Europe, Siberia, and central North America.

Subspecies: A population of a species distinguished from other such populations by certain characteristics.

Succulent: A plant that has thick, fleshy, water-storing leaves or stems.

Sustainable development: Methods of farming or building human communities that meet the needs of the current generation without depleting or damaging the natural resources in the area or compromising its ability to meet the needs of future generations.

T

Taproot: The main root of a plant growing straight downward from the stem.

Territoriality: The behavior displayed by an individual animal, a mating pair, or a group in vigorously defending its domain against intruders.

Troglobyte: A species that lives only in caves.

Tropical: Characteristic of a region or climate that is frost free with temperatures high enough to support—with adequate precipitation—plant growth year round.

Tundra: A relatively flat, treeless plain in alpine, arctic, and antarctic regions.

U

Underbrush: Small trees, shrubs, or similar plants growing on the forest floor underneath taller trees.

Urban sprawl: The spreading of houses, shopping centers, and other city facilities through previously undeveloped land.

U.S. Fish and Wildlife Service (USFWS): A federal agency that oversees implementation of the Endangered Species Act.

V

Vulnerable: A species is vulnerable when it satisfies some risk criteria, but not at a level that warrants its identification as Endangered.

W

Wetland: A permanently moist lowland area such as a marsh or a swamp.

Endangered Species

2nd EDITION

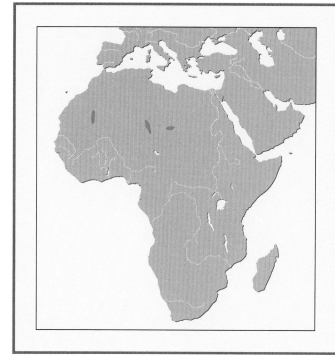

ADDAX
Addax nasomaculatus

PHYLUM: Chordata
CLASS: Mammalia
ORDER: Artiodactyla
FAMILY: Bovidae
STATUS: Critically endangered, IUCN
RANGE: Chad, Mali, Mauritania, Niger

Addax
Addax nasomaculatus

Description and biology

The addax is a large antelope whose coat is gray-brown in winter and almost white in summer. Black hair sprouts from its forehead and from the end of its 10- to 14-inch (25- to 36-centimeter) tail. Two long, thin, spiral horns (each twisting two or three times) extend up and back from the front of the animal's head. An average addax measures about 5 feet (1.5 meters) in length and about 3 feet (1 meter) in height at its shoulder. It weighs between 132 and 287 pounds (60 and 130 kilograms). A female addax usually gives birth to one infant after a gestation (pregnancy) period of eight to nine months.

The addax is at home in a desert environment. It receives all the water it needs from the plants it eats. With its long stride and splayed (spread apart) hooves, the animal easily

An addax is a desert animal that eats plants to receive the water it needs.

crosses vast sandy areas in search of sparse desert vegetation. Addax usually travel at night in groups of 5 to 20.

Habitat and current distribution

In 2000, the population of addax in the wild was estimated at 200 animals. These were found in Africa in small, fragmented groups in remote areas of northeastern Niger, northern Chad, and along the border between Mauritania and Mali.

History and conservation measures

Addax once ranged in Africa from Western Sahara and Mauritania to Egypt and Sudan. Ancient Egyptians domesticated the slow and tame animals. These very traits have led to the animals' present-day decline, as hunters easily capture addax for their prized meat and hide. In 1900, tens of thousands of addax were distributed over most of the Sahara, from Mauritania in the west to Sudan in the east. The population of the species in the 1960s was estimated at slightly less than 10,000, with about 4,000 animals in Chad, about 5,000 in an area extending between Mauritania and Sudan, and 50 more in Algeria. By the early 1970s, the population had been severely reduced to 2,000 animals distributed within a much smaller range in Mauritania, North Mali, Libya, and North Sudan. The International Union for Conservation of Nature and Natural Resources (IUCN) gave the addax an endangered status in 1996 and then upgraded the status to critically endangered in 1999 to more accurately reflect the huge dangers the species faces.

Despite laws protecting the animals, hunting remains a threat. Additional perils currently facing the addax include drought and tourists who destroy addax habitat with their vehicles while tracking and chasing the animals.

In Niger, the 4,943-square-mile (12,810-square-kilometer) Aïr and Ténère National Nature Reserve provides a large protected habitat for addax. Tourism and other human activities are prohibited within the clearly marked park boundaries. Although addax have existed in this area for centuries, their current population is very low. In the early 1990s, political disputes delayed the reintroduction into the reserve of 50 to 75 addax that had been bred in captivity. More than 1,000 addax are currently held in captivity in the United States, Europe, and the Middle East.

ANTEATER, GIANT
Myrmecophaga tridactyla

PHYLUM: Chordata
CLASS: Mammalia
ORDER: Edentata
FAMILY: Myrmecophagidae
STATUS: Vulnerable, IUCN
RANGE: Argentina, Belize, Bolivia, Brazil, Colombia, Costa Rica, Ecuador, French Guiana, Guatemala, Guyana, Honduras, Nicaragua, Panama, Paraguay, Peru, Suriname, Uruguay, Venezuela

Anteater, giant
Myrmecophaga tridactyla

Description and biology

Coarse, shaggy gray hair covers the giant anteater's long, narrow body. A black and silver-white stripe extends across its shoulders and down its back. The giant anteater's neck and head taper to its distinctive long, cylindrical snout. The animal's eyes and ears are small. Its saliva–coated tongue, used to pluck prey from nests, can extend almost 24 inches (61 centimeters). Its powerful front legs and claws allow the animal to break into termite and ant colonies easily, and also provide a means of defense against predators such as pumas and jaguars. An average giant anteater measures 40 to 50 inches (101 to 127 centimeters) from its head to the end of its body and weighs between 40 and 85 pounds (18 and 38 kilograms). Its shaggy tail can reach from 26 to 35 inches (66 to 89 centimeters) long.

4

The giant anteater's home range may extend from 1 to 9.6 square miles (2.6 to 24.9 square kilometers). A single giant anteater exists by itself in the wild and comes in contact with other giant anteaters only to mate. A female giant anteater gives birth to a single infant after a 190-day gestation (pregnancy) period. The infant, which rides on the mother's back and nurses for the first six weeks, stays with the mother for more than a year.

Habitat and current distribution

Although the habitat of giant anteaters extends from Guatemala in Central America to Uruguay in South America, scientists believe these animals are almost extinct over much of this great range. The primary reason is habitat destruction, especially of tropical rain forests.

Although the giant anteater is sometimes killed for its meat and claws, its tail is also highly prized by hunters.

History and conservation measures

Giant anteaters are killed for their meat, for their claws and tails (which are highly prized), and because people wrongly believe they attack dogs, cattle, and humans. The greatest threat to these animals, however, is fire. During dry seasons, large fires sweep through much of central South America. Farmers also set forest fires in order to increase grazing land for their livestock—what is called slash-and-burn agriculture. While almost all other animals escape these fires by running or flying, giant anteaters usually do not. They are slow-moving and their long hair burns easily.

Giant anteaters are protected from hunters in a number of national parks and nature reserves throughout their vast habitat. In Brazil alone, ten parks and three reserves provide safe haven for the animals. Nonetheless, natural and man-made fires recognize no boundaries, so many giant anteaters have burned to death in protected areas.

ARMADILLO, GIANT
Priodontes maximus:

PHYLUM: Chordata

CLASS: Mammalia

ORDER: Edentata

FAMILY: Dasypodidae

STATUS: Endangered, IUCN
Endangered, ESA

RANGE: Argentina, Bolivia, Brazil, Colombia, Ecuador, French Guiana, Guyana, Paraguay, Peru, Suriname, Uruguay, Venezuela

Armadillo, giant
Priodontes maximus

Description and biology

The giant armadillo is the largest member of the armadillo family, which is composed of twenty–one species. Eleven to thirteen moveable bony plates cover a giant armadillo's back, and three to four flexible bands cover its neck. Its body is dark brown, while its head, tail, and a stripe around the bottom of its shell are whitish. A giant armadillo measures 30 to 39 inches (76 to 99 centimeters) from the tip of its nose to the end of its body. Its tail is about 20 inches (50 centimeters) long. It weighs between 44 and 88 pounds (20 and 40 kilograms).

Unlike certain members of the armadillo family, the giant armadillo cannot roll into a ball, protected by its body armor. To escape from danger, the giant armadillo quickly digs itself into the ground using the long claws on its front legs. The

Giant armadillos are not able to roll themselves into a ball like other members of the armadillo family.

animal also uses these claws to dig for ants, termites, worms, spiders, and other insects which it feeds on at night.

The gestation (pregnancy) period of a female giant armadillo is about four months. She gives birth to one or two infants at a time, each weighing about 4 ounces (113 grams), and they nurse for four to six weeks. The life span of a giant armadillo is 12 to 15 years.

Habitat and current distribution

The giant armadillo is found in many South American countries, from Venezuela and Guyana south to Argentina. However, its primary habitat is the Amazonian rain forest.

History and conservation measures

Hunting, human settlement, and agricultural development have all contributed to the giant armadillo's decline. Although laws in Argentina, Brazil, Colombia, Paraguay, Peru, and Suriname protect the animal, it is still hunted for food in some areas. Of greater concern is the destruction of its habitat, as large areas of rain forest are cleared for homes and farms.

National parks and nature reserves in Brazil, Colombia, Peru, and Suriname provide safe habitats for giant armadillos, but rain forest destruction is a continuing problem. Current conservation efforts include plans to move giant armadillos to protected habitats and to breed them in captivity.

ASS, AFRICAN WILD
Equus africanus (equus asinus)

PHYLUM: Chordata

CLASS: Mammalia

ORDER: Perissodactyla

FAMILY: Equidae

STATUS: Critically endangered, IUCN
Endangered, ESA

RANGE: Chad, Djibouti, Egypt, Eritrea, Ethiopia, Somalia, Sudan

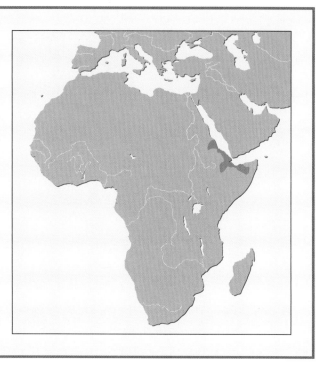

Ass, African wild
Equus africanus (equus asinus)

Description and biology

The African wild ass is one of only seven surviving species of equids (horse family). Of these seven species, five are threatened or endangered. The smallest member of the horse family, the African wild ass stands about 4.5 feet (1.5 meters) tall at the shoulders and weighs about 550 to 600 pounds (250 to 275 kilograms). It has a gray coat with a white belly and a dark stripe up its back. With its long ears and short stubby mane, the African wild ass looks like its cousin, the American domestic donkey, and is in fact the donkey's ancestor. The African ass has strong teeth and sturdy narrow hooves. It eats the tough grasses and shrubs of the desert. Although its teeth wear down from grazing, they continue to grow throughout the life of the animal.

Humans have captured and domesticated, or tamed, the African wild ass to use for work and transportation in parts of Africa since 3000 B.C. .

The African wild ass is most active in the cooler temperatures at dawn, night, and dusk, and takes refuge from the heat during the daytime. Well adapted to the desert, the African ass can go longer without water than any other species of horse. It is also a very skilled runner, and has been seen running at a rate of 31 miles (50 kilometers) per hour.

African wild ass sometimes live alone, but they often join temporary groups. Females generally live with their offspring in herds of about 50 animals. Some males live in their own territory and defend their water sources. They will allow other males and females into their territory, but they remain dominant in it. If a male does not have its own territory, it will usually travel with a small bachelor herd. African wild ass form small herds because the food in the regions in which they live is so scarce it could not support a large number. They communicate with each other through scent and by making vocal calls. The African wild ass mates during the rainy seasons. There is a one-year gestation (pregnancy) period, and females generally bear one offspring at a time. The female African wild ass usually gives birth only every other year, although capable of breeding annually. African wild ass in the wild can live up to about 30 or 40 years.

Habitat and current distribution

The African wild ass lives in desert regions, in hilly and stony areas where grasses and shrubs grow. It avoids sandy regions and needs to be near a water source. In the early 2000s, the surviving members of the species were found mainly in the Horn of Africa (the easternmost projection of the continent), in isolated areas within Ethiopia, the western part of Djibouti, and northern Somalia. It was estimated that there were only a few hundred animals remaining.

History and conservation measures

Humans have captured and domesticated, or tamed, the African wild ass to use for work and transportation in parts of Africa since 3000 B.C. The species was widespread throughout the Horn of Africa for many years. It has been estimated that in 1905 the population of African wild ass in eastern Somalia alone was 10,000 animals. By the 1960s, however, there were only a few hundred survivors in the world.

There are several causes for the decline in the African wild ass population. In Ethiopia and Somalia, the wild ass has been hunted for domestication, for food, and for traditional medicine, as it is believed by some to cure hepatitis. The introduction of modern firearms in the area led to the slaughter of more animals. In the latter part of the twentieth century, warfare and instability in the Horn of Africa led to more (and more deadly) weapons and ammunition being available, and this too led to a reduction in the wild ass population. Animal herders have at times killed wild ass in the belief that the animals were using up grasses and water resources that their domesticated animals needed to survive.

Several conservation projects address the plight of the African wild ass. One of the goals of these programs is to build up the population from a few hundred to 2,500 animals in the wild. More scientific data about the animal is being pursued in the early 2000s. There have been attempts to establish populations of African wild ass in new surroundings, notably in the desert at Hai-Bar, Israel. So far these attempts have not succeeded. African wild ass are legally protected in Sudan, Somalia, and Ethiopia. Conservationists are educating some of the people living in these areas about methods of protecting their resources, including programs to save the African wild ass.

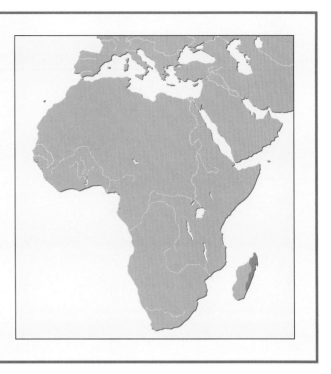

AYE–AYE
Daubentonia madagascariensis

PHYLUM: Chordata
CLASS: Mammalia
ORDER: Primates
FAMILY: Daubentoniidae
STATUS: Endangered, IUCN
Endangered, ESA
RANGE: Madagascar

Aye-aye
Daubentonia madagascariensis

Description and biology

The unusual-looking aye-aye is covered with a coat of coarse blackish-brown hair, which overlays a denser coat of short white hair. The animal has very large, sensitive ears that stick out from its small, rounded head. It has sharp, rodent-like incisor (front) teeth and long, claw-like fingers and toes. An average aye-aye is 15 to 18 inches (38 to 46 centimeters) long from the top of its head to the end of its body. Its bushy tail measures 16 to 22 inches (41 to 56 centimeters) long. The animal weighs between 4.4 and 6.6 pounds (2 and 3 kilograms).

While an aye–aye eats bamboo shoots, sugarcane, and some small animals, most of its diet consists of fruit (especially coconuts) and wood-boring insect larvae. Using its pow-

erful incisors, the aye-aye breaks into coconuts, then scoops out the pulp with its very long, thin middle finger. The aye-aye's large ears allow it to hear insect larvae moving beneath the bark of trees. The animal strips off the bark with its teeth, then crushes and eats the larvae with its middle finger.

Aye-ayes are unusual–looking members of the primate family.

The aye-aye is a nocturnal (active at night) creature. It builds a complex nest in the fork of a large tree for shelter during the day. When active, the animal spends most of its time in trees, often hanging by its hind legs. Biologists (people who study living organisms) know little about the aye-aye's social structure or mating habits. The animal's range is estimated to be 12 acres (5 hectares). A female aye-aye usually gives birth to a single infant every two to three years, and nurses the young aye-aye for up to a year.

Habitat and current distribution

Aye-ayes are found in eastern, northern, and northwestern Madagascar, an island off the southeast coast of Africa. The animals are able to survive in a variety of forest types: deciduous (shedding plants and trees), secondary-growth, and dry scrub (stunted trees and shrubs). They have also been found in coconut groves and mangrove swamps. Although aye-aye are found over a large area of the island, their population numbers are low. Only a few thousand are believed to be alive today.

History and conservation measures

Even though its only natural predator is the fossa, a slender mammal that resembles a cat, the aye-aye was once considered one of the most endangered mammals in Madagascar. The main threat to the aye-aye is habitat destruction. Because it needs large, old trees in which to build its nest, the aye-aye cannot exist in areas that have been cleared of trees. The animal is also at risk because of superstitious fear. Many people on Madagascar believe the aye–aye brings misfortune, even death, to those it meets. For this reason, many local people kill the animal on sight and sometimes eat it. The aye-aye is also killed by local farmers, who believe the animal is a threat to crops.

Even though a number of reserves have been set up for the aye-aye in Madagascar, the protection of these areas has not been enforced. However, under a conservation program begun in 1966, nine aye-aye were released on Nosy Mangabe, a 1,300-acre (520-hectare) island off the east coast of Madagascar. These animals have received special protection, and investigations into the results of the program are ongoing.

BANDICOOT, GOLDEN
Isoodon auratus

PHYLUM: Chordata
CLASS: Mammalia
ORDER: Marsupialia
FAMILY: Peramelidae
STATUS: Vulnerable, IUCN
RANGE: Australia

Bandicoot, golden
Isoodon auratus

Description and biology

The golden bandicoot belongs to the order of mammals known as marsupials, whose young continue to develop after birth in a pouch on the outside of the mother's body. The animal's coarse fur is a mixture of yellow-orange and dark brown hairs, giving it a golden appearance. It has a long, tapering snout and short, rounded ears. An average golden bandicoot measures 9 to 19 inches (23 to 48 centimeters) from the top of its head to the end of its body and weighs about 3 pounds (1.4 kilograms). Its tail is 3 to 8 inches (8 to 20 centimeters) long.

Golden bandicoot are nocturnal (active at night). During the day, they remain in their nests built on the ground, in a hollow, or in a rock pile. At night, the very quick, agile, and aggressive animals search for their diet of insects and worms. Golden bandicoot are solitary animals, so males and females come together only to mate. The female usually gives birth to a litter of four after a gestation (pregnancy) period of almost

Like other members of the marsupial family, female golden bandicoots contain a pouch in which their young finish developing after birth.

two weeks. The young golden bandicoot remain in their mother's pouch for up to eight weeks.

Habitat and current distribution

Golden bandicoot once ranged across one–third of Australia, mainly in grassland habitats. They are now found in a small part of the Kimberleys, a plateau region in northeastern Western Australia, and on a few islands off Australia's coast.

History and conservation measures

Scientists and conservationists (people protecting the natural world) are not quite sure why the number of golden bandicoot has decreased. They believe foxes and cats recently allowed into golden bandicoot territory have become predators of the animals. In addition, fires deliberately set by humans to manage grasslands may have destroyed the animals' natural habitat.

BAT, GRAY
Myotis grisescens

PHYLUM: Chordata
CLASS: Mammalia
ORDER: Chiroptera
FAMILY: Vespertilionidae
STATUS: Endangered, IUCN
Endangered, ESA
RANGE: Central and southeastern
USA

Bat, gray
Myotis grisescens

Description and biology

Contrary to its name, the gray bat is reddish-brown in color. Its forearm measures 1.6 inches (4 centimeters) long, and it weighs 0.35 ounce (10 grams). The gray bat differs from other species of the *Myotis* genus (a group with similar characteristics) in that its wing membrane (a double membrane of skin) attaches to its ankle instead of the side of its foot. The gray bat feeds at night on insects, particularly mayflies and mosquitoes. It roosts in two different types of caves throughout the year.

Female gray bats begin hibernating immediately after mating in the fall; adult males and juveniles follow several weeks later. In late March, the females emerge from hibernation, while the rest emerge about a month later. Using sperm they have stored all winter, female gray bats fertilize their eggs after hibernation, giving birth to a single infant around late May.

Although called the gray bat, these animals are actually reddish–brown in color.

Habitat and current distribution

In summer, while gray bats are raising their young, they roost in caves that have a temperature between 57 and 77°F (14 and 25°C). In winter, during hibernation, the bats roost in caves that have a temperature between 43 and 52°F (6 and 11°C). Gray bats are found in limestone caverns in Alabama, Arkansas, Georgia, Illinois, Indiana, Kansas, Kentucky, Mississippi, Missouri, North Carolina, Oklahoma, Tennessee, and Virginia. In 1980, scientists estimated the gray bat population to be less than 1,600,000.

History and conservation measures

Before the American Civil War (1861–65), millions of gray bats inhabited the southeastern United States. Beginning with the war, bat guano (feces) was used to produce saltpeter (potassium nitrate), a component of gunpowder. When humans entered roosting caves to collect the guano, the bats were disturbed from their normal routine. This was particularly harmful during hibernation. When aroused during this period, a gray bat is forced to use its stored fat and may starve to death before spring.

In modern times, spelunking (cave exploring), tourism, and flooding caused by the construction of dams have all led to the destruction of bat habitat. Between 1960 and 1980, the gray bat population decreased almost 80 percent. Water pollution and pesticides the bats ingested by eating contaminated insects also contributed to this decline.

Since the early 1980s, many bat caves have been protected from human disturbance, and the drop in the number of gray bats seems to have stopped. Without further conservation measures, however, the bats will not reach full recovery.

BAT, TOWNSEND'S BIG-EARED
Plecotus (also Corynorhinus) townsendii

PHYLUM: Chordata
CLASS: Mammalia
ORDER: Chiroptera
FAMILY: Vespertilionidae
STATUS: Vulnerable, IUCN
Endangered, ESA (subspecies
ingens and *virginianus*)
RANGE: Canada, Mexico, USA

Bat, Townsend's big-eared

Plecotus townsendii

Description and biology

The Townsend's big-eared bat is named for its large ears, which are from 1 to 1.6 inches (2.5 to 4 centimeters) long. In contrast, the bat's body length is 1.8 to 2.7 inches (4.5 to 7 centimeters), its tail length is 1.4 to 2.1 inches (3.5 to 5.3 centimeters), and its forearm length is 1.4 to 2 inches (3.5 to 5 centimeters). The average Townsend's big-eared bat weighs between 0.18 and 0.46 ounce (5 and 13 grams).

Townsend's big-eared bats feed primarily on moths, which they locate through echolocation (sonar). In this process, a bat emits high-pitched sounds that echo or bounce off its prey. The bat's sensitive hearing picks up the echo. From that sound, the bat can determine the size, shape, and location of its prey.

Male and female Townsend's big-eared bats come together in late fall or early winter to mate and hibernate. The females store the sperm until early spring, when they fertilize their

eggs. After a gestation (pregnancy) period of 56 to 100 days, they give birth to a single infant, which they nurse until fall.

There are five subspecies of Townsend's big-eared bat, two of which are considered endangered under the Endangered Species Act: the Ozark big-eared bat (*Plecotus townsendii ingens*) and the Virginia big-eared bat (*Plecotus townsendii virginianus*).

Habitat and current distribution

Townsend's big-eared bats are found in forest and desert areas in southwestern Canada, western United States, and Mexico. The bats inhabit caves, abandoned mines, and, sometimes, buildings. They prefer limestone caves, however. Like many other species of bats, Townsend's big-eared bats hibernate in one type of cave while raising their young in another. They will often use these same sites year after year.

The Townsend's big-eared bat is found in forest and desert areas in southwestern Canada, western United States, and Mexico.

The gray and white Ozark big-eared bats are found only in a few caves in Arkansas, Missouri, and Oklahoma. Biologists (people who study living organisms) estimate their population to be under 700. The predominantly gray Virginia big-eared bats are found in eastern Kentucky, southwestern Virginia, and eastern West Virginia. They number approximately 11,000.

History and conservation measures

Human disturbance is the primary reason for the decline in the number of Townsend's big-eared bats. If disturbed while hibernating, the bats will often leave their roosts. Forced to rely on their stored fat for food, the bats often starve to death before winter is over.

The U.S. government has designated as critical habitats those caves known to be occupied by Townsend's big-eared bats. This act prevents federal agencies from carrying out programs that would lead to the disturbance or destruction of these caves. However, this act has not deterred vandals and curious tourists from continuing to enter protected caves.

BEAR, GRIZZLY
Ursus arctos horribilis

PHYLUM: Chordata
CLASS: Mammalia
ORDER: Carnivora
FAMILY: Ursidae
STATUS: Threatened, ESA
RANGE: Canada, USA (Alaska, Idaho, Montana, Washington, Wyoming)

Bear, grizzly
Ursus arctos horribilis

Description and biology

The grizzly bear, a subspecies of the brown bear (*Ursus arctos*), is one of the largest land mammals in North America. An average male grizzly has a head and body length of 6 to 8 feet (1.8 to 2.4 meters), stands 3.5 to 4 feet (1 to 1.2 meters) at its shoulder, and may weigh up to 800 pounds (360 kilograms). The smaller female grizzly weighs between 200 and 400 pounds (90 and 180 kilograms). The grizzly bear is so-named because its thick, light brown to black fur is streaked with gray, giving it a "grizzled" look. Grizzly bears have short, rounded ears, humped shoulders, and long, curved claws.

Although grizzly bears are omnivores (they eat both plants and animals), most of their diet consists of vegetation: fruits, berries, nuts, and the bulbs and roots of plants. They also eat ants and other insects. The meat in a grizzly bear's diet comes from deer or smaller mammals such as elk or moose calves.

Salmon makes up a large part of the diet of grizzly bears that inhabit Alaska and the west coast of Canada.

Grizzly bears store large amounts of fat, which their bodies rely on during their long winter hibernation. Grizzlies build their dens in early fall, often on high, remote mountain slopes underneath the roots of large trees. Once they enter their dens in October or November, they do not emerge for five or six months (females usually emerge one month after the males in the spring).

Male and female grizzly bears usually mate in June or July. After a gestation (pregnancy) period of about six months, a female grizzly gives birth during hibernation to one to three cubs. The infant bears usually weigh 1 pound (.45 kilogram) at birth, but gain as much as 20 pounds (9 kilograms) by the time spring arrives. Female grizzlies nurse their cubs for up to one year, and the cubs remain with their mother for two to three additional years. The average life span of a grizzly bear is 15 to 20 years.

Habitat and current distribution

The grizzly bear's home range is quite large: up to 500 square miles (1,300 square kilometers) for males and 300 square miles (780 square kilometers) for females. That range may extend over a variety of forests, meadows, and grasslands in or near mountains. Grizzlies are active at lower elevations during most of the year. For hibernation, they move to higher altitudes.

In the contiguous United States (the connected 48 states) in the early 2000s, there are five known grizzly bear populations in the states of Idaho, Montana, Washington, and Wyoming. The largest is in Yellowstone National Park (Idaho, Montana, Wyoming) with 400 to 600 bears. Three populations are in Glacier National Park (Montana and Idaho): Northern Continental Divide with 300 to 400 bears; Selkirk with 45 to 50 bears; and Cabinet-Yaak with 30 to 40 bears. A tiny population remains in North Cascades National Park (Washington) with 5 to 30 bears. Wildlife biologists (people who study living organisms) estimate there are over 20,000 grizzly bears in western Canada and over 30,000 in Alaska (where they are called brown bears). British Columbia is currently home to about half of Canada's grizzlies.

History and conservation measures

Grizzly bears used to range over the entire western half of North America, from Mexico up to the Arctic Circle. In 1800, the grizzly bear population in North America exceeded 50,000. By 1975, that number had been reduced to less than 1,000. Habitat destruction and hunting are the two main reasons for this drastic decline. As pioneers moved west during the nineteenth century and settled mountainous regions, grizzly bears were forced out of their natural habitat. These pioneers also shot and trapped grizzlies, believing the animals posed a threat.

As the wild areas of the American west continue to be developed (such as with the building of recreation areas), the survival of grizzly bears will continue to be jeopardized. Even though they are protected by laws, grizzlies are still shot by hunters who mistake the animals for black bears.

During the last decades of the twentieth century, the U.S. government worked with state agencies and Native American tribes in an effort to manage and protect grizzly bear habitat. These efforts were highly successful in areas such as the Yellowstone National Park ecosystem (the system of plant, animals, and microorganisms within their environment), where the grizzly bear population exceeded target levels in the last years of the 1990s. At the turn of the twentieth century, considerable controversy arose over plans to reintroduce grizzlies to Idaho's Bitterroot Mountain ecosystem. The area was once home to a significant population of grizzlies, but none remain in modern times. Because the habitat is so well suited to a recovery program, the U.S. Fish and Wildlife Service developed a detailed reintroduction plan—worked out over six years with the residents and industry representatives of the affected areas in the Bitterroots. In June 2001, however, the secretary of the interior of the United States announced that the plan was to be abandoned. Many wildlife conservationists (people who work to manage and protect nature) protested this disruption in the recovery of the grizzly bear.

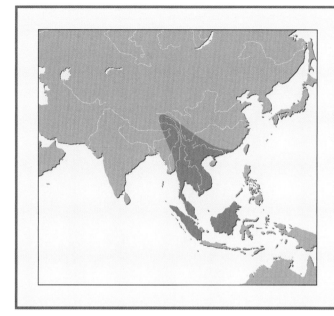

BEAR, SUN
Helarctos malayanus

PHYLUM: Chordata
CLASS: Mammalia
ORDER: Carnivora
FAMILY: Ursidae
STATUS: Data deficient, IUCN
RANGE: Brunei, Cambodia, China, India, Indonesia, Laos, Malaysia, Myanmar, Thailand, Vietnam

Bear, sun

Helarctos malayanus

Description and biology

The smallest member of the bear family, the sun bear has an average head and body length of 3.5 to 4.5 feet (1 to 1.4 meters). Its shoulder height is 26.6 inches (67.5 centimeters) and its weight is between 60 and 140 pounds (27 and 64 kilograms). The animal's short tail extends only 1 to 3 inches (3 to 7 centimeters). The fur on the sun bear's body is very short and black; the fur on its muzzle is almost white. Most animals of this species have a white to yellow-orange horseshoe-shaped marking on their chests.

The sun bear's curved and pointed claws make it an excellent climber. It spends most of its day sleeping or sunning on a platform it builds in trees 7 to 20 feet (2 to 6 meters) above the ground. It uses its strong claws to open bees' nests or to pull back the bark of trees to locate the larvae of wood-boring insects. The sun bear's diet also includes termites and other insects, fruits, birds, and small mammals. Because it is so fond of honey, the sun bear is sometimes called the honey bear.

The sun bear is the smallest member of the bear family and is often called the honey bear because of its fondness for honey.

Sun bears do not hibernate, and they can mate at any time during the year. After a gestation (pregnancy) period of 95 to 240 days, a female sun bear gives birth to one or two cubs.

Habitat and current distribution

Sun bears are found scattered throughout tropical and sub-tropical forests in Southeast Asia.

History and conservation measures

Although biologists (people who study living organisms) are unsure of the total number of existing sun bears, they believe the population of these animals is declining. Throughout their range, the animals are killed and used for food and medicinal purposes. Korean tourists in Thailand seek out special restaurants that serve sun bear meat, believing it will enhance their health. Sun bear cubs are often captured and kept as pets.

A critical threat to sun bears is the destruction of their forest habitat to create agricultural land. A number of reserves have been set up for the animals throughout their range, but biologists do not know if these reserves provide the habitat necessary for sun bear survival.

BISON, AMERICAN
Bison bison

PHYLUM: Chordata
CLASS: Mammalia
ORDER: Artiodactyla
FAMILY: Bovidae
STATUS: Lower risk: conservation dependent, IUCN Endangered, ESA (subspecies *athabascae*)
RANGE: Canada, USA

Bison, American
Bison bison

Description and biology

The American bison (commonly known as the buffalo) has a massive body, humped shoulders, and pointed horns that curve up and in. In winter, its coat is dark brown and shaggy. In the spring, this coat is shed and replaced by one that is short and light-brown. Hair on the head, neck, shoulders, and forelegs remains long and shaggy throughout the year. A beard also hangs from the chin of the animal's huge, low-slung head. An average American bison has a head and body length of 7 to 12.5 feet (2.1 to 3.8 meters) and a shoulder height of 5 to 6.5 feet (1.5 to 2 meters). It weighs between 700 and 2,200 pounds (320 and 1,000 kilograms). The animal's relatively short tail is 12 to 35 inches (31 to 89 centimeters) long and ends in a tuft of hair.

The American bison species is divided biologically into two subspecies: the plains bison (*Bison bison bison*) and the wood bison (*Bison bison athabascae*). The main physical difference between the two is the color of the hair on the shoul-

ders. On the plains bison, this hair is lighter in color than the hair on the rest of its body. The difference in hair color on the wood bison is not so pronounced.

The bison is a fast runner and good swimmer, and has a keen sense of smell. It is active during both day and night, feeding on prairie grasses and sedges (grasslike flowers). Bison usually travel in herds, although some males (bulls) tend to be solitary. Mating season lasts from June to September. The gestation (pregnancy) period of the female American bison is about 285 days. The calves, which are reddish-brown in color when born, may nurse for up to a year.

Habitat and current distribution

In the United States in the early years of the twenty-first century, about 25 herds of plains bison live in parks and

Although once numbering 60,000,000 in the early nineteenth century, the American bison population now numbers less than 40,000.

wildlife reserves, numbering about 16,000 animals. Plains bison are found primarily in Yellowstone National Park in northwestern Wyoming, southern Montana, and eastern Idaho. This herd numbers about 3,600. Additional plains bison are located in other parks and nature reserves. There are an estimated 140,000 animals living on private ranches in the western United States. Wood bison exist in a number of sanctuaries in Canada, including Wood Buffalo National Park in northern Alberta and southern Northwest Territories. The number of Canadian wood buffalo is believed to be more than 5,000.

History and conservation measures

American bison once ranged from Alaska and western Canada into the United States and northern Mexico. Scientists have estimated that in the early nineteenth century more bison—60,000,000 total—than humans existed in North America. These large animals were an essential part of the culture of many Native American people, who depended on the American bison for food and clothing. As American and European settlers moved west during that century, the number of bison began to decline. The animals were hunted for their hides, meat, and tongues, which were considered a delicacy. They were shot from trains for sport. And as part of the American government's strategy to subdue Native Americans, bison were slaughtered by the millions. By the late nineteenth century, only a few hundred of each subspecies remained in the wild.

In 1902, the American government placed a herd of some 40 captive and wild plains bison under protection in Yellowstone National Park. This herd grew into the one that exists in the park today. In 1922, the Canadian government established Wood Buffalo National Park to protect the last surviving wood bison. Unfortunately, plains bison were shortly afterward released into the park, where they mated with the wood bison. The resulting offspring were a hybrid, or genetic mixture, of the two subspecies. In the late 1950s, a small herd of genetically similar wood bison were located in the park. Although scientists allowed these animals to breed only with each other, no one is certain whether any genetically pure wood bison currently exist.

Beginning in 1990, Montana Department of Livestock workers shot plains bison that wandered outside of the boundaries of Yellowstone National Park. Even though the animals are protected within the park, a state-federal agreement gives Montana officials the right to kill bison if they cross onto private land. Both Montana officials and private ranchers feared the bison would infect cattle grazing near the park with brucellosis, a disease that causes cows to abort their calves. Conservationists (people who protect the natural world) claimed that there were no cases of the disease being transmitted from a bison to a cow. Despite the lack of scientific evidence, Montana officials remained fearful. During the harsh winter of 1996–97, more than 1,000 bison that roamed outside of the park in search of food were slaughtered. In the early 2000s, legislation was written in Montana allowing "sport hunting" of the bison that left the park and crossed into Montana. This would mean that private citizens with a permit could shoot bison for sport. The situation was becoming urgent because Yellowstone, with a population of 3,600 bison, had become overcrowded with bison and herds had been traveling out of the park to graze. Conservationists call for better means of controlling the population in the park and more research into the transmission of the brucellosis disease.

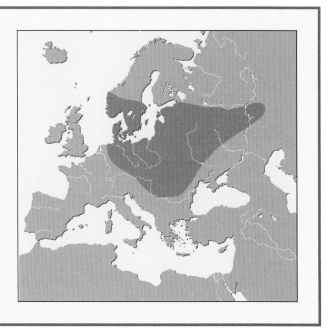

BISON, EUROPEAN
Bison bonasus

PHYLUM: Chordata
CLASS: Mammalia
ORDER: Artiodactyla
FAMILY: Bovidae
STATUS: Endangered, IUCN
RANGE: Belarus, Kyrgyzstan, Lithuania, Poland, Russian Federation, Ukraine

Bison, European

Bison bonasus

Description and biology

European bison (often called *wisent,* from the German word for "bison") are the largest land mammals in Europe but are slightly smaller than their close relative, the American bison. The adult male European bison weighs in the range of 800 to 2,000 pounds (400 to 920 kilograms); the female weighs from 650 to 1,200 pounds (300 to 540 kilograms). A good-sized male has a shoulder height of about 6 to 6.5 feet (1.8 to 2 meters) and his body is about 9 feet (2.75 meters) long. The head is very big, and both males and females have horns. European bison are varying shades of brown, and they have long hair growing from their necks and foreheads and a short beard on their chins. They have a shoulder hump and carry their heads high. In winter, they grow an extra coat of fur to protect themselves from the cold.

Unlike American bison, which live on the plains, European bison live in forests where they can browse (eat) on the

tender shoots, twigs, and leaves of trees and bushes. They generally live close to moist clearings where they graze on grass, moss, herbs, and other greens. During the spring, autumn, and summer, they spend most of their time browsing and grazing. In the primary home of bisons in the Bialowieza Forest, Poland, there is a centuries-old tradition of humans providing hay for the bison to eat in winter. Thus it has become part of the seasonal habit of the species to gather in large groups in winter around the places where the humans have laid out food for them. Today, park wardens provide European bison with hay, oats, and sugar beets in the winter.

Female bison, with their calves and sexually immature young, live in herds of about 20 to 30 animals. Bulls (males) live alone most of the year. When the mating season begins in August each year, the bulls join up with the herds and fight

Early in the twentieth century, hunters killed off the last of the wild European bison, and since then, captured bison raised in zoos have been successfully reintroduced into their natural habitat, where they can be protected.

each other for females. Each mating bull may take up to about a dozen females to mate. When the mating season is over, the bulls go back to living alone. For the females, the gestation (pregnancy) period is about nine months. During calving season, from May to July, the female leaves the herd. Female European bison generally bear one offspring in a season, and occasionally two. In winter, European bison gather into larger groups near their feeding stations. Their life span is about 25 years or longer.

Habitat and current distribution

Today the largest concentration of European bison live in Poland's Bialowieza National Park, which is Europe's last remaining primeval forest (one that has been there since ancient times). The park, which covers an area of about 20 square miles (52 square kilometers), lies within the 220-square-mile (570-square-kilometer) Bialowieza forest. Early in the twentieth century, hunters killed off the last of the wild European bison, and since then, captured bison raised in zoos have been successfully reintroduced into their natural habitat, particulary in Bialowieza, where they can be protected. In the past few decades, European bison have also been either reintroduced or introduced to the wild from captivity in other areas, including Russia, Belarus, Kyrgyzstan, Lithuania, and Ukraine. In 1999, there were an estimated 3,200 European bison in captivity and in the wild.

History and conservation measures

The restoration of the European bison to its natural habitat during the second half of the twentieth century is one of the success stories in the history of animal species protection. Since ancient times, European bison ranged through the deciduous forests (made up of trees that shed their leaves each season) extending from Britain across Europe into Russia. The Bialowieza Forest in what is now Poland was protected for royal hunting from the fifteenth to the eighteenth century; during those centuries the game in the forest was fed by humans. In the nineteenth century, Russia took control of the forests. Overhunting caused a significant reduction in bison, as well as other animals. During World War I (1914–18), a tremendous number of bison were killed by hunters and soldiers, and in the early 1920s the last bison in the wild was killed by a poacher (illegal hunter).

In 1923, the 54 European bison living in zoos represented the entire population of the species. These were placed in breeding programs for several decades. In the 1950s, the animals bred in captivity were released into the wild in Bialowieza, which had been declared a national park in the 1930s. These animals have been carefully protected and have prospered. There are approximately 3,200 animals in existence today, and they are all the descendants of 12 European bison from the breeding-in-captivity programs started in the 1920s. This is potentially a problem for the species in terms of introducing enough genetic diversity (variety of biological units that pass on inherited traits) within the herds in the wild.

The reintroduction of bison into the Bialowieza forests has been so successful that some carefully managed culling (eliminating some of the bison so that the habitat is preserved for the rest) is necessary. There are now programs expanding the bison's range into Belarus, Ukraine, Russia, and beyond. One of the biggest concerns for the preservation of the European bison is to foster genetic variation among thousands of animals with only twelve ancestors.

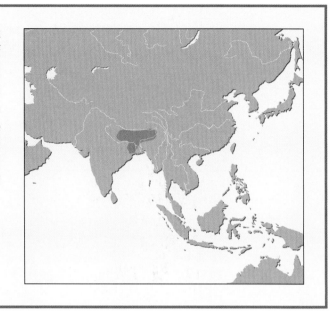

BUFFALO, WILD WATER
Bubalus bubalis

PHYLUM: Chordata
CLASS: Mammalia
ORDER: Artiodactyla
FAMILY: Bovidae
STATUS: Endangered, IUCN
RANGE: Bhutan, India, Nepal, Thailand

Buffalo, wild water

Bubalus bubalis

Description and biology

The wild water buffalo, also known as the Asian or Indian buffalo, is a very large animal, averaging 7.75 to 10 feet (2.4 to 3 meters) long. It stands 5 to 6.25 feet (1.5 to 2 meters) tall at its shoulder and weighs between 1,550 and 2,650 pounds (700 and 1,200 kilograms). Long, coarse hair covers the buffalo's ash gray to black body. Both male and female water buffalo have small ears, thin faces, and widely spread horns. The horns, thick where they emerge from the animal's head, form a semicircle by curving out and back. Ending in a point, these horns may reach a length of 6 feet (2 meters).

The wild water buffalo's diet consists of grasses and other vegetation that grows along the shores of lakes and rivers. Although the animal is fast and aggressive, it can fall prey to tigers. Leopards also often prey on young water buffalo. A female water buffalo gives birth to a single infant after a gestation (pregnancy) period of 310 to 340 days. The infant is then nursed for up to nine months.

Habitat and current distribution

Wild water buffalo inhabit swampy or wet grassland, or river valleys with dense vegetation. The animals like to wallow in mud, which helps protect them against biting insects. To further escape insects, they will often submerge themselves in water so that only their nostrils are exposed.

In 2002, the International Union for Conservation of Nature and Natural Resources (IUCN) estimated that while there are definitely less than 4,000 wild water buffalo left in the wild, the true figure may actually be closer to 200 surviving animals. In contrast, almost 130,000,000 domestic water buffalo, which are used to pull carts and plows, live in India and Southeast Asia. Because of interbreeding between domestic and the larger wild water buffalo, biologists (people who study living organisms) believe that less than 50 of the wild species are genetically pure.

Grass and other vegetation make up the wild water buffalo's diet.

History and conservation measures

Several factors have contributed to the disappearance of wild water buffalo: excessive hunting, the destruction of buffalo habitat to create agricultural land, and diseases transmitted by cattle and other domestic livestock. Two national parks have been set up in India to protect the remaining wild water buffalo.

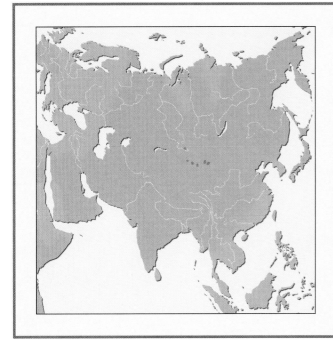

CAMEL, BACTRIAN
Camelus bactrianus

PHYLUM: Chordata
CLASS: Mammalia
ORDER: Artiodactyla
FAMILY: Camelidae
STATUS: Critically endangered, IUCN
Endangered, ESA
RANGE: China, Mongolia

Camel, bactrian

Camelus bactrianus

Description and biology

The bactrian camel and the better–known Arabian camel (*Camelus dromedarius*) are the only two living species of true camel. Whereas the Arabian camel has only one hump, the bactrian camel has two. An average bactrian camel stands 6 to 7.5 feet (1.8 to 2.3 meters) in height and weighs between 1,000 and 1,575 pounds (455 and 715 kilograms). The coat of a wild bactrian camel is short and gray-brown in color; that of a domestic or tame version of the animal is long and dark brown.

The bactrian camel is well adapted to its desert habitat. Its special eyelids help wipe sand from the surface of the animal's eye. Its nostrils close to slits to keep out blowing sand. Its broad, thick-soled feet allow it to move steadily and quickly over shifting sand, achieving speeds up to 40 miles per hour (64 kilometers per hour). The humps of the bactrian camel

Bactrian camels are well adapted to their desert environment. They are able to go for long periods without water by eating plants containing moisture.

store fat like those of other camels. When full, the humps are plump and erect. If the animal has not eaten for a period of time, the humps begin to shrink and sag to one side. Bactrian camels eat mostly low-lying desert shrubs; they also may eat grasses and the leaves of trees growing near water. The camels may go without drinking water for long periods of time only if they receive enough moisture from the plants they eat.

Male bactrian camels fight for the opportunity to mate with female bactrian camels. The competitions between males are quite fierce and some end in death. A dominant male will gather a group of 10 to 20 females with which to mate. After a gestation (pregnancy) period of almost 13 months, a female bactrian camel gives birth to a single infant, usually in March or April. The infant camel, weighing about 80 pounds (36 kilograms) at birth, nurses for at least its first year.

Habitat and current distribution

Wild bactrian camels inhabit desert and steppe (semiarid, grass-covered plain) areas in lowland and mountain regions. In Mongolia, they are found in and around the Great Gobi National Park, a protected area of the Gobi Desert located in southwestern Mongolia. Biologists (people who study living organisms) estimate that 350 camels live in this area. In China, an estimated 600 wild bactrian camels are found in the western provinces of Xinjiang (Sinkiang) and Gansu (Kansu).

History and conservation measures

Humans in China and Mongolia probably began to use bactrian camels as pack animals to carry supplies as far back as 2500 B.C. Up until the beginning of the twentieth century, the range of wild bactrian camels extended from Asia Minor to northern China. As human populations grew in this large area, the camels were confined to a smaller and smaller range.

Habitat loss continues to be a major threat to the bactrian camel. Both Chinese and Mongolian governments have declared the camel a protected species. Several reserves have been established to safeguard the animals: the Great Gobi National Park in Mongolia, the Annaba Nature Reserve in Gansu, and the Altun Mountain Nature Reserve in Xinjiang. However, wolves continually prey on bactrian camels in the Gobi Park, and those camels that stray outside of the park are often killed for food by humans. In 2000, China established a new park, the Arjin Shan Lop Nur Nature Reserve. The population is still in decline, and interbreeding with domestic camels has further reduced the population of genetically pure wild bactrian camels.

In 2002, the International Union for Conservation of Nature and Natural Resources (IUCN) raised the status of the wild bactrian camel from endangered to critically endangered. A series of five expeditions into China and Mongolia in the late 1990s produced data showing that the species faces a population size reduction of at least 80 percent within the next three generations due to continued hunting, increased killings by wolves, and breeding with domestic camels throughout the area. In China, illegal mining, gas-pipe installation, and proposed industrial development are rapidly destroying camel habitat. Because of the extreme threat to the survival of the species, conservation programs have become urgent. In 2002, there were only 15 wild bactrian camels in captivity in China and Mongolia. The species breeds slowly, so it is essential to begin breeding-in-captivity programs without delay in order to save the species from possible extinction in the next few decades.

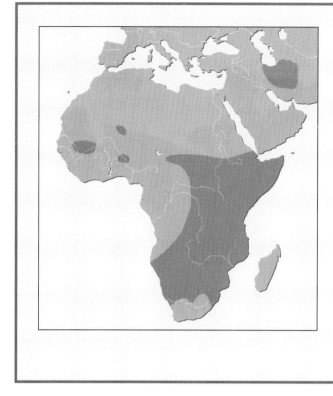

CHEETAH
Acinonyx jubatus

PHYLUM: Chordata
CLASS: Mammalia
ORDER: Carnivora
FAMILY: Felidae
STATUS: Vulnerable, IUCN
Endangered, ESA
RANGE: Afghanistan, Algeria,
Angola, Benin, Botswana, Burkina
Faso, Cameroon, Central African
Republic, Chad, Congo, Egypt,
Ethiopia, India, Iran, Jordan, Kenya,
Libya, Malawi, Mali, Mauritania,
Morocco, Mozambique, Namibia,
Niger, Nigeria, Pakistan, Saudi
Arabia, Senegal, Somalia, South
Africa, Sudan, Swaziland, Tanzania,
Togo, Uganda, Western Sahara,
Zambia, Zimbabwe

Cheetah
Acinonyx jubatus

Description and biology

"Cheetah" comes from the Hindu word *chita,* meaning "spotted one." Round black spots cover the cheetah's tawny fur and a black streak runs down each cheek. An average cheetah measures 4.5 to 5 feet (1.4 to 1.5 meters) long and stands between 27 and 34 inches (69 and 86 centimeters) high at its shoulder. Its tail extends 24 to 32 inches (61 to 81 centimeters). It weighs between 80 and 145 pounds (36 and 66 kilograms).

Cheetahs are the world's fastest land animal. They are capable of bursts of speed up to 70 miles per hour (110 kilometers per hour), but they usually cannot keep up this top speed for more than 1500 feet (455 meters).

A cheetah prowling for prey, which may include gazelles, wildebeest, antelope, warthogs, hares, and ground birds.

Unlike other cats, a cheetah cannot retract its claws. This physical feature allows the animal to dig into the ground as it runs, giving it speed. Whereas leopards and tigers ambush their prey, cheetahs chase their prey down. Because they exert themselves so much when catching prey, cheetahs often have to rest for up to half an hour before they can eat. Typical cheetah prey includes gazelles, wildebeest, antelope, warthogs, hares, and ground birds.

Male cheetahs often live with their male littermates (brothers) in groups called coalitions. Much more solitary, female cheetahs join their male counterparts only to mate. After a gestation (pregnancy) period of 90 to 95 days, a female cheetah gives birth to a litter of one to eight cubs, which she nurses for three months. Because she must provide her cubs with fresh kill almost every day, a female cheetah's hunting territory may cover as much as 310 square miles (800 square kilometers). She will frequently bring small, live prey to her cubs to help them develop hunting skills.

Habitat and current distribution

Cheetahs prefer to inhabit savannas and other arid (dry), open grasslands. The animals are now restricted to Africa south of the Sahara Desert. The largest number of cheetahs is found in Namibia and East Africa. Wildlife biologists (people who study living organisms) estimate that the total population ranges from 5,000 to 12,000. A small group of cheetahs numbering about 200 was found recently in northern Iran.

History and conservation measures

Cheetahs once ranged over Africa, Arabia, the Middle East, and northern India. Since they can be tamed, cheetahs have been kept for centuries by kings and noblemen as pets and hunting animals. In the mid-1950s, the cheetah population was estimated to be 28,000. Within twenty years, however, that number was cut in half.

Hunting and habitat destruction are the main causes for this drastic decline. Although cheetahs are legally protected in most countries, poachers still hunt them for their fur, which remains popular in Asia and Europe. Farmers also kill cheetahs, believing the animals might harm their livestock. As grassland is converted into pasture and agricultural land, cheetahs are confined to smaller and smaller areas, limiting their hunting ability.

Reserves have been set up in Africa, but in these protected areas cheetahs face fierce competition from predators such as lions and hyenas. Some African countries like Namibia have tried to introduce cheetahs into areas where they would face few animal or human predators.

CHIMPANZEE
Pan troglodytes

PHYLUM: Chordata
CLASS: Mammalia
ORDER: Primates
FAMILY: Pongidae
STATUS: Endangered, IUCN
Endangered, ESA
RANGE: Burundi, Cameroon,
Central African Republic, Congo,
Congo Republic, Côte d'Ivoire,
Equatorial Guinea, Gabon,
Gambia, Ghana, Guinea, Guinea-
Bissau, Liberia, Mali, Nigeria,
Rwanda, Senegal, Sierra Leone,
Sudan, Tanzania, Uganda

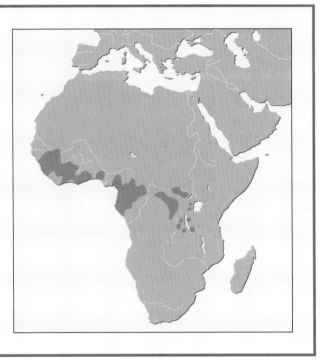

Chimpanzee

Pan troglodytes

Description and biology

Chimpanzees, gorillas, and orangutans are all considered great apes. Of the three, chimpanzees are the most closely related to humans. Chimpanzees and humans share 98 percent of the same genetic makeup. In addition, the two groups share many social and psychological traits. Researchers have documented chimpanzees making and using tools, expressing complex emotions, forming bonds and friendships, and communicating using sign language.

An average chimpanzee stands 5 feet (1.5 meters) tall and weighs about 150 pounds (68 kilograms). Since its arms are longer than its legs, a chimpanzee walks on the ground using the soles of its feet and the knuckles of its hands. Most of its body is covered with long, black hair. A chimpanzee's hair-

Because they are most closely related to humans, chimpanzees are often used as research subjects in medical experiments.

less face can range in color from almost white to almost black. The hair around a chimpanzee's face grays with age, and older chimpanzees often become bald.

Highly social mammals, chimpanzees live in communities made up of 30 to 60 members. During the day, the animals often travel on the ground. At night, they stay in nests they build in treetops. A chimpanzee's diet consists mainly of fruit, but they also eat insects, leaves, flowers, bark, seeds, tree resin, eggs, and meat. At times, chimpanzees band together to hunt animals such as antelopes and monkeys.

Mating between male and female chimpanzees takes place anytime during the year. Unlike many other animal species, female chimpanzees do not have to mate with the dominant male in their group. Instead, females often mate with males of their choosing. After a gestation (pregnancy) period of 230 to 240 days, a female chimpanzee gives birth to a single infant. During the course of her life, an average female chimpanzee will give birth to fewer than five infants. Bonds between mothers and infants are very strong, and some last a lifetime.

Habitat and current distribution

A few centuries ago, several million chimpanzees existed in the equatorial regions of Africa. They inhabited a range of ecosystems, from dense forests to open savannas. Now, estimates vary, but it is thought that there are between 200,000 and 225,000 chimpanzees in the wild, and many believe these estimates are high. Only 10 present-day African nations have chimpanzee populations above 1,000.

About 5,000 chimpanzees exist in captivity worldwide. Over one-half of these are used as subjects in medical research. The rest are zoo exhibits, entertainment props, and private pets.

History and conservation measures

Habitat destruction, disease, and expanding human populations have led to the decline in the number of chimpanzees. Mining has destroyed the chimpanzee habitat in the diamond districts of Sierra Leone and the iron districts of Liberia. The cutting of forests for timber has destroyed the animals' habitat in Uganda. And the conversion of forests into agricultural land has threatened chimpanzees in Rwanda and Burundi.

Certain laws prohibit the hunting and sale of chimpanzees, but these laws are not enforced. Many chimpanzees are caught and traded illegally. For each chimpanzee shipped overseas, ten die during transport due to mistreatment and malnutrition. Two sanctuaries exist in Gambia and Zambia for orphaned chimpanzees and those seized from illegal traders. Most African nations have passed laws and have set aside areas to protect chimpanzees. However, as human populations in Africa continue to grow, many of these reserves may be used to fill human needs.

In 2003, a group of scientists and conservationists called for an upgrade in the status of chimpanzees from endangered to critically endangered. Data coming from Gabon and the Republic of Congo, where most of the world's chimpanzees live, reveals that the ape population there has decreased by half between 1983 and 2000. The reasons for the decline were continued hunting and outbreaks among chimpanzees and gorillas of the Ebola virus, a very deadly and contagious virus that was discovered in Africa during the 1970s and afflicts humans as well. The group of scientists warned that chimpanzees and gorillas are in greater jeopardy of extinction than had been formerly realized. They called for greater enforcement of laws against hunting and capturing chimpanzees and an increased focus on research of the Ebola virus in primates.

CHINCHILLA, SHORT-TAILED
Chinchilla brevicaudata

PHYLUM: Chordata
CLASS: Mammalia
ORDER: Rodentia
FAMILY: Chinchillidae
STATUS: Critically endangered,
IUCN
Endangered, ESA
RANGE: Argentina, Bolivia, Chile,
Peru

Chinchilla, short-tailed
Chinchilla brevicaudata

Description and biology

The short-tailed chinchilla is a nocturnal (active at night) rodent with soft fur, large ears, and a bushy tail. It is one of two species of chinchilla—the other is the long-tailed chinchilla (*Chinchilla langiera*). An average chinchilla has a head and body length between 9 and 15 inches (23 and 38 centimeters) and a tail length between 3 and 6 inches (7.5 and 15 centimeters). Female chinchillas weigh up to 28 ounces (794 grams), while the smaller males weigh up to 18 ounces (510 grams). A chinchilla's silky fur is mostly gray in color. The animal's hind legs are much larger than its front legs, making it an agile jumper.

A chinchilla's diet includes leaves, seeds, fruits, and other vegetation. While eating, it often stands erect and holds the

The demand for the short–tailed chinchillas' fur has lead to the animals becoming endangered.

food with its forepaws. A female chinchilla may give birth to up to six infants at a time.

Habitat and current distribution

Short–tailed chinchillas prefer to live in the mountainous regions of Argentina, Bolivia, Chile, and Peru at elevations over 6,560 feet (2,000 meters). They live among crevices and rocks in barren areas covered with dense shrubs and grasses. The number of short-tailed chinchillas in the wild is unknown, but centuries of hunting has severely reduced their population.

History and conservation measures

Humans have prized chinchilla fur since the days of the Incas, native Quechuan people of Peru who established an empire in South America in the fifteenth century. Between 1895 and 1900, 1,680,000 chinchilla skins were exported from the country of Chile alone. Coats made from the animal's soft fur have sold for over $100,000. Since the 1920s, millions of chinchillas have been raised on farms for use in the fur industry.

Before laws were passed protecting wild chinchillas, hunters almost made the animals extinct. Reserves have been established to provide wild short-tailed chinchillas with a protected habitat, but illegal hunting still threatens their survival.

CIVET, MALABAR LARGE SPOTTED
Viverra civettina

PHYLUM: Chordata
CLASS: Mammalia
ORDER: Carnivora
FAMILY: Viverridae
STATUS: Critically endangered, IUCN
Endangered, ESA
RANGE: India

Civet, Malabar large spotted

Viverra civettina

Description and biology

The Malabar large spotted civet is nearly identical to, or is in fact the same species as, the large spotted civet (*Viverra megaspila*). Adults of this species usually weigh about 18 to 20 pounds (8 to 9 kilograms). Their long gray coats are mottled with large black spots. They have long tails banded in black and a black crest of long fur down their backs. Although most civets look like cats, the Malabar large spotted civet more closely resembles a dog with its long legs and dog-like head.

Malabar civets stay hidden in the thickets during the day and forage for food at night. They have never been seen in trees, and probably obtain their food on the ground. They are thought to eat eggs, small mammals, and some vegetation. Solitary animals, they can become aggressive when they encounter members of their own species. Female Malabar large spotted civets usually have from one to four offspring at a time, and they raise their young in the cover of thickets in the woods.

Habitat and current distribution

The original home of the Malabar large spotted civet was in the Western Ghats, a mountain range in southwest India. The species lived in the wooded plains and natural forests surrounding the mountains. Today the Malabar large spotted civet is one of the rarest mammals of the world. In 1999, it was estimated that there were less than 250 surviving adult animals in the wild. Small, scattered populations are thought to exist in certain areas of South Malabar.

History and conservation measures

At one time the Malabar large spotted civet roamed about southwest India in the districts of Malabar and Travancore. As more and more humans moved into the area, clearing it for residential, industrial, and agricultural purposes, the forests have nearly disappeared. With the elimination of its habitat, the Malabar large spotted civet population declined drastically. By the 1960s, the species was thought to be extinct. However, members of the species were found in the late 1980s, and some isolated groups are still known to exist. One of the reasons for the disappearance of the Malabar civet was that they were once hunted as a source of "civet musk," a product used in perfumes. The largest threat to the species, however, is the deforestation of its original habitat in the Western Ghats, which forces the population into tiny isolated areas. The refuge of the last remaining Malabar civets during the last decades of the twentieth century was the area's cashew plantations, which are not weeded and therefore provide the dense thickets the animals can use as their homes. These are now being cleared for rubber plantations.

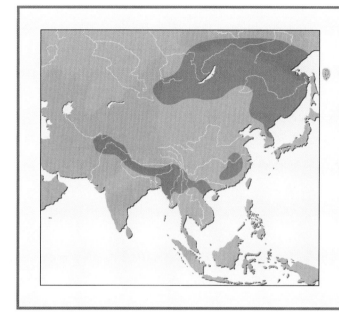

DEER, MUSK
Moschus spp. (all species)

PHYLUM: Chordata

CLASS: Mammalia

ORDER: Artiodactyla

FAMILY: Moschidae

STATUS: Vulnerable, IUCN
(*Moschus moschiferus*)
Endangered, ESA (all species)

RANGE: Afghanistan, Bhutan,
China, India, Mongolia, Myanmar,
Nepal, North Korea, Pakistan,
Russia, South Korea, Vietnam

Deer, musk

Moschus spp. (all species)

Description and biology

Musk deer are so-named because the males of the species have a gland, called the pod, that develops in the skin of their abdomen. This gland produces a waxy substance called musk, which may be used by males to attract females. An average musk deer has a head and body length of 28 to 39 inches (71 to 99 centimeters), stands 20 to 24 inches (51 to 91 centimeters) at its shoulder, and weighs between 15 and 40 pounds (7 and 18 kilograms). The musk deer's hair is long and coarse. It varies in color from dark to golden brown, depending on the species.

The hind legs of a musk deer are almost one-third larger than its front legs. This helps to make the animal a quick and agile jumper. Unlike most other deer, musk deer have no antlers. The upper canine teeth of male musk deer grow into narrow, pointed tusks that curve down and backward from the animal's mouth. Males use these 2.5- to 3-inch (6.3- to

Musk deer are often killed by hunters in order to obtain the animals' musk, which is used in perfumes and medicines.

7.6 -centimeter) teeth when fighting each other over the right to mate with females.

Mating takes place in November and December. A male musk deer pursues a female until she is too exhausted to run anymore. After a gestation (pregnancy) period of 150 to 198 days, a female musk deer gives birth to one or two infants, which are born with spotted coats.

Musk deer feed on leaves, flowers, twigs, mosses, grasses, and lichen (an organism formed by algae and fungus growing together) during morning and evening hours. Predators of musk deer include the lynx, wolf, fox, and yellow-throated marten (mammal related to the weasel and the mink).

Habitat and current distribution

Musk deer inhabit wet forests in the Himalayas, eastern Asia, and Siberia. During summer, the animals can be found in mountain forests ranging over 8,500 feet (2,600 meters) in elevation. They prefer dense vegetation and brush so they can easily find shelter during the day.

Wildlife biologists (people who study living organisms) are unsure of the total number of all species of musk deer in existence. They believe the population to be between 30,000 and 100,000. Of the five main species of musk deer, the Siberian musk deer (*Moschus moschiferus*) is the most threatened.

History and conservation measures

Humans have hunted musk deer not for their meat or hide, but solely for their musk, which is used in perfumes and medicines. Hunting and habitat destruction endanger the present-day survival of all musk deer species.

Musk deer do not have to be killed in order to extract their musk. A program to raise the animals and extract their musk without causing injury began in China in the late 1950s. After the program proved successful, similar programs were implemented in India, Nepal, and Russia.

DEER, SWAMP
Cervus duvauceli

PHYLUM: Chordata
CLASS: Mammalia
ORDER: Artiodactyla
FAMILY: Cervidae
STATUS: Vulnerable, IUCN
Endangered, ESA
RANGE: India, Nepal

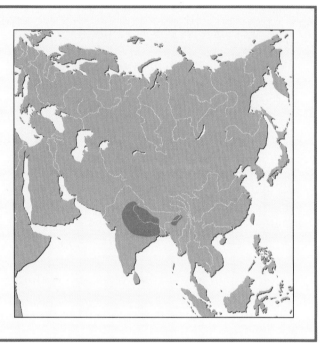

Deer, swamp

Cervus duvauceli

Description and biology

The swamp deer is a large member of the deer family. The animal has an average head and body length of 4 to 6 feet (1.2 to 1.8 meters), measures about 4 feet (1.2 meters) in height at its shoulder, and weighs between 375 and 620 pounds (170 and 280 kilograms). In winter, the swamp deer's coat is brown on the top part of its body and paler on its underside. In summer, the entire coat lightens in color. Male swamp deer are often darker overall than females. Swamp deer feed on grasses and aquatic plants, and their main predators are tigers and leopards.

In central India, swamp deer are known as barasingha, which means six-pointer. However, their 36- to 40-inch (91- to 102-centimeter) antlers can have 10 or more points. Antlers are solid, bony outgrowths of a deer's skull. The stem of an

antler is called the beam, while the branches are called the tines. Most male deer grow and shed antlers annually.

Like male deer of other species, male swamp deer use their antlers when competing with each other over the right to mate with females. A dominant male may mate with as many as 30 females during mating season, which lasts from September to April. After a gestation (pregnancy) period of 225 to 250 days, a female swamp deer gives birth to a single infant.

Habitat and current distribution

Swamp deer are found scattered throughout Nepal and northern, central, and far eastern India. Almost 5,000 swamp deer inhabit the marshy grasslands and floodplains of the northern regions. In the remaining habitat areas, about 600 swamp deer live in drier woodlands and fields.

Although often called barasingah (six–pointer) in India, swamp deers can have ten or more points on their antlers.

History and conservation measures

Scientists estimate that thousands of swamp deer lived along the major rivers of India during the nineteenth century. Now, most swamp deer live in protected reserves such as the Sukla Phanta Preserve in Nepal, the Dudhwa National Park in northern India, and the Kanha National Park in central India.

Habitat destruction has been the leading cause for the decline in the population of swamp deer. Illegal hunting and competition from other deer species for food and habitat also continue to threaten its existence.

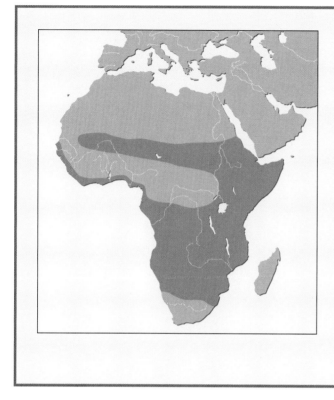

DOG, AFRICAN WILD
Lycaon pictus

PHYLUM: Chordata
CLASS: Mammalia
ORDER: Carnivora
FAMILY: Canidae
STATUS: Endangered, IUCN
Endangered, ESA
RANGE: Algeria, Angola, Benin,
Botswana, Burkina Faso, Burundi,
Cameroon, Central African
Republic, Chad, Congo, Congo
Republic, Côte d'Ivoire, Eritrea,
Ethiopia, Gabon, Gambia, Ghana,
Guinea, Kenya, Malawi, Mali,
Mozambique, Namibia, Niger,
Nigeria, Rwanda, Senegal, Sierra
Leone, Somalia, South Africa,
Sudan, Swaziland, Tanzania, Togo,
Uganda, Zambia, Zimbabwe

Dog, African wild

Lycaon pictus

Description and biology

The African wild dog, also called the African painted wolf,
has a streaked, multicolored coat. The tan, black, and white
pattern varies between individual dogs, but each animal's
head is usually dark. An African wild dog has large rounded
ears, which it uses to signal other dogs and to control body
temperature by radiating (giving off) heat. Its 12- to 16-inch
(30- to 41-centimeter) tail ends in a plume that is white-
tipped. The dog's legs are long and thin. An average African
wild dog has a head and body length of 30 to 44 inches (76
to 112 centimeters) and a shoulder height of 24 to 31 inches
(61 to 79 centimeters). It weighs between 37 and 79 pounds
(17 and 36 kilograms).

An African wild dog and her pups in their den. A female wild dog can give birth to up to 16 pups, but probably only half of these will survive infancy.

African wild dogs have a tightly knit social structure. They form packs of 2 to 45 members that hunt cooperatively. Prey includes impalas, antelopes, gazelles, zebras, wildebeest, and warthogs. The dogs are swift runners and can reach speeds up to 40 miles (64 kilometers) per hour. Their hunting range varies widely from 600 to 1,500 square miles (1,555 to 3,885 square kilometers).

In a pack, all males are related to each other and all females are related to each other, but males and females are not related. Male and female groups often travel from packs to join new ones. In most cases, mating takes place between the dominant male and dominant female in a pack. After a gestation (pregnancy) period of 69 to 72 days, a female African wild dog gives birth to up to 16 pups. About half of these pups do not survive infancy. All members of the pack care for the pups, which are allowed to eat first after the pack makes a kill.

Habitat and current distribution

African wild dogs are found throughout Africa south of the Sahara Desert. The animals prefer to inhabit grasslands, savannas, or open woodlands. Biologists (people who study living organisms) estimate that about 5,000 African wild dogs currently exist in the world.

History and conservation measures

African wild dogs were once common throughout the African continent. At the beginning of the twentieth century, packs of 100 or more dogs roamed the Serengeti Plain in northern Tanzania. Today, the total number of African wild dogs on the Serengeti is fewer than 60.

As the human population in Africa has grown, wild dog habitat has decreased. The animals have also suffered because of the widespread—but unfounded—belief they are pests. In many areas in Africa, people have shot, poisoned, and trapped them. The greatest threat to African wild dogs, however, is increased contact with domestic dogs. Canine diseases such as distemper and rabies run rampant when introduced into an African wild dog pack.

The breeding of African wild dogs in zoos has been moderately successful.

DOLPHIN, CHINESE RIVER
Lipotes vexillifer

PHYLUM: Chordata
CLASS: Mammalia
ORDER: Cetacea
FAMILY: Platanistidae
STATUS: Critically endangered, IUCN
Endangered, ESA
RANGE: China

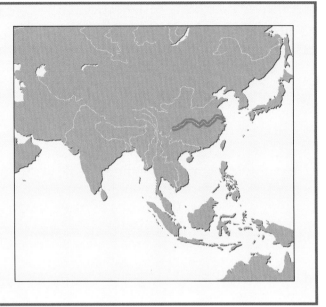

Dolphin, Chinese river

Lipotes vexillifer

Description and biology

The Chinese river dolphin, also known as baiji, is one of the most rare and endangered cetaceans (pronounced si–TAY–shuns; the order of aquatic mammals that includes whales, dolphins, and porpoises). It has an average overall length of 6.75 to 8.25 feet (2 to 2.5 meters) and weighs between 220 and 500 pounds (100 and 230 kilograms). Its body color is blue-gray on top and almost white underneath.

Chinese river dolphins have very poor eyesight, which is an evolutionary result of the muddy conditions of the water in which they live. Since the dolphins could not use their vision, they lost it over the course of time. The species adapted to this loss by developing the ability to use echolocation (sonar). In this process, the dolphin emits a sound wave that bounces off objects and is echoed or reflected back to the dolphin. Like bats, Chinese river dolphins use echolocation to navigate and to find prey.

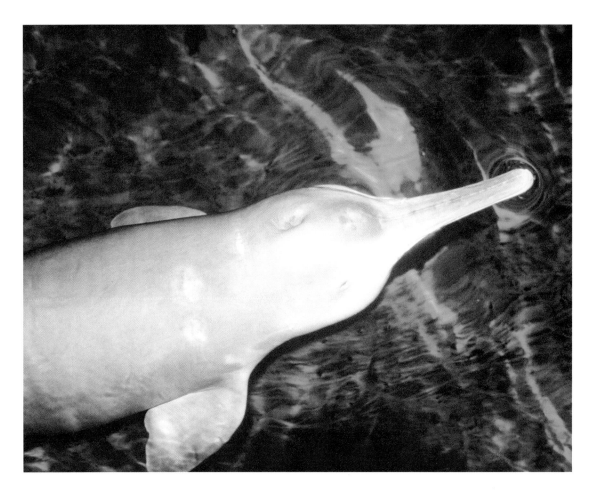

The dolphins usually travel in pairs or in groups of up to ten. The mating season for Chinese river dolphins occurs between March and May and again between August and October. A female dolphin gives birth to a single calf after a gestation (pregnancy) period of 10 to 11 months. During its first year, the young dolphin may swim behind its mother or the mother may carry it with her flipper.

Habitat and current distribution

Chinese river dolphins are found only in the Changjiang (Yangtze River) in China. They inhabit the middle and lower reaches of the main river and often congregate where fish gather, such as around sandbanks or where tributaries and lakes connect to the main river. Scientists estimate that the entire population of Chinese river dolphins is less than 200.

Chinese river dolphins have very poor eyesight, which is an evolutionary result of the muddy conditions of the water in which they live. Dolphins adapted by developing the ability to use echolocation (sonar) to navigate and to find prey.

DID YOU KNOW?

On August 8, 1997, the Beijing Natural History Museum opened the world's first major museum exhibition on the Chinese River dolphin. *Baiji: Treasure in the Yangtze River* featured slide programs, puppet shows, and media news stories on the plight of the baiji and the deteriorating conditions of the Yangtze River. The exhibition ran for three months, then traveled to museums in other Chinese cities throughout 1998. The baiji exhibit was to be the first in a yearly series of endangered species exhibits sponsored by the Beijing museum.

History and conservation measures

Many factors have led to the current critically endangered status of the Chinese river dolphin. Fishermen on the Changjiang often try to snag bottom-feeding fish by dragging hooks along the river's bottom. This illegal fishing method accounts for about one-half of the known Chinese river dolphin deaths. Other dolphins are killed by boat propellers, especially in the lower region of the river where boat traffic is dense. A number of dolphins are killed when construction crews use explosives to build dams along the river. When built, dams and other barriers on the Changjiang destroy the dolphins' habitat and food sources, leading to further deaths.

Since the late 1970s, the Chinese government has tried to protect the Chinese river dolphin. Programs are being developed to establish reserve areas on the river where fishing and fast boat traffic would be prohibited. Unless drastic conservation measures are taken, however, the Chinese river dolphin will become extinct in the wild.

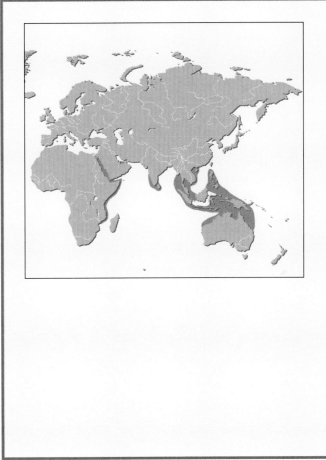

DUGONG
Dugong dugon

PHYLUM: Chordata
CLASS: Mammalia
ORDER: Sirenia
FAMILY: Dugongidae
STATUS: Vulnerable, IUCN Endangered, ESA
RANGE: Indian and Pacific Oceans: Australia, Bahrain, Bangladesh, Cambodia, China, Djibouti, Egypt, Eritrea, Guam, India, Indonesia, Iran, Iraq, Israel, Japan, Jordan, Kenya, Democratic People's Republic of Korea, Korea, Republic of, Kuwait, Madagascar, Malaysia, Maldives, Mauritius, Micronesia, Mozambique, Myanmar, New Caledonia, Oman, Palau, Papua New Guinea, Philippines, Saudi Arabia, Singapore, Solomon Islands, Somalia, South Africa, Sri Lanka, Sudan, Taiwan, Tanzania, Thailand, United Arab Emirates, Vanuatu, Vietnam, Yemen

Dugong
Dugong dugon

Description and biology

Dugongs are very large sea mammals, sometimes called "sea cows." They have been familiar to humans for centuries, particularly because, for some reason, these ungainly creatures gave rise to the mermaid myths of the past. Adult dugongs, both male and female, range in size from 8 to 13 feet (2.4 to 4 meters). They weigh between 500 and 1,100 pounds (230 to 500 kilograms) and have a big roll of fat around their bodies.

Dugongs are gray or rusty brown in color; their young, called calves, are born a creamy beige and then darken as they grow. Although dugongs breathe air into their lungs like land mammals, they live in the ocean and never come onto land. They are able to stay underwater for up to about six minutes at a time, but their dives usually last only one to three minutes before they come up for air. They have nostrils near the top of their long snouts on a large lip that can reach up to the water's surface to make breathing easier. Dugongs have a broad flat tail with a notch at its center and paddle-shaped flippers. They flap their tails in an up-and-down motion to propel them through the water, steering and balancing with their flippers.

Dugongs are herbivores (plant eaters) who graze on sea grasses on the ocean floors in warm shallow waters. Although their eyesight is poor, they have bristles on the lips of their snouts that help them find the grasses they eat. They spend a good deal of their time grazing.

Dugongs are social animals. At one time they were known to travel in large herds of several hundred or even thousands of animals. Since their numbers have declined, they usually travel in herds of about six animals. Not much is known about this shy species, but evidence suggests that lasting bonds form between mated dugongs and also that there are distinct family groups within the larger herd. Aggressive behavior is not normal. Dugongs make whistling sounds among themselves that communicate fear; calves make a bleating sound. Mating takes place throughout the year. Females give birth to one offspring at a time, and they generally give birth only once every three to seven years. A newborn calf is delivered in shallow water, and is able to swim immediately to the surface for air. The offspring will stay with the mother for about a year. Sexual maturity occurs at about 10 years of age or later. Dugongs in the wild can live to be up to 70 years old. Because they live a long time and breed at a slow rate, they cannot recover quickly from population declines and they are thus more threatened by them.

Habitat and current distribution

Scientific data on dugong distribution are not very advanced. Dugongs prefer to live in undisturbed, isolated areas in shallow waters of tropical seas with abundant sea grass beds. They are found in the Pacific and Indian Oceans within a very

wide range, but the populations within this range are scattered. Currently there are populations of dugong in waters around Australia, New Guinea, Sri Lanka, Indonesia, the Pacific Islands, the Persian Gulf, the Red Sea, and off the coast of east Africa. The number of dugong worldwide was estimated at the end of the 1990s at approximately 100,000. Australia has the largest population. Many areas report significant declines in the population.

Dugongs are herbivores (plant-eaters) who graze on sea grasses on the ocean floors in warm shallow waters.

History and conservation measures

The dugong is reported in the literature of the ancient world: it was seen in Greece, in Egypt, and in the Mediterranean, but there have not been dugong in those areas for centuries. Dugong populations have disappeared from their former habitats off several island groups in the Indian Ocean.

They are declining around Guam and along the mainland coast of eastern Asia. A very serious decline has occurred along the coasts of India, southwestern Asia, Africa, and Madagascar. The Torres Strait off Australia, where the dugong has always been abundant, has also lost significant numbers due to overhunting. Aboriginal and Torres Strait Islanders, indigenous (native) people of Australia for whom the animal is a traditional food, are exempt from laws against hunting dugong, and kill an estimated 750 animals a year.

Dugongs have natural enemies, but their biggest threat comes from humans and is largely due to hunting. Dugong meat is said to taste like tender veal. Dugong hide has been used to make good-quality leather. There is also a strong market for dugong oil, bones, and teeth. Dugongs are still legally hunted in some parts of their range. Humans also kill the dugong by accident. Coastal areas in which the dugong have lived are increasingly being used for residential, recreational, and agricultural purposes. Shark nets set up around beaches to protect swimmers from predators trap and kill dugongs regularly. Gill nets used by fisherman also trap the dugong. Increasing boat traffic has taken a toll. Pollution has resulted in the loss of sea grass beds essential to their survival. Other enemies to the dugong are sharks and some other sea predators. Hurricanes at sea sometimes strand dugongs.

In Australia dugongs are protected and there are a number of programs in progress to restore the sea grass beds and protect the natural habitat of the dugong. Net fishing has been banned in dugong areas, and fishermen have been required to take a course on endangered species in order to stop unnecessary accidents. Many of Australia's indigenous communities have agreed to stop hunting the animal and are educating their populations about dugong management. At beaches, alternatives to shark nets are being used to protect swimmers without endangering dugong. Further research about the species is underway. Worldwide, protection of the dugong and its habitat is inconsistent.

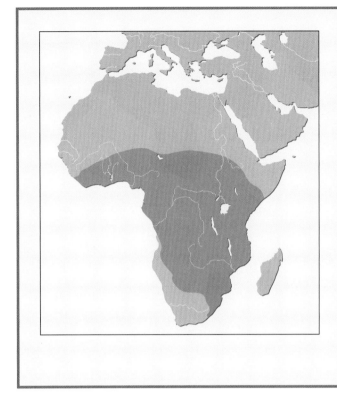

ELEPHANT, AFRICAN
Loxodonta africana

PHYLUM: Chordata

CLASS: Mammalia

ORDER: Proboscidea

FAMILY: Elephantidae

STATUS: Endangered, IUCN Threatened, ESA

RANGE: Angola, Benin, Botswana, Burkina Faso, Cameroon, Central African Republic, Chad, Congo, Congo Republic, Côte d'Ivoire, Equatorial Guinea, Ethiopia, Gabon, Ghana, Guinea, Kenya, Liberia, Malawi, Mali, Mauritania, Mozambique, Namibia, Niger, Nigeria, Rwanda, Senegal, Sierra Leone, Somalia, South Africa, Sudan, Tanzania, Togo, Uganda, Zambia, Zimbabwe

Elephant, African
Loxodonta africana

Description and biology

The African elephant is the world's largest living land mammal. An average adult male stands 10 feet (3 meters) tall at its shoulder and weighs between 11,000 and 13,000 pounds (5,000 and 5,900 kilograms). Females are a little shorter in height and weigh about 8,000 pounds (3,600 kilograms). The animal's thick and loose skin is dark, muddy gray in color. Its large ears, up to 42 inches (107 centimeters) in diameter, hold many prominent veins. To cool its blood during the heat of the day, the African elephant flaps its ears vigorously. Its long, white tusks are actually elongated incisor teeth. It has only four other teeth, all molars, that it uses to grind down food. These teeth are replaced up to six times as they wear

Even though conservation efforts have been established, African elephants continue to be in danger due to illegal hunting for their ivory tusks.

away periodically during an average elephant's seventy-year life span.

Besides its tusks, a unique feature of the elephant is its trunk, which is an extension of its nose and upper lip. The animal uses its trunk for drinking, bathing, smelling, breathing, feeling, greeting, communicating, and grasping. The African elephant has two fingerlike tips at the end of its trunk that are sensitive enough to pick up very small objects.

African elephants are herbivores (plant-eaters), consuming tree bark, fruits, grasses, and leaves of trees and shrubs. They require approximately 300 to 400 pounds (135 to 180 kilograms) of food and 50 gallons (190 liters) of water a day. The animals never stray far from a source of water, which they use for drinking, bathing, and cooling. After bathing each day, the elephants coat themselves in dust and dirt for protection against insects.

Elephants are social animals that form strong family ties. Family units or herds are made up of females (called cows) and their young (calves). The entire herd is led by an older cow called the matriarch, to which all other members of the herd are related. When a member of the herd dies, other members "grieve" over the loss, covering the dead elephant with leaves and twigs and staying by the grave for hours.

Older male elephants (bulls) live by themselves or with other males in small groups called bachelor herds. They associate with females only to breed. After a gestation (pregnancy) period of almost two years, a female elephant gives birth to a single calf, which weighs between 200 and 300 pounds (90 and 136 kilograms). Other females are often present during the birth and help keep predators away. The calf nurses for at least two years and remains dependent on the mother for four to five years.

Habitat and current distribution

African elephants are found in most areas of Africa south of the Sahara Desert. Those elephants living in central or western Africa inhabit forest areas, while the elephants in the eastern and southern regions of the continent live in savanna and bush habitats. In 1998 elephant specialists estimated the African elephant population on the entire continent of Africa to be a "definite" 301,773 animals, or a "speculative" total of 487,345 animals. Since many areas were not surveyed and because elephants in the forests are difficult to count, these figures are rough.

History and conservation measures

African elephants have been hunted for centuries for their tusks, which are composed of ivory. This substance has been used to make items ranging from jewelry to piano keys. The animals once ranged in northern Africa up to the Mediterranean coast, but they became extinct there during the European Middle Ages (450–1450).

As the human population in Africa continues to grow, the elephant's habitat continues to shrink. In the late 1970s, African elephants numbered approximately 1,500,000. Less the 20 years later, that number has been decreased by two-thirds.

The greatest threat to the future of African elephants continues to be poaching, or illegal killing. Steps have been taken to protect the animals from poachers. Several African countries have established elephant conservation programs. National parks and reserve areas have been set aside to safeguard the animals and allow tourists to see them in their natural habitat.

In 1989, the Convention on International Trade in Endangered Species of Wild Fauna and Flora (CITES; an international treaty to protect wildlife) adopted a ban on the sale of elephant ivory. The international market for ivory immediately decreased. In June 1997, that ban was lifted when a majority of CITES member nations voted to allow the African countries of Botswana, Namibia, and Zimbabwe to sell 59 tons of stockpiled elephant tusks to Japan. The sale, estimated to bring in $30,000,000, was allowed as a reward for the conservation efforts of the three countries. Opponents of the sale believed it would simply encourage renewed African elephant slaughters by poachers.

ELEPHANT, ASIAN
Elephas maximus

PHYLUM: Chordata
CLASS: Mammalia
ORDER: Proboscidea
FAMILY: Elephantidae
STATUS: Endangered, IUCN
Endangered, ESA
RANGE: Bangladesh, Bhutan,
Brunei, Cambodia, China, India,
Indonesia, Laos, Malaysia,
Myanmar, Nepal, Sri Lanka,
Thailand, Vietnam

Elephant, Asian
Elephas maximus

Description and biology

The Asian elephant, also known as the Indian elephant, is smaller than its relative, the African elephant. An average male Asian elephant weighs up to 11,500 pounds (5,220 kilograms) and stands 8.5 feet (2.6 meters) tall at its shoulder. Females of the species are slightly shorter in height and weigh up to 6,000 pounds (2,270 kilograms). The elephant has an arched back and a flat forehead. Its ears are smaller and its trunk shorter and smoother than those of the African elephant.

The Asian elephant's trunk, which is an extension of its nose and upper lip, has one fingerlike tip at the end that is used to grasp food and other items. Elephants also use their trunks for drinking, bathing, smelling, breathing, feeling, greeting, and communicating. All of the animals can create a variety of sounds with their trunks, from rumbling noises to the well–known trumpeting sound.

Unlike African elephants, only some male Asian elephants (and no females) have tusks, which are enlarged incisor teeth. Like its relative, the Asian elephant has four molar teeth, which are replaced up to six times during its lifetime. When the final set of teeth are worn out, the elephant can no longer chew its food, and it dies of starvation.

Asian elephants feed on more than 100 species of plants, including grasses, leaves, twigs, roots, and bark. The animals spend 17 to 18 hours foraging for the 330 pounds (150 kilograms) of food they require each day. They need large areas of forest habitat to supply this food, but they never travel far from a source of water, which they use daily for drinking and bathing.

Elephants have a close and complex social structure. Related females (mothers, daughters, sisters) and their young form herds headed by an older related female, called the matriarch. Older males live singly or together in a small group known as a bachelor herd. The relationships elephants form with each other last a lifetime, which is up to 70 years. When a member of a herd dies, the other members cover the dead body with leaves and twigs, then remain at the site for hours.

Males and females associate with each other only for mating and sometimes for feeding. After a gestation (pregnancy) period of 18 to 22 months, a female Asian elephant gives birth to a single calf. The calf nurses and remains dependent on its mother for three to four years.

Habitat and current distribution

Asian elephants once ranged from Iraq to southern China. They now occupy the forests and jungles of India, Sri Lanka, China, Indonesia, and southeast Asia. Biologists (people who study living organisms) estimate that about 55,000 Asian elephants remain in the wild, occupying a habitat of only about 190,000 square miles (492,000 square kilometers). The largest population is found in India.

History and conservation measures

Humans have domesticated Asian elephants for centuries, using them to carry people and goods. The elephants have been used extensively in the timber industry, carrying items such as logs with their trunks.

Because many Asian elephants do not have tusks, they have not been hunted to supply the ivory trade as much as African elephants have (tusks are composed of ivory, a substance that has been used to make items ranging from jewelry to piano keys). Nevertheless, the Asian elephant faces greater threats to its existence than its African relative.

Deforestation, the loss of forests as they are cut down to produce timber or to make land available for agriculture, has had a devastating impact on Asian elephants. The animals need large forest areas to supply their daily food needs. Growing human populations in the region (in India alone, the human population has more than tripled in the twentieth century) have converted vast areas of forested land into farmland. As a result, much of the elephant's habitat has been reduced, and they are forced to live in pockets of forest surrounded by cultivated land.

Although not commonly hunted for their tusks, Asian elephants are in greater risk of extinction than their larger relatives because of habitat loss due to deforestation.

Seeking food, they often eat crops planted on farms that were once their feeding grounds. This brings them into greater conflict with humans.

Asian elephants are still used in the Asian timber industry. Unless protected areas for the animals and human populations stabilize in the region, the continued survival of Asian elephants is in jeopardy.

FERRET, BLACK–FOOTED
Mustela nigripes

PHYLUM: Chordata

CLASS: Mammalia

ORDER: Carnivora

FAMILY: Mustelidae

STATUS: Extinct in the wild, IUCN Endangered, ESA

RANGE: USA (reintroduced in Arizona, Colorado, Montana, New Mexico, South Dakota, Utah, and Wyoming)

Ferret, black-footed
Mustela nigripes

Description and biology

The black–footed ferret is a member of the weasel family (other members include weasels, martens, fishers, otters, minks, wolverines, and skunks). Similar in size to a mink, the back–footed ferret has a long, slender body covered in short, pale yellow fur. On its throat and belly, the fur is nearly white. The animal has a brownish head, a brownish–black mask across its eyes, black feet and legs, and a black tip on its tail. An average black–footed ferret has a body length of 18 to 22 inches (46 to 59 centimeters) and a tail length of 4.5 to 5.5 inches (11.5 to 14 centimeters). It weighs 18 to 36 ounces (510 to 1,021 grams).

Black–footed ferrets prey on prairie dogs and live in prairie dog burrows. They hunt at night and are rarely active above ground during the day. Ferrets also eat mice, voles, ground squirrels, gophers, birds, and insects. They are preyed upon by great–horned owls, golden eagles, coyotes, and badgers.

Although still extremely endangered, the once thought to be extinct black–footed ferret is beginning to make a comeback due to successful captive–breeding programs.

Ferrets are solitary animals. They move around a territorial range of about 100 acres (40 hectares), which they mark with musk from scent glands. Males often have a larger range than females. The two sexes come together only to mate in March and April. After a gestation (pregnancy) period of 41 to 45 days, a female black–footed ferret gives birth to three to five infants, called kits. The kits do not come out of the burrow until they are six weeks old. Then the mother separates the kits into different burrows, where they learn to take care of themselves. By early fall, they are on their own. Most kits do not survive their first year, and most adult ferrets do not live more than a few years.

Habitat and current distribution

Black–footed ferrets once ranged throughout the Great Plains—from Texas to southern Saskatchewan, Canada, and from the Rocky Mountains to the Dakotas, Nebraska, and Kansas. Considered one of the most endangered mammals in the United States, the black–footed ferret did not exist in the wild between 1987 and 1991.

History and conservation measures

When American pioneers moved west across the plains in the nineteenth and early twentieth centuries, they destroyed prairie dog habitat in order to create land for livestock and agriculture. The use of poison and hunting and habitat destruction reduced the prairie dog population by 90 percent. As prairie dogs and their habitat disappeared, so did the food sources and habitat for black–footed ferrets. A severe plague of canine distemper (viral disease) in the 1950s further reduced the small number of remaining black–footed ferrets.

Because no black–footed ferrets were found in the wild between 1972 and 1981, the animal was thought to be extinct. However, in 1981, a small population of ferrets was discovered near Meeteetse, Wyoming. The population increased over the next few years, but an outbreak of canine distemper in 1985 severely threatened the survival of the species.

In 1987, the U.S. Fish and Wildlife Service (USFWS) placed the last 18 known wild black–footed ferrets in a captive breeding facility. The goal of this program is to maintain a breeding population of black–footed ferrets in captivity and to return their offspring to the wild. In 1991, 49 captive–bred, young ferrets were released into the Shirley Basin in Wyoming. Several of these animals survived the winter and bred successfully. Since 1991, 200 captive–bred ferrets have been released in Wyoming.

The captive breeding programs that followed have been highly successful. By 1998, the captive breeding programs were producing record–breaking numbers of kits, many of which were reintroduced to the wilderness. In 1998 alone, 94 kits were released in South Dakota's Conata Basin/Badlands National Park. Montana received 77 kits in two sites, Arizona received 29, New Mexico 7, and 10 went to an experimental area in Colorado and Utah. Ferrets have also been successfully released in the wild in Mexico. All of these reintroduced ferret populations have produced healthy numbers of litters in the wild. Between South Dakota and Montana, an estimated 100 kits were born in the wild in 1998 alone. In the fall of 2002, ferrets were released at a new managed prairie dog/black–footed ferret site on the Rosebud Sioux Reservation in South Dakota. The tribe has been active in conservation of the prairie ecosystems (the ecological community, including plants, animals, and microorganisms, considered together with their environment), and will take a leading role in ferret recovery on their lands, where a population of 200–400 ferrets is expected.

The U.S. Fish and Wildlife Service reports that there are limited sites in North America with suitable prairie dog populations to support the self–sustaining ferret population currently being released in the wild. Further work on managing prairie dog populations and their habitat is needed in order to keep up the progress made on the recovery of the black–footed ferret in the wild.

FOX, ISLAND GRAY
Urocyon littoralis

PHYLUM: Chordata
CLASS: Mammalia
ORDER: Carnivora
FAMILY: Canidae
STATUS: Lower risk: conservation dependent, IUCN
Proposed Endangered, ESA
RANGE: USA (California)

Fox, island gray
Urocyon littoralis

Description and biology

While the island gray fox is mostly gray, its belly and throat are white, and the sides of its neck and the underside of its tail are rust. Black markings often accent its face and limbs. An average island gray fox has a head and body length of 20 inches (50 centimeters) and stands roughly 5 inches (13 centimeters) tall at its shoulder. Its tail can extend in length from 4.5 to 11.5 inches (11.4 to 29.2 centimeters). It weighs between 3 and 6 pounds (1.3 and 2.7 kilograms).

The island gray fox hunts for food primarily in the early morning and late evening. Insects and fruits constitute the main portion of its diet, with small mammals, birds, reptiles, and eggs making up the remainder.

Male and female foxes come together to mate between December and March. A female island gray fox usually gives birth to a litter of one to eight pups after a gestation (pregnancy)

The island gray fox is found only on the six largest Santa Barbara Islands (also known as the Channel Islands) that extend along the southern coast of California

period of 50 to 60 days. The mother nurses her pups for six weeks while the father hunts for food in a range of about 3 square miles (7.7 square kilometers).

Habitat and current distribution

The island gray fox lives in a variety of habitats, including grassland, coastal scrub, sand dune, and forest areas. It is found only on the six largest Santa Barbara Islands (also known as the Channel Islands) that extend along the southern coast of California. Scientists believe that the Channel Islands split off from mainland California some 11,500 years ago and that the islands then broke apart from each other over the next 2,000 years. The island foxes evolved separately from mainland foxes and from each other, forming unique subspecies on each island.

History and conservation measures

A study of island gray foxes was begun in 1993 by biologists (scientists who study living organisms) on San Miguel Island. This has revealed that the population of island gray foxes on the island has declined from 450 animals in 1994 to fewer than 40 animals. It is believed that similar declines have occurred on the other islands. Destruction of its limited habitat is the main threat to the animal's continued existence. Other threats include competition for food from feral (once domesticated, now wild) cats and possible diseases from domestic dogs.

The remoteness of the Santa Barbara Islands makes protection of the island gray fox difficult. The U.S. Navy is attempting to eliminate feral cats on the islands of San Clemente and San Nicolas. Also, the Los Angeles Zoo is considering establishing a program to breed island gray foxes in captivity.

GAZELLE, DAMA
Gazella dama

PHYLUM: Chordata
CLASS: Mammalia
ORDER: Artiodactyla
FAMILY: Bovidae
STATUS: Endangered, IUCN
Proposed Endangered, ESA
RANGE: Algeria, Chad, Libya,
Mali, Mauritania, Morocco, Niger,
Senegal, Sudan, Western Sahara

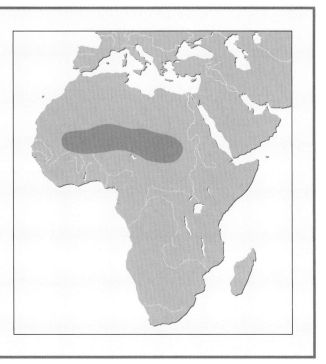

Gazelle, dama

Gazella dama

Description and biology

The dama gazelle, a graceful antelope found in the Sahara Desert region of Africa, has long legs, a long neck, and ringed horns curved back in the shape of a lyre (musical instrument). Its neck and a portion of its back are reddish brown in color, while the rest of its body is white (including one spot on the inside of its neck). An average dama gazelle has a head and body length of 40 to 67 inches (102 to 170 centimeters) and measures 35 to 42 inches (89 and 107 centimeters) high at its shoulder. Its tail, white with a black tip, extends 9 to 12 inches (23 to 30 centimeters). The animal weighs between 90 and 185 pounds (41 and 84 kilograms).

Like most species of gazelle, the dama gazelle has keen senses of hearing and smell. It grazes on shrubs and trees such as acacia and desert date. This gazelle travels alone or in small

groups in search of food. A female dama gazelle gives birth usually to one infant after a gestation (pregnancy) period of 160 to 220 days.

A female dama gazelle nursing her young.

Habitat and current distribution

Once populous in the countries of Libya and Morocco, the dama gazelle is now virtually extinct in northern Africa. The animal currently ranges across several countries in central and western Africa. A few thousand are found in Mali, Chad, and Niger. Only very small and scattered populations survive in other African countries.

In its range, the dama gazelle inhabits the arid (dry) grassy zone between the Sahara and the Sahel (an semiarid area south of the Sahara). It prefers to live on stony or rocky terrain, especially around the edges of hills.

History and conservation measures

Like many other gazelle species, the dama gazelle is vanishing from its traditional range because of illegal hunting, habitat destruction, and competition for food from domestic livestock.

Although protected areas exist in the dama gazelle's range, such as the Ouadi Rime–Ouadi Achim Faunal Reserve in Chad and the Aïr and Ténère National Nature Reserve in Niger, they afford the animal little security. Illegal hunting, especially from motor vehicles, occurs inside and outside the reserves. The need to feed an expanding human population also threatens the animals. Dama gazelle habitat is disappearing as irrigation and other agricultural methods have turned African deserts and grasslands into farmland. Facing competition from grazing livestock, dama gazelles have been forced to move south of their usual range in search of food. Such movement has brought the animals into even greater contact with humans. The result has been increased hunting.

The future of the dama gazelle is not certain, but some recovery programs are underway. The species was extinct in Senegal, but it has been reintroduced there. By 1997, there were at least 25 animals living in Senegal as part of a semi–captive breeding program.

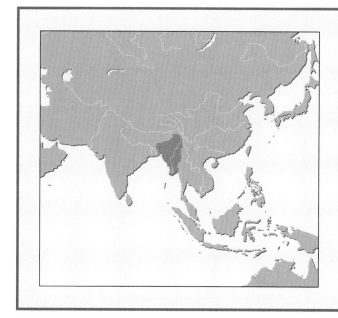

GIBBON, HOOLOCK
Bunipithecus hoolock

PHYLUM: Chordata
CLASS: Mammalia
ORDER: Primates
FAMILY: Hylobatidae
STATUS: Endangered, IUCN
RANGE: Bangladesh, China, India, Myanmar, Laos, Thailand

Gibbon, hoolock
Bunipithecus hoolock

Description and biology

Gibbons are apes, related to gorillas and chimpanzees, but they are known as "lesser apes" because of their small size. There are 13 or more kinds of gibbons. Hoolock gibbons are the second–largest kind, generally growing to about 13 pounds (6 kilograms). Adults are about 24 to 35 inches (60 to 90 centimeters) long and have no tail. Male hoolocks have black fur with white eyebrows, while females have beige or red–brown fur with dark brown eyebrows and cheek areas.

Gibbons are amazing acrobats when it comes to brachiating, or swinging by their arms among the treetops. Hoolocks' bodies are built for this movement. They have very long arms and long, hook–shaped hands. They swing by their arms from one branch to another, with their hand forming a hook on the limb. They are capable of leaping long distances through the air from branch to branch or running atop the leaves in the treetops. Their diet is made up mainly of fruit and leaves,

Hoolock gibbons generally sleep sitting up in one or two favored treetops. When they need to come down from the trees, hoolocks walk on two feet in an upright position.

along with some insects and flowers. Figs are a favorite food. Hoolocks are diurnal, meaning they roam the forests during the day and sleep at night. A family of hoolocks generally sleeps sitting up in one or two favored treetops. When they need to come down from the trees, hoolocks walk on two feet in an upright position.

Most gibbons live in family units consisting of two parents with several immature offspring. They are monogamous (when the male and female become partners, they remain together for life). Gibbons generally give birth to one offspring at a time. Baby hoolock gibbons are born with no hair and depend upon their mothers for warmth. The offspring usually stay with their parents until they are six to nine years old and have reached sexual maturity. Each gibbon family group lives within its own specific territory, usually about 30 to 50 acres (12 to 20 hectares) in area, which they defend from the intrusion of other gibbons. The life span of a gibbon in the wild is not known, but is probably about 30 to 40 years.

Hoolocks, like other gibbons, are very musical mammals, with a distinctive form of vocal communication displayed in half–hour–long morning songs performed by the family each day. The male and female partners sing a kind of duet together, and then other members of the family may join in to sing solos. These morning songs communicate to other gibbons that the hoolock family's area is claimed and will be defended, and may also serve as mating calls from the younger family members. The folklore of the indigenous (native) people of Southeast Asia includes many stories about this magical music of the rain forests. Unfortunately, these morning songs also inform hunters of the location of the gibbon families.

The only known enemy to hoolock gibbons is the human being.

Habitat and current distribution

Gibbons have lived in the forests of Southeast Asia for millions of years. The hoolock is found in tropical (a climate warm enough year–round to sustain plant life) and subtropical evergreen forests, and in mountain forests produced by seasonal monsoons (heavy rainfalls accompanying high winds). Currently hoolocks live in Myanmar (formerly Burma), Bangladesh, the northeastern part of India, and the southwestern part of China. There are two subspecies of hoolock gibbons, the eastern and western. They are divided by the Chindwin River in Myanmar. Hoolocks range from the Brahmaputra River (in Bangladesh, India, and China) on the west to the Salween River (in China and Myanmar) on the east.

History and conservation measures

The habitat in which hoolock gibbons live is shrinking rapidly. The tropical and subtropical forests are being cut down and burned in order to make way for tea plantations and other crops, for logging and taking out other fuel, and also for human settlement.

As their habitat is fragmented by the clearing of forests, hoolock gibbons become more vulnerable to humans, since they must come down from the treetops to cross from one food source to the next. Humans hunt hoolocks for food and to sell as pets, and gibbon bones and meat are valued in some traditional Asian medicines. Among some groups in Myanmar, for example, it is believed that eating the dried hands and legs of hoolocks will promote fertility (the ability to have children) in women.

In 1977, biologists (scientists who study living organisms) estimated the hoolock gibbon population at more than 500,000 animals. Ten years later, it was down to 170,000. By 2000, the hoolock gibbon population had been severely reduced. In India (where there were about 80,000 hoolocks in the early 1970s), there were only about 5,000 animals in 2000; there were less than 200 hoolocks in China, and 200 in Bangladesh. There is no current data about hoolock gibbons in Myanmar.

Preserving the remaining rain forest habitat and eliminating hunting of hoolock gibbons are key factors in the effort to save the species from extinction in the wild. Since the 1990s, some sanctuaries and reserves have been created within hoolock gibbon habitats. China and India have laws protecting gibbons, but the enforcement is not strict and poachers (illegal hunters) continue to profit from killing hoolocks in the wild.

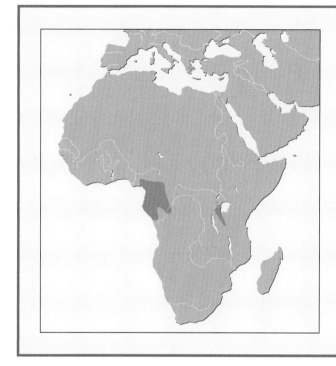

GORILLA
Gorilla gorilla

PHYLUM: Chordata

CLASS: Mammalia

ORDER: Primates

FAMILY: Hominidae

STATUS: Endangered, IUCN
Endangered, ESA

RANGE: Angola, Cameroon,
Central African Republic, Congo,
Congo Republic, Equatorial
Guinea, Gabon, Nigeria, Rwanda,
Uganda

Gorilla
Gorilla gorilla

Description and biology

The gorilla is considered the most intelligent land animal other than humans. It is the largest of the living primates, an order of mammals that includes lemurs, monkeys, chimpanzees, orangutans, and human beings. When standing on its hind legs, an average male gorilla measures 5 to 5.75 feet (1.5 to 1.75 meters) high. It can weigh between 300 and 500 pounds (136 and 227 kilograms). Females are smaller, measuring about 5 feet (1.5 meters) in height and weighing between 200 and 250 pounds (91 and 114 kilograms). The color of a gorilla's coat varies from brown–gray to black. In males, the hair on the back begins to turn silver after 10 years of age. Males also have a large bone on top of their skull (called the sagittal crest) that supports their massive jaw muscles and gives them their distinctive high

The largest of the living primates, gorillas are considered the most intelligent land mammals after humans.

forehead. Both sexes have small ears, broad nostrils, and a black, hairless face.

Gorillas are active during the day, foraging for a variety of vines, herbs, leaves, fruit, roots, and bark. During the wet season (April to June), the animals may move as little as 1,500 feet (457 meters) a day in search of food. During the dry season (July to August), they may travel almost 1 mile (1.6 kilometers). At night, gorillas build individual nests from branches and leaves in trees or on the ground.

Highly social animals, gorillas form groups of 5 to 10 members, although larger groups have been documented. An average group is composed of a dominant mature male (called a silverback) and several females and their young. When young males in the group become mature (at about age 11), they leave to form their own groups. Young females also leave upon reaching maturity (at about age 8), joining lone males or other groups.

Breeding between males and females can take place any time during the year. After a gestation (pregnancy) period of 250 to 270 days, a female gorilla gives birth to a single infant. She will carry her infant for the first few months of its life, after which time it will begin to crawl and then walk. The young gorilla will remain dependent on its mother for up to three years. Almost half of all infant gorillas die. Female gorillas successfully raise only two to three young during their lives.

Scientists have recognized three subspecies of gorilla: the western lowland gorilla (*Gorilla gorilla gorilla*), the eastern lowland gorilla (*Gorilla gorilla graueri*), and the mountain gorilla (*Gorilla gorilla berengei*).

Habitat and current distribution

All three gorilla subspecies prefer forest habitats. The western lowland gorilla is found in Nigeria, Cameroon, Central African Republic, Río Muni (the portion of Equatorial Guinea on the African mainland), Gabon, Congo Republic, and Angola. Its population is estimated to be about 35,000. The eastern lowland gorilla, having a population between 3,000 and 5,000, is found primarily in eastern Congo. The mountain gorilla is found in the Virunga Mountains, a range of volcanic mountains stretching across eastern Congo, southwestern Uganda, and northwestern Rwanda. With a population of about 600, the mountain gorilla is the most endangered of the three gorilla subspecies.

History and conservation measures

Hunting has been the leading threat to gorillas for years. The animals are killed for use as food or trapped for use as pets. Although current international agreements ban the selling or trading of gorillas as pets, illegal capture of the animals continues.

As human populations swell in Africa, increasing numbers of gorillas are hunted for their meat, known as bush meat. A hunter can receive $30 for the remains of a 400–pound (180–kilogram) male gorilla. Female gorillas are also slaughtered, and their infants are captured and sold to private collectors or zoos. Sometimes hunters make more money for live infant gorillas than for the remains of dead adults.

The destruction of African forests is another serious threat to gorillas. More and more of their habitat has been cleared to create farms and to supply European and Asian timber companies. Logging roads, built deep into the forests, also allow hunters easy access to remaining gorillas.

In 2003, a group of scientists and conservationists called for an upgrade in the status of gorillas from endangered to critically endangered. Data coming from Gabon and the Republic of Congo, where 80 percent of the world's gorillas live, reveal that the ape population there has decreased by half between 1983 and 2000. The reasons for the decline were continued hunting and outbreaks among gorillas and chimpanzees of the Ebola virus, a very deadly and contagious virus discovered in Africa in the 1970s that also afflicts human beings. The group of scientists warn that gorillas are in peril of becoming extinct in the wild. They called for greater enforcement of laws against hunting and capturing gorillas and an increased focus on research of the Ebola virus in primates.

African countries within the gorilla's range are trying to establish conservation programs for the animal. These efforts, though, are often thwarted by limited finances and social and political unrest. A successful program has been the Mountain Gorilla Veterinary Project, which provides health care for injured and sick mountain gorillas in Rwanda, Congo, and Uganda. It is one of the few programs in the world to provide treatment to an endangered species in its natural habitat.

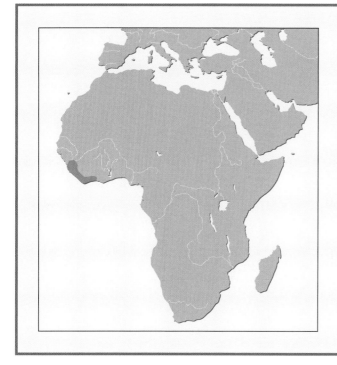

HIPPOPOTAMUS, PYGMY
Hexaprotodon liberiensis

PHYLUM: Chordata
CLASS: Mammalia
ORDER: Artiodactyla
FAMILY: Hippopotamidae
STATUS: Vulnerable, IUCN
RANGE: Côte d'Ivoire, Guinea, Guinea–Bissau, Liberia, Nigeria, Sierra Leone

Hippopotamus, pygmy
Hexaprotodon liberiensis

Description and biology

The pygmy hippopotamus is smaller and more piglike in appearance than its larger relative, the common hippopotamus. Its skin color is generally black, with a greenish tinge on the top of its back. Its belly is cream or yellow–gray. Its eyes are on the side of its round head instead of on top as in the common hippo. An average pygmy hippo has a head and body length of 5 to 5.5 feet (1.5 to 1.7 meters) and a shoulder height of 30 to 39 inches (76 to 99 centimeters). Its tail extends 6 inches (15 centimeters). It weighs between 355 and 600 pounds (161 and 272 kilograms). By contrast, an average common hippo weighs between 2,425 and 5,720 pounds (1,100 and 2,597 kilograms).

The pygmy hippo is a solitary animal, spending much of its time on the shore near swamps and rivers. It goes in the

The pygmy hippopotamus and its larger relative, the common hippopotamus, are often hunted for their meat and hides.

water only occasionally. Like the common hippo, the pygmy hippo has glands beneath its skin that secrete a pink, sweat–like substance. This biological fact has inspired the myth that hippos "sweat blood." This pink substance helps to regulate the hippo's skin temperature. Because its skin is sensitive to the sun, the pygmy hippo seeks shelter during the day in thickets and other forested areas. It feeds at night on leaves, shoots, grasses, roots, and fruits.

Male and female pygmy hippos usually mate in the water at any time during the year. After a gestation (pregnancy) period of 188 days, a female pygmy hippo gives birth to one calf. She then nurses that calf for eight months.

Habitat and current distribution

Pygmy hippos inhabit lowland forests. They are found in the tropical region of western Africa, primarily in the country of Liberia. Wildlife biologists (people who study living organisms) estimated that the pygmy hippo population in Liberia in the early 1980s was several thousand. No estimates have been made since then, but the population has almost certainly decreased.

History and conservation measures

Deforestation and hunting are the major threats to pygmy hippopotami. Africans hunt the animal and its larger relative for their meat and hides, which are used to make whips and shields. Very few conservation efforts exist for the pygmy hippopotamus. Between 350 and 400 pygmy hippos are held in captivity throughout the world.

PHYLUM: Chordata
CLASS: Mammalia
ORDER: Artiodactyla
FAMILY: Suidae
STATUS: Critically endangered,
IUCN
Endangered, ESA
RANGE: Bhutan, India, Nepal

Hog, pygmy
Sus salvanius

Description and biology

The pygmy hog is the smallest of all pig species. An average adult pygmy hog is 25 inches (63.5 centimeters) long, stands 10 inches (25 centimeters) tall at its shoulder, and weighs 19 pounds (8.6 kilograms). Its short tail measures only 1 inch (2.5 centimeters). Its hide is covered with coarse dark brown or black bristles. Because of its small, bullet–like shape, the animal is extremely agile.

Male pygmy hogs are larger than their female counterparts and have exposed tusks. The normally solitary males interact with the females only during mating season. A female pygmy hog gives birth to a litter of two to six infants, usually in late April or May, after a gestation (pregnancy) period of about 100 days. Both males and females build and use their nests throughout the year.

Habitat and current distribution

Pygmy hogs inhabit dense, tall grasslands. They are found primarily in two wildlife sanctuaries in northwestern Assam (a state in far eastern India): Manas Wildlife Sanctuary and Barnadi Wildlife Sanctuary. Scientists estimate the total number of pygmy hogs to be no more than 300. The actual number may be far less.

History and conservation measures

The pygmy hog is one of the most endangered mammals in the world. Destruction of the animal's habitat is the main reason. Farmers routinely set fire to grassland forests to clear them for agricultural use. Many pygmy hogs are killed because they cannot escape the extensive fires. Those that do escape

The pygmy hog is one of the most endangered mammals on Earth because of habitat loss. If this habitat loss continues, the pygmy hog will probably face extinction soon.

are forced onto very small grassland areas where they are sometimes killed by unexpected fires or onto tea plantations where they are often killed by hunters.

The international wildlife community and the Indian government have focused much attention on the pygmy hog's plight. In 1985, the International Union for Conservation of Nature and Natural Resources (IUCN) placed the pygmy hog on its first list of the 12 most threatened species in the world. The Indian government has given the animal the maximum legal protection allowed under its Indian Wild Life Protection Act. In 1986, the United Nations Educational, Scientific, and Cultural Organization (UNESCO) designated the Manas Wildlife Sanctuary as a World Heritage Site.

All these measures have done little to stop the destruction of pygmy hog habitat. If grassland fires in their habitat are allowed to continue unchecked, pygmy hogs will face extinction.

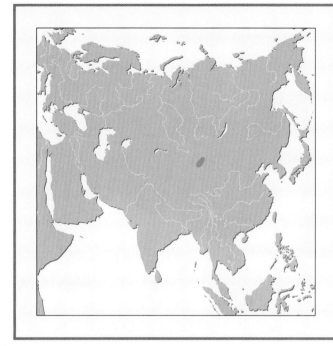

HORSE, PRZEWALSKI'S
Equus przewalskii

PHYLUM: Chordata
CLASS: Mammalia
ORDER: Perissodactyla
FAMILY: Equidae
STATUS: Endangered, ESA
RANGE: China, Kazakhstan, Mongolia

Horse, Przewalski's

Equus przewalskii

Description and biology

Przewalski's horse is the last truly wild horse. Slightly smaller than most domestic horses, it has a compact body with a thick neck and large head. The color of its upper body is dun (a dull grayish brown), while its belly and muzzle are much lighter. The horse has a dark stripe along its backbone and a dark, plumed tail. The dark hair on its head and along its neck (the mane) is short and stands erect. Unlike the domestic horse, Przewalski's horse sheds its mane and the short hairs at the base of its tail annually.

An average Przewalski's horse may reach 8 feet (2.4 meters) in length and stand 4 to 4.5 feet (1.2 to 1.4 meters) high at its shoulders. It may vary in weight between 440 and 750 pounds (200 and 340 kilograms). The horse feeds primarily on grass and other low vegetation.

Przewalski's horse is considered extinct in the wild since there are no genetically pure specimans remaining.

Groups of Przewalski's horses are headed by a dominant stallion (male), which is responsible for breeding with most of the group's females. The females usually give birth to a single foal (infant) between April and June, after a gestation (pregnancy) period of 330 to 340 days. The foals may nurse for up to two years.

Habitat and current distribution

Przewalski's horses prefer open grassland, steppe (vast, semiarid grass–covered plain), and semidesert areas. The last possible sighting of Przewalski's horse in the wild was in 1968. Chinese biologists (people who study living organisms) believe there may be a small population of horses inhabiting northeastern Xingiang (an autonomous region in northwestern China). It is more likely that this group is extinct.

Over 1,000 Przewalski's horses are currently held in captivity in zoos and reserves around the world.

History and conservation measures

Przewalski's horse was discovered in 1878 by Russian geographer and explorer Nikolai Mikhailovich Przhevalsky (1839–1888). Scientists believe the horse once ranged from western Mongolia to northern Xingiang and western Kazakhstan.

By 1900, hunting and competition with domestic horses for food and water greatly reduced the Przewalski's horse population. By the 1950s, the remaining animals were seen in a small area between southwestern Mongolia and northwestern China called the Takhin–Shara–Nuru (mountain of the yellow horses). The Przewalski's horse was last seen in the wild in 1968.

The International Union for Conservation of Nature and Natural Resources (IUCN) listed the species as extinct in the wild in 1996. However, the Przewalski's horse has become a great success story in the ongoing efforts to preserve species through reintroduction to the wild. In 1992, 16 horses bred in captivity and chosen for their genetic (inherited) traits were slowly and carefully reintroduced to the wilderness at Hustai National Park in Mongolia. By 2000, 84 horses had been reintroduced and 114 foals had been born in the wild. In the early 2000s, a population of around 142 Przewalski's horses roamed freely in the park, and the animals appeared to be doing better each year they spend in the wild. They are being very carefully watched and protected as they adapt to the original habitat of the species.

PHYLUM: Chordata
CLASS: Mammalia
ORDER: Carnivora
FAMILY: Hyaenidae
STATUS: Endangered, ESA
RANGE: Angola, Botswana, Mozambique, Namibia, South Africa, Zimbabwe

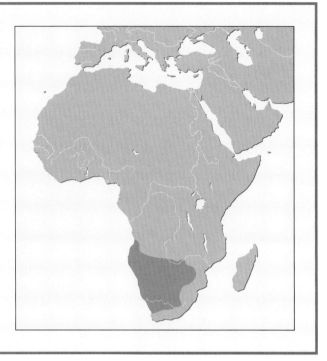

Hyena, brown
Hyaena Brunnea

Description and biology

The brown hyena, also known as the strand wolf, has a long, brown, shaggy coat with lighter underparts. Its face and legs are gray to black. An average brown hyena measures 43 to 53 inches (109 to 135 centimeters) long and stands 25 to 35 inches (64 to 89 centimeters) high at its shoulder. It weighs between 82 and 104 pounds (37 and 47 kilograms). Males are larger than females.

The brown hyena feeds primarily on the remains of prey killed by other predators. With its strong teeth and jaws, the animal can crush and eat bone. It also feeds on insects, eggs, fruits, and an occasional small animal or bird that it kills. Although it has acute vision and hearing, the brown hyena lo-

cates its prey by scent. Lions and spotted hyenas are the animal's main predators.

Brown hyenas sleep during the day and hunt at dusk or during the night. While on its nightly hunting expedition, a brown hyena will normally cover about 19 square miles (49 square kilometers). Some have been known to travel over 31 square miles (80 square kilometers).

Although often solitary in their habits, brown hyenas will form clans of up to 10 members. Male and female brown hyenas mate at any time during the year. After a gestation (pregnancy) period of 90 to 100 days, a female will give birth to 1 to 5 cubs. In a communal den (dwelling place shared by all members in a clan), cubs may suckle from females other than their mother. All members of the clan help to feed the cubs by carrying food to the den.

Brown hyenas are often killed because of the false belief that they are a threat to livestock.

Habitat and current distribution

In southern Africa, brown hyenas inhabit arid (dry) areas such as rocky deserts with thick brush, open grassland and scrub (land covered with stunted trees and shrubs), and semi-deserts. They sleep in dense vegetation, under sheltering rocks, or in burrows dug by other animals.

History and conservation measures

Scientists do not know the exact number of existing brown hyenas, but they believe the animals' range and population has been greatly reduced. Of the six African countries where brown hyenas can be found, only Botswana and Zimbabwe host sizable populations.

Many humans dislike brown hyenas because of their foul stench and their cry (which sounds like maniacal laughter). Brown hyenas are often killed by humans for these reasons and because the animals are seen as a threat to livestock. Since brown hyenas feed on carrion (decaying flesh of dead animals), this last view is utterly false.

Brown hyenas are given protection in several conservation areas in the Kalahari, an arid plateau region stretching about 100,000 square miles (259,000 square kilometers) in Botswana, Namibia, and South Africa. The animals are also protected along the coastal regions of the southern Namib Desert in western Namibia.

JAGUAR
Panthera onca

PHYLUM: Chordata

CLASS: Mammalia

ORDER: Carnivora

FAMILY: Felidae

STATUS: Near threatened, IUCN Endangered, ESA

RANGE: Argentina, Belize, Bolivia, Brazil, Colombia, Costa Rica, Ecuador, French Guiana, Guatemala, Guyana, Honduras, Mexico, Nicaragua, Panama, Paraguay, Peru, Suriname, USA, Venezuela

Jaguar
Panthera onca

Description and biology

The jaguar is the largest living member of the cat family in North and South America and the third largest in the world. Its coat ranges from yellow–brown to auburn and is covered with black spots and rosettes, or rings, encircling spots. An average adult jaguar has a head and body length of 4 to 6 feet (1.2 to 1.8 meters) and a tail length of 18 to 30 inches (46 to 76 centimeters). It stands about 2.5 feet (0.7 meter) high at its shoulder and weighs between 100 and 250 pounds (45 and 115 kilograms). Of the big cats, only the jaguar and the snow leopard do not seem to roar.

Jaguars are good swimmers, runners, and tree climbers. Their diet includes fish, frogs, turtles, small alligators, iguanas, peccaries (mammals related to the pig), monkeys, birds,

A jaguar leaping for its prey. Jaguars are good runners, swimmers, and tree climbers.

deer, dogs, and cattle. Jaguars are solitary mammals and are quick to defend their chosen hunting territory. For male jaguars, this territory ranges between 8 and 80 square miles (20 and 207 square kilometers); for females, it ranges between 4 and 27 square miles (10 and 70 square kilometers).

Male and female jaguars come together only to mate. In tropical areas, mating takes place at any time during the year. In areas with cooler climates, jaguars mate in the spring. After a gestation (pregnancy) period of 90 to 110 days, a female jaguar gives birth to a litter of one to four cubs. She raises the cubs on her own, and they may stay with her for up to two years.

Habitat and current distribution

Jaguars are found in parts of Mexico, Central America, South America as far south as northern Argentina, and the southwestern United States. Because the animals are secretive and rare, biologists (people who study living organisms) have not been able to determine the exact number remaining in the wild, but in 1998 it was estimated that the jaguar population in the world was less than 50,000 breeding adults. The largest remaining population of jaguars is believed to live in the Amazonian rain forest.

Jaguars live in a variety of habitats, including tropical and subtropical forests, open woodlands, mangroves, swamps, scrub thickets, and savannas.

History and conservation measures

The jaguar once inhabited areas as far north as the southern United States. It is now extinct over much of its former range. The primary reason for the animal's decline was ruthless hunting, both for sport and for the jaguar's prized coat. In the early to mid–1960s, spotted cat skins were in great demand. International treaties have all but eliminated the commercial trade of cat pelts.

Jaguars now face the threat of habitat destruction. The clearing of forests to build ranches and farms has rapidly eliminated the animals' original habitat. Forced to live next to farmland, jaguars are often killed by farmers because they prey on domestic animals.

Small populations of jaguars are protected in large national parks in Bolivia, Brazil, Colombia, Peru, and Venezuela. Smaller reserves and private ranches in these areas provide protection to isolated pairs or families. The jaguar has been bred successfully in zoos.

KANGAROO, MATSCHIE'S TREE
Dendrolagus Matschie

PHYLUM: Chordata
CLASS: Mammalia
ORDER: Diprotodontia
FAMILY: Macropodidae
STATUS: Endangered, IUCN
RANGE: Papua New Guinea

Kangaroo, Matschie's tree
Dendrolagus Matschie

Description and biology

Matschie's tree kangaroo, also known as Huon tree kangaroo, is a marsupial (marsupial young are born undeveloped and are initially carried in a pouch on the outside of their mothers' body) in the Macropodidae family, which consists of more than fifty kinds of kangaroos. It is one of ten kinds of tree kangaroos, all living in Australia and nearby islands. The Matschie's tree kangaroo is usually about 20 to 35 inches (51 to 90 centimeters) long in its head and body; its large tail is 16 to 37 inches (41 to 94 centimeters) long. Females are slightly larger than males, with females weighing about 17 pounds (8 kilograms) and males about 15 pounds (7 kilograms). Their coats are usually reddish brown or dark brown, but their belly, face, part of their tail, and feet are yellow. Fur on their necks and backs grows in an opposite direction to the rest of their fur, allowing the kangaroo to shed rain when it gets into the right position.

Matschie's tree kangaroos are arboreal (they live in trees) and nocturnal (they are active mainly at night and sleep during the day). Their bodies are similar to those of other kinds of kangaroos, except they are designed for getting around in trees. Unlike ground kangaroos, their hind limbs are the same length as their front limbs, and the front limbs are big and strong for tree climbing. They have large feet with pads that keep them from slipping on wet branches, and a long heavy tail that helps them to balance their weight. They have long claws, and their feet can turn sideways in order to grasp branches. Matschie's tree kangaroos are capable of jumping long distances—up to 30 or 40 feet—but they generally climb up and down trees slowly and carefully. Their large eyes aid in judging distances when they leap from branch to branch. Their diet consists of leaves and fruit.

Matschie's tree kangaroos are solitary animals. Each individual lives within its own home range, but a male's home range may overlap several females' home ranges. They mate throughout the year. The female gives birth to one offspring after a 35– to 45–day gestation (pregnancy) period. The "joey," or newborn infant, unformed and only about an inch long, nurses in the pouch for about 350 days as it develops and then stays with its mother until it is about a year and a half old. The life span of a Matschie's tree kangaroo is thought to be about 14 years.

Habitat and current distribution

Matschie's tree kangaroos live in mountainous tropical rain forest areas in the Huon Peninsula in eastern Papua New Guinea and in the island of Umboi and the western tip of New Britain Island, both off Papua New Guinea. It is estimated that there are about 1,400 animals in the wild. Because

DID YOU KNOW?

How can scientists know so much about animals that are difficult or impossible to observe in the wild? Conservationists studying the Matschie's tree kangaroo use a variety of scientific and research methods to obtain data. One of the methods used to understand the population—how many, where, how dense—is called distance sampling. First, the researchers locate Matschie's tree kangaroo dung (excrement) and record the distances between specimens and measure how much they find. They can then determine an estimated population density (how many animals exist within a measured area) by using statistics, a form of math in which numbers are collected, analyzed, and interpreted. Animal dung is also used in the lab in genetic studies (biological studies dealing with heredity and the variation among living things). Through modern procedures the dung samples can be used to identify individual animals in a region and to learn about the size of their home ranges. Another method of studying the animals is to set up remotely triggered cameras along animal trails to record their patterns. In addition, the scientists interview local people about their experiences with Matschie's tree kangaroos to learn about things like their history in the area and their eating habits. Further studies include a survey of the biodiversity (the variety of all life forms) in the Huon peninsula, and habitat mapping, which can provide geographical information on the best spots for conservation.

Matschie's tree kangaroos live in inaccessible places, scientific study of the species is difficult and not very advanced.

History and conservation measures

Matschie's tree kangaroos are hunted by the people of Papua New Guinea for their meat and fur. Hunters in the past used dingos (Australian wild dogs) to locate tree kangaroos by their scent and then to pull them out of the trees. When guns were introduced in Papua New Guinea, hunters became much more efficient, and the population of Matschie's tree kangaroos began to decline. At the same time, the species is threatened by the destruction of its habitat in the Huon Peninsula due to logging, mineral and oil exploration, and farming. Because the Matschie's tree kangaroo only lives in this one unique area, its chances of survival are very slim unless this habitat is preserved. Papua New Guinea's traditional communities control the use and management of the nation's natural resources.

In 1996, the Tree Kangaroo Conservation Program (TKCP) formed to promote the management and protection of tree kangaroos and their habitat while at the same time working to meet the needs of the local people. Since conservation (protection of the natural world) depends on educating the traditional landowners about the value of biodiversity (the variety of forms of life on Earth) and the need to use sustainable development practices (methods of farming or building communities that do not deplete or damage the natural resources of an area), the program has focused on education. It has been very successful. By the end of December 2001, 50,000 acres (20,250 hectares) of land had been pledged by local land owners to establish a wildlife management area, and the TKCP expects to increase this area to 150,000 acres (60,725 hectares) in the near future.

Matschie's tree kangaroos are arboreal (they live in trees) and nocturnal (they are active mainly at night and sleep during the day).

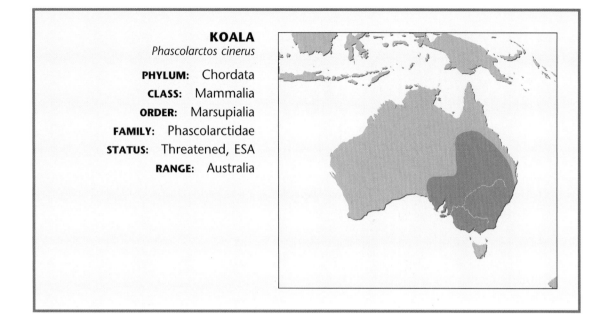

KOALA
Phascolarctos cinerus

PHYLUM: Chordata
CLASS: Mammalia
ORDER: Marsupialia
FAMILY: Phascolarctidae
STATUS: Threatened, ESA
RANGE: Australia

Koala

Phascolarctos cinerus

Description and biology

Although the koala is often called a "koala bear" and is noted for its teddy bear looks, it is not a member of the bear family. Rather, it is a marsupial—an animal related to wombats, opossums, and kangaroos. (Marsupials differ from other mammals in that the females carry their undeveloped young in pouches on their abdomen.) Koalas are small and round, with little eyes and a big black nose. They have no tail. Adults range from about 24 to 35 inches (61 to 90 centimeters) in length and weigh about 10 to 30 pounds (4.5 to 13.5 kilograms). Males are much larger than females. Koalas have soft, thick gray fur with brown tinges and a white undercoat, with white patches on the chest, neck, and ears. The fur acts as a rain repellant and provides warmth. Koalas living in southern Australia, where winters are colder, have longer fur.

Koalas are arboreal (they live in trees) and nocturnal (active during the night). They have a keen sense of balance and are very muscular, with strong, well–developed limbs for climbing in trees. Their padded hands and feet are also well adapted to the arboreal life. Their front paws have five fingers with very long claws. Two of the fingers are opposable (capable of being pushed against the other fingers). The back paws also have long claws and one opposable thumb. Koalas slowly climb up tree trunks and branches by gripping them, first with the front claws, then the back. Often, to go from tree to tree, a koala will descend to the ground, where it is most vulnerable to its predators and to injury.

Koalas are herbivorous, meaning they eat only plants. Their diet consists mainly of eucalyptus (gum tree) leaves. Some types of eucalyptus leaves are poisonous, so koalas are highly selective about which leaves they will eat. They use their keen sense of smell to select their food. Their digestive systems are adapted to detoxify the poisons and to obtain energy from the eucalyptus leaves, which are low in nutrients. Koalas sleep an average of 18 to 20 hours per day. They have a very low metabolic rate (method of breaking down nutrients to create energy) and by sleeping long hours and remaining fairly inactive, they are able to save energy. Koalas drink very little water, as the eucalyptus leaves provide them with fluids.

Koalas are territorial animals. Although they are solitary, they live in a complex social world that is evenly distributed throughout eucalypt forests. Each individual animal has its own home range, where it will live its whole life. The home range must have the right kind of eucalyptus for the koala to eat and it must be located within a stable community of koalas. An individual koala's territory will usually overlap several other koala territories, and some socializing occurs in the shared areas, though there is little interaction outside of mating season. Koalas can communicate with each other over large distances by means of a deep bellow. Males bellow, sometimes in place of fighting, to communicate their social and physical position. Females bellow, though far less than males, either to signal aggression or as a part of a mating routine. Koalas communicate fear, annoyance, and intimacy with other sounds. Also, the male uses scent–marking during mating season, rubbing his large sternal (near the breastbone) gland against tree trunks to communicate his space and dominance.

During mating season, males begin to bellow aggressively. They mate with several females during the season. The female koala gives birth to a single offspring after a gestation (pregnancy) period of 34 to 36 days. The undeveloped baby, called a "joey," weighs only a couple of ounces and is delivered directly into the mother's pouch, where it will stay, constantly nursing, for six to seven months. When koala young leave the pouch, they stay with their mother, riding on her back, until they are about one year old. For the next two to three years, they will remain in the mother's home range. After that, they go off to find their own home ranges. Koalas in the wild can live from 13 to 18 years.

Habitat and current distribution

Koalas live in eucalyptus forests ranging from northern Queensland to southern Victoria and southeastern South Australia. However, by most estimates about 80 percent of the eucalyptus forests where koalas have historically lived have now been cleared, and the remaining koalas live in increasingly fragmented areas. Because the koala is dependent on certain types of eucalyptus leaves for food, the loss of the eucalyptus forests means a decline in the koala population no matter how much they are otherwise protected. According to the Australian Koala Foundation, there are about 40,000–80,000 koalas left in the wild, although there is controversy about these numbers.

History and conservation measures

There were millions of koalas in Australia in 1788, when European settlement began. Although indigenous (native) Australians hunted koalas for food, the koala population remained stable until a market developed in Europe for the thick and soft koala fur. During the last decades of the nineteenth century and the first decades of the twentieth approximately 3 million koalas were killed for their fur. In 1927, the Australian government banned hunting or intentionally killing a koala without special permission. By that time the population had been reduced from millions to thousands.

Since the 1930s, koalas have been protected from hunters, but their habitat has been swiftly destroyed. The land along the eastern shores of Australia, once teeming with eucalyptus forests, has been cleared for farming; towns and cities have

Koalas live in eucalyptus forests ranging from northern Queensland to southern Victoria and southeastern South Australia.

grown up around the farms. Today, with 80 percent of the eucalyptus forests gone, the remaining 20 percent of the forests in which the surviving koalas live are for the most part privately owned. Koalas have suffered heavily from the destruction of their habitat and from the fragmentation caused by roads, farms, and towns that restrict movement. This makes it difficult or impossible for the individuals within a koala population to reach one another. Koalas are regularly killed and injured by dogs and by cars. Fires and weed infestations have further ruined the eucalyptus groves that are so important to their survival. The stresses of living in these fragmented and dangerous conditions have led to large outbreaks of disease among koalas, including infections in their reproductive systems that cause infertility (inability to bear young).

Numerous recovery programs have been initiated in the early 2000s with the mission to stop further clearance of koala habitat areas, to restore and protect certain habitat areas that have been damaged or destroyed, to restrain dogs, to control traffic on roads in koala areas, and to educate area residents on the management of koalas. Research programs on disease, breeding, and genetics are also in place.

KOUPREY
Bos sauveli

PHYLUM: Chordata

CLASS: Mammalia

ORDER: Artiodactyla

FAMILY: Bovidae

STATUS: Critically endangered, IUCN
Endangered, ESA

RANGE: Cambodia, Lao People's Democratic Republic, Thailand, Vietnam

Kouprey
Bos sauveli

Description and biology

The kouprey, also called the Cambodian forest ox, the gray ox, or the wild forest ox of Indochina, is one of the most rare species of wild cattle and may be the most endangered large mammal in the world. Kouprey were not known to humans until 1937, and there has been no close observation of a kouprey for nearly 50 years. Most of the information we have on the species today comes from a zoologist who studied and filmed the animal in the wild for two months in 1957.

Kouprey are massive animals, weighing from 1,500 to 2,000 pounds (700 to 900 kilograms). They stand between 5.5 and 6.5 feet (1.7 and 2 meters) tall at the shoulder, and their bodies are about 7 feet (2.15 meters) long. They have long legs and humped backs. Kouprey are born brown but turn gray as they mature, and males then turn black or very dark brown as they get older. Both males and females have white patches on their shoulders, legs, and hindquarters. Males have horns that are wide–spreading and arch forward and upward with a distinctive splintered fringe, growing to about 32 inches (80 centimeters) long. Female horns are about 16 inches (40 centimeters) long. Adult male kouprey have a very large dewlap, a sack of skin that hangs about 16 inches (40 centimeters) from the base of the neck, sometimes reaching down to the ground.

Kouprey live and travel in herds. Females and their young form separate herds from the male herds. The animals graze (eat grass in the meadows and fields) and browse (feed on the tender shoots and leaves of bushes and trees) during the early part of the day. During the night they travel, sometimes great distances. The whole herd forms a tight circle in the early afternoon to sleep. April is the mating season, and females give birth to one offspring sometime between December and February. The kouprey's life span in the wild is thought to be about 20 years.

Habitat and current distribution

The kouprey's habitat is comprised of low, rolling hills covered in a mixture of open forest and dense monsoon (heavy rain) forest. The range of the kouprey has been thought to be Cambodia, the Lao People's Democratic Republic, Thailand, and Vietnam, but many wildlife biologists (people who study living organisms) now believe that the species is extinct in all its former habitats with the exception of small, fragmented populations in Cambodia. The total remaining population is thought to be about 250 animals and declining.

History and conservation measures

As far as is known to humans, kouprey have always had a low population. When first discovered in 1938, there were an estimated 800 kouprey. From a high of 1,000 animals in 1940, the population went into a decline. By 1970, there were only 30 to 70 kouprey left in the world. There are many reasons for the decline in population, but war was a major factor. The war in Vietnam, which began soon after World War II (1939–45) and lasted three decades, is thought to have decimated the kouprey in that country. During the war kouprey were hunted without restriction by locals and by the military. They were killed by land mines, and their habitat was destroyed. In Thailand, poaching (illegal hunting) was responsible for a major population decline. In all areas, loss of habitat due to illegal logging and slash–and–burn farming and disease transmitted from domestic stock took a heavy toll. Laos and Cambodia have experienced periods of violent political upheaval, making it difficult to initiate conservation programs or send out expeditions to study the species in the wild. Kouprey are now legally protected in all of the countries in their range, however, and Cambodia has some conservation programs in progress.

LEMUR, MONGOOSE
Eulemur mongoz

PHYLUM: Chordata
CLASS: Mammalia
ORDER: Primates
FAMILY: Lemuridae
STATUS: Vulnerable, IUCN
Endangered, ESA
RANGE: Comoros, Madagascar

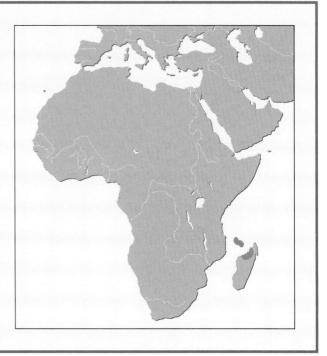

Lemur, mongoose
Eulemur mongoz

Description and biology

Lemurs are mammals with monkey–like bodies and limbs. They are found only on Madagascar (large island lying in the Indian Ocean off the eastern coast of the African country of Mozambique) and adjacent islands. The mongoose lemur is one of only two lemur species found on both Madagascar and Comoros (group of islands between northeastern Mozambique and northwestern Madagascar). It is covered with long, soft fur and has a ruff (projecting growth of fur) around its neck and ears. The upper bodies of male mongoose lemurs are gray in color. The mongoose lemur has a pale face with bushy, red-dish brown cheeks. The upper bodies of females are gray–brown. They have a dark face with bushy, white cheeks. Both sexes are white underneath.

Although living on reserves, the mongoose lemur is still in jeopardy of extinction because conservation laws are not enforced.

An average mongoose lemur has a head and body length of 12 to 17 inches (30 to 43 centimeters) and weighs 4.5 to 6.6 pounds (2 to 3 kilograms). The tail of the mongoose lemur is longer than its body, extending 16 to 25 inches (40 to 64 centimeters).

Mongoose lemurs are active either at night or during the day, depending on the season and area. Their diet is mainly composed of flowers, fruit, and leaves. Family groups are made up of a male, a female, and their infants. Female mongoose lemurs normally give birth to one infant in mid–October after a gestation (pregnancy) period of 128 to 135 days.

Habitat and current distribution

The mongoose lemur inhabits dry deciduous (shedding plants and trees) forests on northwestern Madagascar and humid forests on the Comoros islands of Anjouan and Mohéli. The lemurs on the Comoros are probably descendants of lemurs brought to the islands by fishermen from Madagascar.

History and conservation measures

Biologists (people who study living organisms) believe the number of mongoose lemurs in existence is declining. In Madagascar, the animals are found only in the protected area of Ankarafantsika. The reserve, however, is not well managed to provide protection for the wildlife it harbors. Nearby residents are continually clearing forested land around (and even within) the reserve to obtain lumber and to create agricultural land for livestock and crops.

On the islands of the Comoros, laws have been passed to protect the mongoose lemurs, but little has been done to enforce them. An increase in the number of cyclones (violent windstorms) that have hit the islands recently has also taken its toll on the animals.

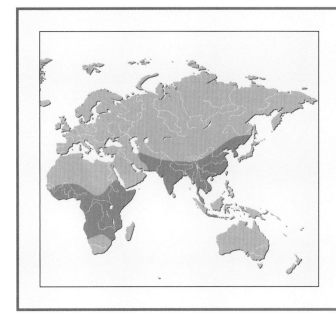

LEOPARD
Panthera pardus

PHYLUM: Chordata
CLASS: Mammalia
ORDER: Carnivora
FAMILY: Felidae
STATUS: Endangered, ESA
Threatened, ESA (parts of Africa)
RANGE: Africa (south of the
Sahara Desert), southeastern Asia

Leopard
Panthera pardus

Description and biology

A large member of the cat family, the leopard is known for its light to tawny brown coat patterned with black spots and rosettes, or rings. Unlike those of the jaguar, the rosettes of the leopard never have spots inside them. Some leopards are born with a black coat that still has the characteristic spotting. Found mainly in southern Asia, these cats are commonly (but incorrectly) called black panthers. An average leopard has a head and body length of 38 to 75 inches (97 to 191 centimeters) and weighs 65 to 155 pounds (30 to 70 kilograms). Its tail can reach a length of up to 3 feet (1 meter).

Leopards are solitary mammals that hunt primarily at night. Their diet includes monkeys and other small mammals, birds, rodents, and insects. Good climbers, leopards often store their dead prey in trees. They cover a home range of about 4 to 20 square miles (10 to 51 square kilometers) in search of food.

Male and female leopards come together only to mate, which can occur at any time during the year. After a gestation (pregnancy) period of 90 to 105 days, a female leopard gives birth to a litter of three to five cubs. She alone cares for the cubs, hiding them until they are six to eight weeks old. The young leopards nurse for several months and may stay with the mother for 18 to 20 months.

Habitat and current distribution

Leopards have the ability to adapt to almost any environment. As long as prey is available, these cats inhabit areas ranging from semidesert to dense rain forest. They are found in Africa south of the Sahara Desert and in southeastern Asia.

Leopards are considered endangered throughout their range. The only exception is the region south of the African countries of Gabon, Congo, Congo Republic, Uganda, and Kenya. Because leopards are more numerous here, they are considered only threatened.

History and conservation measures

Like most spotted cats, the leopard has been a victim of the fur trade. Although global treaties protect the leopard, poachers still hunt the animal to sell on the international market. In Africa, it is legal to hunt leopards for sport.

Contact between humans and leopards has not favored the animals. As more and more of their habitat has been converted to farm and ranch land, leopards have been forced to prey on domestic livestock. In response, farmers and ranchers have actively sought to poison the animals.

Leopards have protection only in national parks, where they are considered a tourist attraction.

Because of the demand for leopard fur, the animals are often illegally hunted. It is this hunting that has led to the leopards' endangered status.

LEOPARD, SNOW
Panthera uncia (or uncia uncia)

PHYLUM: Chordata

CLASS: Mammalia

ORDER: Carnivora

FAMILY: Felidae

STATUS: Endangered, IUCN
Endangered, ESA

RANGE: Afghanistan, Bhutan,
China, India, Kazakhstan,
Kyrgyzstan, Mongolia, Nepal,
Pakistan, Russia, Tajikistan,
Uzbekistan

Leopard, snow
Panthera uncia

Description and biology

The snow leopard, or ounce, has a beautiful coat of long, pale gray fur with white underneath. Its coat is patterned with solid black spots on its head and legs and dark gray rosettes (rings) on the rest of its body. The animal is smaller than its closest relative, the leopard. An average snow leopard has a head and body length of 48 to 56 inches (122 to 142 centimeters) and weighs 132 to 165 pounds (60 to 75 kilograms). Its heavy, thickly furred tail measures 32 to 40 inches (81 to 102 centimeters). The snow leopard has thick chest muscles for climbing and large, heavily padded forepaws for walking through snow. An excellent leaper, the animal can jump as far as 50 feet (15 meters) in a single bound.

Snow leopards usually hunt at dusk or at night. While their preferred prey is the bharal (a goatlike mammal), they

also hunt yak, marmots, musk deer, and domestic livestock. An individual snow leopard's home range extends from 5 to 15 square miles (13 to 39 square kilometers).

Like other big cats, snow leopards are solitary animals. Males and females come together only to mate in late winter. After a gestation (pregnancy) period of 98 to 103 days, a female snow leopard gives birth to one to four cubs. The cubs nurse for at least two months and remain dependent on their mother for up to a year.

Habitat and current distribution

Snow leopards inhabit mountain ranges in central Asia. Their entire range covers a massive area of almost 1,000,000 square miles (2,590,000 square kilometers). However, these rare and endangered animals sparsely populate this area.

Two snow leopards from the Cincinnati Zoo. Unless the animals' natural habitat is preserved, they may fall victim to extinction.

Biologists (people who study living organisms) estimated in 1996 that the snow leopard population was below 2,500 breeding adults in the wild and declining.

Snow leopards are normally found in dry alpine and subalpine regions above 9,840 feet (3,000 meters). During summer months, when their prey moves to higher pastures, snow leopards may climb to an altitude of 13,000 feet (3,960 meters).

History and conservation measures

Along with other spotted cats, the snow leopard has long been hunted for its prized coat. Although current international treaties protect the animal, poachers still hunt down the snow leopard and sell it illegally. Because some of the animal's habitat is not easy to reach, officials have a difficult time enforcing the snow leopard's protective rights.

Snow leopards are also threatened by human development. As human populations have grown in the region and snow leopard habitat has been converted into agricultural land for livestock, the animal's traditional prey has become scarce. Forced to feed on domestic animals, the snow leopard has become a target for angry farm and ranch owners.

Unless large areas of its natural habitat are preserved, the continued existence of the snow leopard is in jeopardy.

LYNX, IBERIAN'S
Lynx pardinus (also felis pardina)

PHYLUM: Chordata
CLASS: Mammalia
ORDER: Carnivora
FAMILY: Felidae
STATUS: Critically endangered, IUCN
Endangered, ESA
RANGE: Portugal, Spain

Lynx, Iberian

Lynx pardinus (also felis pardina)

Description and biology

The Iberian lynx, also known as the Spanish lynx, is the most endangered wild cat species in the world and the only cat to be included in the critically endangered category set out by the International Union for Conservation of Nature and Natural Resources (IUCN). There are two types of lynx in Europe: the Iberian lynx and the Eurasian lynx. Iberian lynx are about half the size of Eurasian lynx, with females weighing about 20 pounds (9 kilograms) and males 29 pounds (13 kilograms). Their body length is between 30 and 40 inches (75 and 100 centimeters) and shoulder height is 18 to 28 inches (45 to 70 centimeters). Iberian lynx are spotted and deep yellow or brown, with short tails and black tufts of fur at the tops of their ears. They are nocturnal (active during the night). In winter, their fur grows thicker and they remain active, taking shelter in caves or trees when the weather is severe. With a keen sense of vision and smell, the

The Iberian lynx, also known as the Spanish lynx, is the most endangered wild cat species in the world.

Iberian lynx is a good hunter. Its diet consists mainly of rabbits, but may also include small or baby deer, small mammals, and ducks. When the lynx kills its prey, it drags it away to eat elsewhere, burying anything that is left over for the next day.

Lynx are solitary animals. Each Iberian lynx, male and female, has its own home range, an area it knows thoroughly and patrols on a regular basis but does not necessarily defend. Within its home range, the lynx lives within a territory, which may range in size from 2.5 to 6 miles (4 to 9.5 kilometers) in diameter, which it does defend from other lynx. Female lynx generally only have one mate per season; males may have more than one. Females give birth to two or three offspring at a time. The mother stays with her young until she mates again the next year. The offspring will then remain within the mother's territory for about another year before going off to establish their own territory. Iberian lynx have a life span of about 13 years.

Habitat and current distribution

Iberian lynx live in woodlands or other areas of dense vegetation near open pastures where they can hunt for rabbits. An extreme reduction in rabbits and the intrusion of human settlement in the twentieth century have drastically reduced the population, which now lives in a few isolated areas in Spain and Portugal, in the southern part of the Iberian peninsula. In 2002, wildlife biologists (people who study living organisms) estimated that there were less than 300 Iberian lynx left. If the Iberian lynx becomes extinct, it will be the first wild cat species to be lost in thousands of years.

History and conservation measures

Iberian lynx have lived throughout Spain and Portugal for centuries, particularly in cork oak forests. In the early twentieth century, the introduction of wheat farming in these regions damaged the habitat for the rabbits, causing in turn a decline in the number of Iberian lynx. In the early 1950s, myxomatosis, a contagious disease, killed a very large proportion of Spain's rabbit population. The loss of the main food in its diet reduced the Iberian lynx population further. Iberian lynx had long prospered in the habitat provided by cork oak forests, but in the 1990s cork became less marketable and many of these forests were cut down. Humans built vacation homes and roads in previously remote lynx territories, further destroying their habitat. Humans have also illegally hunted lynx and accidentally maimed them in snares meant for other animals. Lynx have been hit by cars on the new roadways. But the loss of the rabbit population has been the biggest factor threatening the species.

Restoration of the rabbits in the effected areas of Spain and Portugal is the first step in the attempt to save the Iberian lynx from extinction. Preserving the natural habitat, such as the cork oak forests, is equally important. Because much of the lynx's natural habitat is privately owned, it is necessary for private landowners to become involved in conservation efforts. With so few Iberian lynx left, efforts have been made to protect the two known remaining populations. A captive breeding program has been initiated, but in 2002 it had not yet produced any offspring. Little is known about breeding lynx in captivity.

MANATEE, WEST INDIAN
Trichechus manatus

PHYLUM: Chordata

CLASS: Mammalia

ORDER: Sirenia

FAMILY: Trichechidae

STATUS: Vulnerable, IUCN
Endangered, ESA

RANGE: Bahamas, Belize, Brazil,
Colombia, Costa Rica, Cuba,
Dominican Republic, French
Guiana, Guatemala, Guyana, Haiti,
Honduras, Jamaica, Mexico,
Nicaragua, Panama, Puerto Rico,
Suriname, Trinidad and Tobago,
USA (Florida, Georgia), Venezuela

Manatee, West Indian

Trichechus manatus

Description and biology

The West Indian manatee, also known as the Florida manatee, is a large marine mammal with a rounded, heavy gray body and a horizontally flattened tail. An average West Indian manatee has a combined body and tail length of 8 to 13 feet (2.4 to 4 meters) and weighs 800 to 3,500 pounds (360 to 1,590 kilograms). It has small eyes and no ear pinnas (external flaplike portions). The animal's nostrils are on the upper surface of its snout and can be tightly closed by valves when the manatee is underwater. Manatees often rest just below the water's surface, coming up to breathe every 15 or 20 minutes. They use their flexible flippers almost like hands for eating, moving through seagrass, touching, holding a nursing calf, and even hugging other manatees.

The manatee is the only marine mammal that feeds solely on vegetation. It eats a variety of aquatic plants, including water hyacinths, hydrillas, and seagrasses. The manatee is often called a sea cow because it grazes on marine seagrass meadows. It uses its split upper lip to grasp food and pull it into its mouth. Primarily a nocturnal (at night) feeder, the animal can consume up to 100 pounds (45 kilograms) of food a day.

Manatees have no particular breeding season, but most births seem to occur in spring and early summer. After a gestation (pregnancy) period of 13 months, a female manatee gives birth to one calf, which is about 4 feet (1.2 meters) long and weighs 60 pounds (27 kilograms). Even though it begins grazing on vegetation within a few months, the calf continues to nurse from its mother for one to two years.

Even though newly born manatees begin grazing on vegetation within a few months, the calf continues to nurse from its mother for one to two years.

Habitat and current distribution

The West Indian manatee is found in the coastal waters and rivers of Florida and Georgia, Central America, and the West Indies. It prefers to inhabit slow–moving rivers, river mouths, bays, lagoons, coves, and other shallow coastal areas. It is at home in all types of water environments: fresh, brackish (slightly salty), and salt. The manatee requires warm water and will migrate great distances between winter and summer grounds.

The total number of West Indian manatees in existence is unknown, but a statewide survey in Florida in early 1997 listed the manatee population there at just over 2,220.

History and conservation measures

Native Americans hunted manatees for centuries, using the animals' flesh, bones (for medicine), and hide (for leather). When Spanish explorers began colonizing Caribbean islands in the sixteenth century, manatee hunting increased. Biologists (people who study living organisms) believe this hunting is responsible for the manatee's initial decline.

Natural events, such as sudden changes in water temperature, also can be deadly to manatees. In the 1980s, three abnormally cold winters in Florida lowered water temperatures throughout the state. In water below 60°F (15°C), manatees become sluggish, stop eating, and eventually die. Many manatees perished during those cold Florida winters.

The greatest continued threat to manatees, however, comes from humans. Many manatees drown each year from being trapped in fishing nets. Others are drowned or crushed by flood gates or canal locks. Some are injured by discarded fishing lines, hooks, and trash. The majority of manatee deaths in Florida are caused by collisions with speeding boats. Those animals that survive such collisions bear lifelong propeller scars.

In 1978, the Florida legislature passed the Florida Manatee Sanctuary Act, which designated the entire state a refuge and sanctuary for the animal. Manatee protection zones have been established in which boats are required to reduce their speed. In areas declared manatee refuges, no boats, swimmers, or divers are allowed. In other countries in the West Indian manatee's range, public education programs have been launched to raise awareness about the animal's plight.

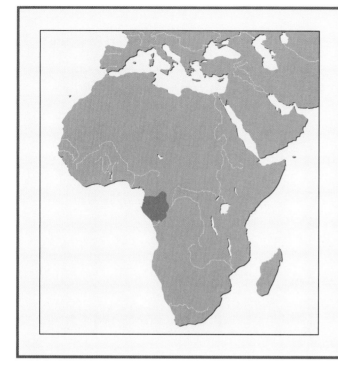

MANDRILL
Mandrillus sphinx

PHYLUM: Chordata

CLASS: Mammalia

ORDER: Primates

FAMILY: Cercopithecidae

STATUS: Vulnerable, IUCN
Endangered, ESA

RANGE: Cameroon, Congo
Republic, Equatorial Guinea,
Gabon

Mandrill
Mandrillus sphinx

Description and biology

Related to the baboon, the mandrill is the largest member of the monkey family. An average male has a head and body length of 31 inches (79 centimeters), a shoulder height of 20 inches (51 centimeters), and a tail length of 3 inches (8 centimeters). It weighs 119 pounds (54 kilograms). Females are considerably smaller.

Male mandrills are considered the most colorful of all mammals. While the animal's body fur is mainly dark brown, its bare areas (face and buttocks) are dazzlingly colored. Bright blue ridges line its face on either side of its nose. Its doglike muzzle is bright red. Black fur surrounds its close-set, yellow-brown eyes. Its beard and the edges of its mane are pale yellow. The pads on its buttocks are bright red, blue, and purple. The coloring on females and infants is not as brilliant.

The most colorful of all mammals, the mandrill is the largest member of the primate family.

Mandrills are active during the day, foraging for fruits, buds, leaves, roots, insects, fungus, and seeds. When food is scarce, the animals sometimes raid crops from nearby farms and plantations. At night, they sleep in trees.

Social animals, mandrills form groups of 20 to 40 members headed by a single male. The home range of a single group may be between 12 and 19 square miles (31 and 48 square kilometers). Little is known about the mandrill's reproductive habits. Most female mandrills give birth between December and April after a gestation (pregnancy) period of about 170 days.

Habitat and current distribution

Mandrills are found in the tropical forests and thick bush areas south of the Sanaga River in southwestern Cameroon, Rí Muni (the portion of Equatorial Guinea on the African mainland), western Gabon, and southwestern Congo Republic.

Since mandrills avoid contact with humans, they are difficult to observe in the wild. Biologists (people who study living organisms) are, therefore, unsure of the total number currently in existence.

History and conservation measures

The mandrill population has drastically declined in the late twentieth century due to habitat destruction and hunting. It is relatively easy to hunt mandrills because they emit loud calls. Hunters sometimes use dogs to chase the animals up trees before shooting them down.

Local people hunt the mandrill for food in all countries in its range. Much of the animal's forest habitat has been logged for its timber or cleared to create farmland. Although the animal is found in several reserves, including the Campo Reserve in Cameroon and the large Lopé Okanda Reserve in Gabon, it receives little protection. Hunting, logging, and the building of settlements still take place within many of these areas. In Rí Muni, the mandrill receives no protection and is considered extremely rare.

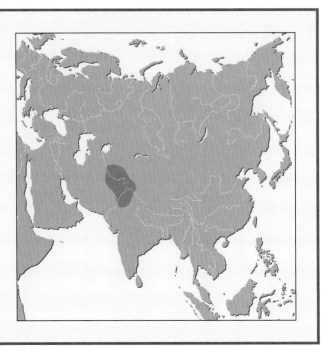

MARKHOR
Capra falconeri

PHYLUM: Chordata
CLASS: Mammalia
ORDER: Artiodactyla
FAMILY: Bovidae
STATUS: Endangered, IUCN
Endangered, ESA
RANGE: Afghanistan,
India, Pakistan, Tajikistan,
Turkmenistan, Uzbekistan

Markhor

Capra falconeri

Description and biology

The markhor is one of the largest members of the goat family. An average markhor has a head and body length of 55 to 70 inches (140 to 195 centimeters) and a shoulder height of 26 to 40 inches (66 to 102 centimeters). Its tail measures 3 to 5.5 inches (8 to 14 centimeters). The animal may weigh between 70 and 240 pounds (30 and 110 kilograms). Males are substantially larger than females.

Male markhors have unique corkscrew–shaped horns that are very thick and heavy. They also have a large beard and a long, shaggy mane at the base of their neck. If a female has a beard, which is rare, it is small. The coat of both sexes varies in length and color with the seasons. In summer, a markhor's coat is short and reddish brown. In winter, it is long, silky, and gray.

Markhors are active during the day, grazing on grasses and herbs or browsing (feeding on the tender shoots, twigs, and leaves) on shrubs and low trees. Wolves, leopards, and snow leopards often prey on the markhor.

Males generally live by themselves, while females and young live in groups of 10 to 12. During the winter mating season, males compete with each other over the right to mate with females. After a gestation (pregnancy) period of

Markhor | **147**

about 155 days, a female markhor gives birth to one or two young.

Habitat and current distribution

Markhors inhabit rocky areas, open forested slopes, and meadows in the rugged mountains of central Asia. Their range extends from the western end of the Himalayas in northwestern India to southern Tajikistan and Uzbekistan.

There are three subspecies of the markhor: the Kabal markhor (*Capra falconeri megaceros*), the straight–horned markhor (*Capra falconeri jerdoni*), and the Tajik markhor (*Capra falconeri heptneri*). Kabal and straight–horn markhors are found primarily in Afghanistan and Pakistan. Tajik markhors occupy southern Uzbekistan and Tajikistan. With population numbers ranging from 700 to just over 3,000, all three subspecies are in danger of extinction.

History and conservation measures

Excessive hunting, primarily for the markhor's horns, is the main reason for the animal's decline. As the human population increases in the markhor's range, so does the destruction of its habitat. Trees are cut down for timber, forested land is cleared to create agricultural land, and domestic sheep and goats compete with the markhor for food.

Twenty–seven protected areas have been established in the markhor's range. The level of safety in these areas, however, is limited by political unrest and military activity in the region. In addition, most markhor populations are very small and often isolated from each other, making conservation efforts difficult.

MARMOSET, WHITE–EARED
Callithrix aurita

PHYLUM: Chordata
CLASS: Mammalia
ORDER: Primates
FAMILY: Callitrichidae
STATUS: Endangered, IUCN
Endangered, ESA
RANGE: Brazil

Marmoset, white-eared

Callithrix aurita

Description and biology

The white–eared marmoset, also known as the buffy–tufted ear marmoset, is a small monkey, about 7 to 9 inches (18 to 23 centimeters) long and weighing only about 9 to 11 ounces (257 to 314 grams). The white–eared marmoset is a member of the Callitrichidae family, which includes 26 species of marmosets and tamarins from the tropical forests of Central and South America. They are some of the world's smallest primates. The white–eared marmoset is black with white spots on the forehead and tail and very long white hair coming out of its ears. The species is diurnal (active during the daytime) and arboreal (lives in the trees). Its diet consists of fruit and insects, such as ants, termites, and caterpillars, and some small animals. It may also eat tree gum when other foods are not available. It has claws instead of nails on its fingers

The white–eared marmoset is a social animal. It usually lives in a small group consisting of two to thirteen members.

and toes for climbing in trees. It moves about on all four limbs when on the ground. The white–eared marmoset can also leap through the forest.

The white–eared marmoset is a social animal. It usually lives in a small group consisting of two to thirteen members. Each group has its own territory, which may be 1 to 13 acres in diameter. The group sleeps together in the branches of a tree or in dense vegetation (plant life) on the ground. The white–eared marmoset is monogamous—males and females remain partners for life. Living groups are centered around one dominant monogamous couple; other members tend to come and go over the course of time. Only the dominant female in the group breeds. She will give birth to one to four offspring—but usually twins—after a gestation (pregnancy) period of 140 to 148 days. The young are then raised cooperatively by the members of the living group. Males as well as females care for the young in this family arrangement. Marmosets' life spans are about 11 to 17 years.

The white–eared marmoset has several means of communication. It makes high–pitched trills to signal alarm. It opens and closes its mouth, making a lip–smacking sound, to initiate sexual behavior or to convey aggression. Sometimes it puts its tongue in and out of its mouth rhythmically along with the lip smacking. When threatened, it will raise its eyebrows. Scent is also used by a female to mark a male before mating takes place.

Habitat and current distribution

The white–eared marmoset occurs in coastal mountain rain forest regions, above 3,000 feet in altitude, along the Atlantic coastline of southeastern Brazil. The area includes parts of Minas Gerais, Rio de Janeiro, and Sao Paulo. Marmosets in the wild are difficult for humans to observe, and their current population numbers are not known.

History and conservation measures

The largest threat to the white–eared marmoset is the deforestation (cutting down of trees) in the Brazilian rain forests and tropical forests. Brazil's Atlantic rain forest region has long been home to hundreds of thousands of species. It is a huge area of more than a half million square miles. In the last five centuries, however, the area has been overwhelmed by an overflowing human population. Into the 1970s, the Brazilian government promoted clearing the forests to harvest the lumber and to make way for sugar, coffee, and cocoa plantations, cattle grazing, and industry. Nearly 93 percent of the natural forests and wilderness have been lost. White –eared marmosets live, therefore, in small, fragmented areas. They are at risk from human capture as well, as they are prized as pets in Europe and elsewhere, and they are used for testing in medical and scientific laboratories. During the 1990s, with severely declining populations, it appeared that the white–eared marmoset would be extinct within 20 years. Breeding–in–captivity programs were thought to be the greatest hope for the preservation of the species.

DID YOU KNOW?

The Atlantic rain forest in Brazil has an average rainfall of 78 inches (2,000 millimeters) per year. Before being cleared, it teems with life and has an extraordinarily high level of biodiversity (variety of life forms). The luxuriant growth is due to tiny micro–organisms, or fungi, from which the plant–life gets its nutrients.

When farmers clear the rain forest to make room for coffee plantations, there is rich growth there. But after the land has been cleared, the fungi that feeds the vegetation dies, and the soil is too poor to keep up the coffee harvests for long. The farmers then have to clear more land to grow coffee. This cycle gets particularly bad in poor economic times, such as the 1980s and the early 2000s. Although the Brazilian government prohibited clearing of rain forests in 1988, the rate of cutting has actually accelerated. From 1990 to 1995 1,235,000 acres (500,000 hectares) were cleared in the Atlantic rain forest.

Since the 1980s, the Brazilian government changed its policies. Concerned citizen groups have made a tremendous difference in conservation efforts. Marmosets are now protected by the government, and cutting down the rain forests has been prohibited. To assure enforcement of these new laws, one nongovernmental organization, SOS Atlantic Forest, launched a satellite survey of the rain forests, to reveal and record illegal forest clearing. Another Brazilian group, the Pro–Bocainan Association, has championed restoring the management of Bocaina National Park, which had been only been protected by unenforced laws and had for years been subjected to great exploitation. Bocaina has 275,000 acres (111,336 hectares) of coastal mountain rain forest and is part of the largest remaining stretch of the marmoset's original habitat. With many organizations and private citizens working on behalf of the tiny primates, there was reason to hope that the marmoset populations were on the road to recovery in the early 2000s.

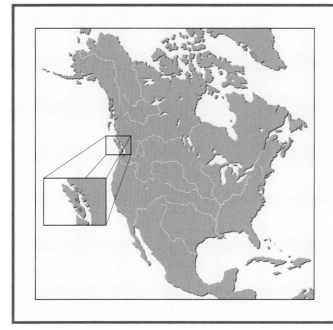

**MARMOT,
VANCOUVER ISLAND**
Marmota vancouverensis

PHYLUM: Chordata

CLASS: Mammalia

ORDER: Rodentia

FAMILY: Sciuridae

STATUS: Endangered, IUCN
Endangered, ESA

RANGE: Canada (Vancouver
Island)

Marmot, Vancouver Island
Marmota vancouverensis

Description and biology

Marmots are ground–living rodents of the squirrel family, closely related to the chipmunk, ground squirrel, and prairie dog. The woodchuck is the best–known North American marmot species. The Vancouver Island marmot has coarse fur and a bushy tail 4 to 10 inches (10 to 25 centimeters) long. Its deep brown coat is darker than that of most marmots. An average Vancouver Island marmot has a head and body length of 12 to 23.5 inches (30 to 60 centimeters) and weighs between 6.5 and 16.5 pounds (3 and 7.5 kilograms).

Vancouver Island marmots feed on plants, especially the flowering parts. They hibernate for six to nine months in a den, huddled together in a family group of about eight members. Male and female Vancouver Island marmots mate after emerging from hibernation, usually in April or May. After a gestation (pregnancy) period of four to five weeks, a female marmot gives birth to a litter of two to six young.

Conservation efforts to save the Vancouver Island marmot have been successful. The population has increased considerably since the programs were implemented in the 1970s.

Habitat and current distribution

This species of marmot is found only on Vancouver Island, off the southwest coast of British Columbia, Canada. It inhabits the higher regions of the coastal mountains that mark the central and southern parts of the island. Most of the known groups of marmots are found in a small area between Green Mountain and Butler Peak in the island's southern section. In the mid–1980s, biologists (people who study living organisms) estimated that the population of Vancouver Island marmots numbered 231.

The marmots prefer to inhabit steep, rocky slopes and open meadows at elevations between 3,280 and 6,560 feet (1,000 and 2,000 meters).

History and conservation measures

The Vancouver Island marmot was discovered in 1911. Since that time, its population has declined, probably as a result of contact with humans. Extensive logging and the building of recreation areas such as ski resorts have destroyed some marmot habitat. Hunting of the animal, more common in the past, continues even today.

The Vancouver Island Marmot Preservation Society has led recent conservation efforts to save the animal. The organization has spurred the Canadian government to conduct scientific field research on the species and to establish captive breeding programs, among other actions. The society's efforts have been successful. The population of Vancouver Island marmots has increased since the 1970s.

MINK, EUROPEAN'S
Mustela lutreola

PHYLUM: Chordata
CLASS: Mammalia
ORDER: Carnivora
FAMILY: Mustelidae
STATUS: Endangered, IUCN
RANGE: Austria, Belarus, Bulgaria, Czech Republic, Estonia, Finland, France, Georgia, Germany, Greece, Hungary, Latvia, Lithuania, Moldova, Republic of Netherlands, Poland, Romania, Russian Federation, Slovakia, Spain, Ukraine

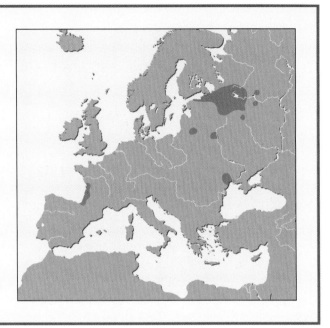

Mink, European

Mustela lutreola

Description and biology

Minks belong to the weasel family, which also includes ermine, skunks, martens, wolverines, and otters. There are two types of mink within the family, the European and the American mink. The European mink, now very rare, is smaller than the American and has a wide white area around its mouth. European minks have blackish–brown to light–brown fur. They change their fur twice a year. Males weigh about 1.6 pounds (740 grams) and females weigh about 0.9 pound (440 grams). Minks live near water. They have partly webbed feet that aid them in swimming and diving. They are nocturnal (active at night) creatures that hunt on ground and under water for their food. Their diet consists of small mammals, birds, frogs, mollusks, crabs, fish, and insects. They have a keen sense of smell that helps in their hunting. European minks live in burrows taken from water voles or among the roots of trees.

European minks are solitary animals. Each mink has its own territory near a river or a stream, which it will defend from intruding members of its species. The minks check their borders regularly, marking them with their scent. Mating takes place in February and March each year, and after a five- to ten-week gestation (pregnancy) period females give birth to two to seven young in April or May. The females raise their offspring for the first three or four months of their lives. After that the offspring go off on their own. They are mature at about ten months old and they generally live about six years in the wild, and up to twelve years in captivity.

Habitat and current distribution

European minks live on the banks of fresh waterways, such as lakes, creeks, and rivers, where there is heavy vegetation

European minks live on the banks of fresh waterways, such as lakes, creeks, and rivers, where there is heavy vegetation (plant growth).

(plant growth). Although the species was once common throughout Europe, today it exists mainly in parts of Russia and a few other Eastern European countries, where it is rapidly declining. A few small populations can be found in France and Spain. In 1997 there were an estimated 40,000 European mink in Eastern Europe and 100 to 1,000 in Western Europe. The species is extinct in much of its former habitat.

History and conservation measures

One of the reasons for the decline in the population of the European mink was the introduction of the American mink into its native regions. The American mink was imported into Europe in 1926 for fur farming. Some of the American population escaped into the wild, where it multiplied and rapidly spread throughout Europe. The American mink competed for food and shelter with the European mink.

Other causes of the decline of the species are the loss of natural habitat due to human settlement, hunting, and pollution. Since the 1990s, predictions of the extinction of the species have motivated numerous Eastern and Western European conservation efforts to preserve the European mink in the wild and to breed it in captivity. Crucial to the survival of the species is the conservation of its original habitats in Russia, France, Spain, Estonia, and Byelorussia, along with the creation of new habitats and conservation areas. Efforts are underway to get rid of the population of American mink in the wild in some European areas.

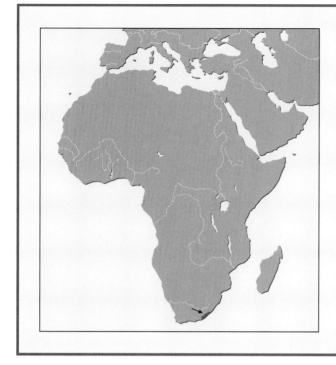

MOLE, GIANT GOLDEN
Chrysospalax trevelyani

PHYLUM: Chordata
CLASS: Mammalia
ORDER: Insectivora
FAMILY: Chrysochloridae
STATUS: Endangered, IUCN
RANGE: South Africa

Mole, giant golden

Chrysospalax trevelyani

Description and biology

There are 17 species of golden moles, all found in Africa. The giant golden mole, the largest, rarest, and most endangered of the golden moles, is about 8 inches (20 centimeters) long and weighs as much as 19 ounces (538 grams). Its fur is shiny and reddish–brown. Giant golden moles have tiny eyes that are covered by skin, making them blind. Their ears, too, are tiny and hidden in fur.

The giant golden mole spends most of its time below ground, where it digs systems of tunnels. It builds hills in the ground that serve as doors into its underground chambers. The giant golden mole eats crickets, cockroaches, grasshoppers, worms, snails, and other invertebrates. One of the items on its diet is the giant earthworm, found only in South Africa and the longest known species of earthworm in the world at

4 or 5 feet (1.5 meters) long. The giant golden mole rarely comes up from underground, except when heavy rains wash out its tunnels and force it to the surface. At these times, the mole is particularly vulnerable to dogs. The giant golden mole hibernates in winter, burrowing among the roots of trees. It moves slowly but stays in motion all the time it is awake in order to keep its body temperature normal. When it sleeps, its body twitches to keep up the body temperature. A mother giant golden mole generally gives birth to two, but sometimes only one, offspring at a time.

Habitat and current distribution

Giant golden moles live in South Africa in a few areas in the Cape Province from King William's Town and East London to Port St. John in Transkei. They live in forests where there is leaf litter and dense shrubs. Because these moles are so rare and remain underground and hidden most of the time, they are difficult to study. Wildlife biologists (people who study living organisms) do not know how many giant golden moles remain in the world today.

History and conservation measures

The forests in which the giant golden mole lives are being cleared and damaged by human settlement and the overgrazing of domestic herds. Where there are humans, there are also dogs, which are predators (hunters) of giant golden moles. It is believed that some of the remaining population of giant golden moles has found refuge from dogs and human activities in Dwesa Nature Reserve, Transkei, but little is known about this rare species.

MONKEY, CENTRAL AMERICAN SQUIRREL
Saimiri oerstedii

PHYLUM: Chordata
CLASS: Mammalia
ORDER: Primates
FAMILY: Cebidae
STATUS: Critically endangered, IUCN
Endangered, ESA
RANGE: Costa Rica, Panama

Monkey, Central American squirrel
Saimiri oerstedii

Description and biology

The Central American squirrel monkey is also known as the red–backed squirrel monkey because of the short, thick reddish fur covering its back, limbs, and tail. The fur on the rest of its body, including its face, is white. An average Central American squirrel monkey has a head and body length of 9 to 14 inches (23 to 36 centimeters) and weighs between 1 and 2.4 pounds (0.5 and 1.1 kilograms). The tail, which is not prehensile (adapted for grasping or holding by wrapping around something), measures 14 to 18 inches (36 to 46 centimeters) long.

The Central American squirrel monkey spends most of its time in trees and feeds on fruit and insects. Groups of 10 to

161

A female Central American squirrel monkey with her baby. The infant will remain with its mother for almost a year.

40 monkeys live together, often combining with other groups to form very large societies. Some groups inhabit forest areas as small as 2 acres (0.8 hectare). Others may occupy as much as 50 to 100 acres (20 to 40 hectares).

Males often fight with each other over the right to mate with a female. After a gestation (pregnancy) period of 152 to 170 days, a female Central American squirrel monkey gives birth to a single infant. It clings to its mother after birth and remains dependent on her for almost a year.

Habitat and current distribution

Central American squirrel monkeys are found only in western Panama and southern Costa Rica. Biologists (people who study living organisms) have estimated that the Costa Rican population numbers 3,000. The number of monkeys living in Panama is unknown. In these two regions, the animals prefer to inhabit forests, woodlands, and areas dominated by shrubs and low, bushy trees.

History and conservation measures

The population of Central American squirrel monkeys has decreased greatly since the 1950s. The primary reason is due to deforestation (the loss of forests as they are rapidly cut down to produce timber or to make land available for agriculture). Much of the squirrel monkey's habitat has been converted to banana plantations, cattle ranches, and rice and sugar cane farms.

Costa Rican farmers have transformed this land through slash–and–burn agriculture, a process whereby a forest is cut down and all trees and vegetation are burned to create cleared land. Although this process clears land quickly, it robs the soil of essential nutrients. The land does not stay fertile for very long. Thus, farmers must continually clear new land in order to grow crops.

The Panamanian government passed a land reform law in the 1950s that required land owners to make profitable use of their forested land or be forced to give up that land. As a result, forests—and squirrel monkey habitat—were destroyed to create money–making farms.

The monkeys have also faced the threat of capture. Up through the 1970s, they were taken from their forest habitat and exported around the world for use as pets and in medical research. International treaties now ban the sale and trade of the animals.

Central American squirrel monkeys are protected in the Corcovado National Biological Reserve in southern Costa Rica.

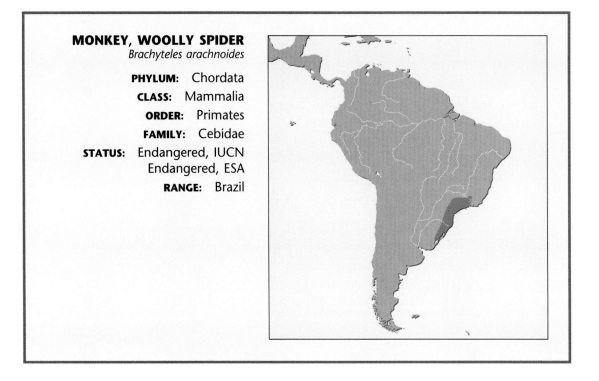

MONKEY, WOOLLY SPIDER
Brachyteles arachnoides

PHYLUM: Chordata
CLASS: Mammalia
ORDER: Primates
FAMILY: Cebidae
STATUS: Endangered, IUCN
Endangered, ESA
RANGE: Brazil

Monkey, woolly spider
Brachyteles arachnoides

Description and biology

The woolly spider monkey, or muriqui, is the largest species of New World (Western Hemisphere) monkey. It has an average head and body length of 18 to 25 inches (46 to 64 centimeters) and weighs between 26 and 33 pounds (12 and 15 kilograms). Its prehensile (able to grasp or hold something by wrapping around it) tail is longer than its body, measuring 25 to 32 inches (64 to 81 centimeters) long. The animal's head is round and small in relation to its body. Its limbs are long. The fur on its body is thick and gold in color. The fur on its face, arms, and legs is black, although sometimes it may be pink or mottled (spotted or streaked).

The woolly spider monkey lives in the crown of the tallest trees and has never been seen on the ground. It moves through the trees by swinging from branch to branch with

its arms. It feeds during the day on leaves, seeds, fruits, and insects.

Most woolly spider monkeys form social groups of 2 to 4 members, although groups of up to 20 or more have been observed in the wild. Mating between males and females may take place at any time. After a gestation (pregnancy) period of four to five months, a female woolly spider monkey gives birth to a single infant.

Habitat and current distribution

The woolly spider monkey prefers to inhabit undisturbed tropical and rain forests. Its range extends only over the southeastern Brazilian states of São Paulo, Espírito Santo, Rio de Janeiro, and Minas Gerais. Biologists (people who study living organisms) estimate that 200 to 400 of the animals currently exist in the wild.

History and conservation measures

The woolly spider monkey once ranged over all Atlantic coastal forests of eastern and southeastern Brazil. It is estimated that the monkey's population in the sixteenth century numbered almost 500,000. By 1972, that population had dropped to 2,000. Today, the animal is almost extinct, and in 2000 the International Union for Conservation of Nature and Natural Resources (IUCN) raised the status of the species from endangered to critically endangered. The woolly spider monkey is, according to the IUCN, one of the most threatened primates remaining in existence in the Atlantic forests of southeastern Brazil.

Since the 1800s, the human population in this region of Brazil has swelled enormously. To feed the growing numbers of people, large tracts of forest have been cleared over the years to provide pasture land for cattle and to create coffee, sugar cane, and cocoa plantations. Logging of these forest areas for their valuable timber has also taken its toll. Only two percent of the original forest cover remains in this region.

In the past, woolly spider monkeys were hunted for food. Although currently protected by law, many may still be taken by hunters in some areas.

Small, isolated groups of the animals exist in protected areas. In the state of Minas Gerais, about 50 monkeys live on a private coffee plantation called Fazenda Montes Claros. Another group lives on Fazenda Barreiro Rico, a private ranch in São Paulo. Woolly spider monkeys may also be found in the Biological Reserve of Nova Lombardi in Espírito Santo and in other state and national parks in the region.

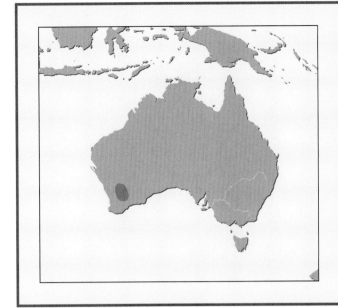

NUMBAT
Myrmecobius fasciatus

PHYLUM: Chordata
CLASS: Mammalia
ORDER: Marsupialia
FAMILY: Myrmecobiidae
STATUS: Vulnerable, IUCN
Endangered, ESA
RANGE: Australia

Numbat

Myrmecobius fasciatus

Description and biology

The numbat, also known as the banded anteater, is a very unusual Australian marsupial. Marsupials are an order of mammals whose young continue to develop after birth in a pouch on the outside of the mother's body. Most marsupials are nocturnal (active at night). The numbat, however, does not have a true pouch in which its young develop and it is diurnal (pronounced die–ER–nal; active during the day).

Resembling a squirrel in size, an average numbat has a head and body length of 9 inches (23 centimeters) and a tail length of 7 inches (18 centimeters). It weighs between 14 and 21 ounces (397 and 595 grams). The numbat's coat is reddish brown with white flecks. A series of white stripes stretches across its back all the way to its bushy tail. A dark stripe runs across the animal's eye from its ear to its long, flattened snout.

The numbat feeds chiefly on termites. It uses its sharp–clawed forefeet to dig into termite colonies it finds in fallen

Unlike other marsupials, the numbat does not have a pouch for its young to develop in and is active during the day. Most marsupials are nocturnal or active during the night.

branches. It then uses its long, sticky tongue to remove the termites, which it swallows whole. The animal has a home range of 50 to 120 acres (20 to 48 hectares). At night, it builds a sheltering nest of leaves, grass, and bark in hollow logs or in burrows it digs for itself.

The normally solitary male and female numbat come together only to mate. A female numbat gives birth to four young, usually in January or February. Since she does not have a pouch, her young attach themselves to her nipples and cling to the surrounding hair. They stay attached for six months. Afterward, the female places her young in various nests she has built, moving them between those nests by carrying them on her back. The young numbats eventually leave their mother's home range by November or December.

Habitat and current distribution

Numbats prefer to live in forests dominated by eucalyptus trees that are prone to attack by termites. The animals are currently found only in southwestern Western Australia. Biologists (people who study living organisms) estimate that less than 2,000 numbats exist in the wild.

History and conservation measures

The numbat once ranged throughout southern Australia. Slowly it began to disappear from eastern areas until, by the 1960s, it was found only in the southwestern region of the country. The numbat population continued to decline until 1980, when the Australian government realized that red foxes that had been introduced into numbat habitat were preying on the animals. Since then, the government has controlled the number of foxes in the region and the numbat population has recovered slightly. The Australian government is also trying to relocate numbats to their former eastern habitats.

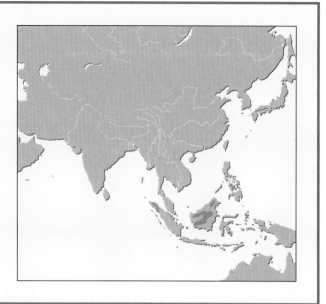

ORANGUTAN
Pongo pygmaeus

PHYLUM: Chordata
CLASS: Mammalia
ORDER: Primates
FAMILY: Hominidae
STATUS: Endangered, IUCN
Endangered, ESA
RANGE: Brunei, Indonesia,
Malaysia

Orangutan

Pongo pygmaeus

Description and biology

The only great ape found in Asia, the orangutan is the largest living arboreal (tree–dwelling) ape. In the Malay language, its name means "forest person" or "man of the woods." With its long, powerful arms and hands and feet that can grasp branches, the animal moves easily from tree to tree. The orangutan's reddish brown coat is long and soft. It has small ears, a bulging snout, and a high forehead. An average orangutan has a head and body length of 30 to 40 inches (76 to 102 centimeters) and a shoulder height of 45 to 60 inches (114 to 152 centimeters). It weighs between 85 and 220 pounds (39 and 100 kilograms). Males are much larger and heavier than females.

Orangutans spend 95 percent of their lives in trees. During the day, the animals feed primarily on fruit. They also eat leaves, insects, bark, and young birds and squirrels. Each night, they build a nest in a tree 35 to 80 feet (11 to 24 meters) above

One of the greatest threats to orangutans is their capture to be used as pets. Some childless human couples will even "adopt" the animals and dress them in clothes.

the ground. Their home range varies from 1 to 4 square miles (2.5 to 10 square kilometers).

The orangutan is a solitary animal. The only bond formed is between a mother and her infant. Mating, which can occur at any time during the year, is the only time males and females interact. They stay together for a few days to a few months until the female is pregnant, then they split up. After a gestation (pregnancy) period of 233 to 270 days, a female gives birth to one young. She raises the infant alone, keeping it constantly with her for the first year. She nurses the infant for up to three years. During a normal life span of 40 years, a female will bear only 4 or 5 offspring.

Habitat and current distribution

The orangutan inhabits a variety of forest habitats, including swampy coastal forests, mangrove forests, and mountain forests. It is found only on the Southeast Asian islands of Sumatra (part of the country of Indonesia) and Borneo (divided among Malaysia, Indonesia, and Brunei). In the mid–1990s, biologists (people who study living organisms) estimated that 12,000 to 20,000 orangutans existed on Borneo, while another 9,000 lived on Sumatra.

History and conservation measures

For thousands of years, the orangutan has been a victim of human abuse. Early humans considered it a food source and hunted it to the point of extinction in many areas. Orangutans once ranged throughout Southeast Asia. They now live on only 2 percent of that original range.

The greatest threat to orangutans is habitat destruction. The relentless clearing of rain forests to create plantations on the islands has reduced their habitat by 90 percent in the last 50 years. The animals are driven into forest areas that are too small to support them. Seeking food, the orangutans often wander onto nearby plantations. They are then killed or injured by workers protecting the crops.

In late 1997, orangutans and other wildlife in Southeast Asia suffered terribly from devastating wildfires and smoke that swept across the region. The fires resulted from man–made and natural causes. Farmers in the region rely on slash–and–burn agriculture, a process whereby a forest is cut down and all trees and vegetation are burned to create cleared land. When the El Niño weather pattern delayed the seasonal monsoon rains, hot and dry conditions fanned the fires. Many orangutans died in the fires or from smoke inhalation. Others were killed by frightened villagers as they escaped the burning forests. In 2000, the Indonesian news agency announced that the population of orangutan in Indonesia had dropped by one–third in the three years after the fires, noting that the animals had still not recovered. Individual orangutans were still found wandering outside their former habitat.

Another major threat to orangutans is capture. Thousands of females have been slaughtered so their offspring could be captured and sold as pets. Some childless couples even raise the animals as children, dressing them in human clothes. In the late 1980s and early 1990s, the demand for orangutan pets was especially strong in Taiwan, where a children's television show featured a pet orangutan. Of those infants that are captured in the wild, up to 50 percent die during transport.

Several protected reserves have been established in the orangutan's range, including the Gunung Lueser National Park in northern Sumatra and the Tanjung Puting National Park in Borneo. Conservationists and wildlife researchers have also established camps to help train orangutans that were once pets to return to their natural habitat. However, most of these orangutans have spent too much time among humans and cannot exist in the wild. In 2002, there was some good news. An expedition into the remote wilds of Borneo discovered a large and previously unknown population of the species, comprising perhaps the largest remaining orangutan population. But as clearing of the forests continues at a rapid rate, this population, too, is in jeopardy.

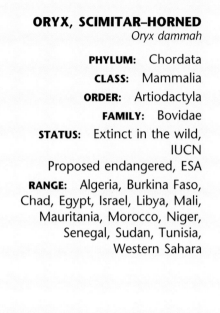

ORYX, SCIMITAR–HORNED
Oryx dammah

PHYLUM: Chordata

CLASS: Mammalia

ORDER: Artiodactyla

FAMILY: Bovidae

STATUS: Extinct in the wild, IUCN
Proposed endangered, ESA

RANGE: Algeria, Burkina Faso, Chad, Egypt, Israel, Libya, Mali, Mauritania, Morocco, Niger, Senegal, Sudan, Tunisia, Western Sahara

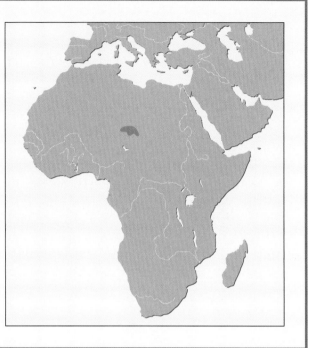

Oryx, scimitar-horned

Oryx dammah

Description and biology

The scimitar–horned oryx is a small, horselike antelope. It is so–named because its two horns, which extend back from its head in a long sweeping arc, are similar in shape to scimitars, which are curved, single–edged Asian swords. Most of its body is nearly white in color. Its neck and small portions of its face are dark brown. This oryx has short, rounded ears, large hooves, and a tuft of hair below its chin and at the end of its tail. It also has a short mane extending from its head over its shoulders.

An average scimitar–horned oryx has a head and body length of 60 to 90 inches (152 to 229 centimeters) and weighs 250 to 460 pounds (114 to 209 kilograms). Its tail measures 18 to 35 inches (46 to 89 centimeters) long, while its horns extend 30 to 55 inches (76 to 140 centimeters).

174

Scimitar–horned oryx often gather in herds of 20 to 40 members. During the day, the herds travel over great distances to feed on grass and other desert vegetation. The animals are often preyed upon by hyenas and large cats.

A scimitar–horned oryx with its horns that resemble a scimitar, a type of Asian sword.

Mating may take place between males and females at any time, but births seem to peak during early spring and early fall. Female scimitar–horned oryx give birth to a single infant after a gestation (pregnancy) period of 220 to 253 days.

Habitat and current distribution

Scimitar–horned oryx inhabit the rolling dunes and grassy plains of the desert regions in northern Africa. In 1996, it was reported that a few oryx remained in the wild in Chad. After that there were no more sightings, and in 1999 the International Union for Conservation of Nature and Natural

Resources (IUCN) listed the scimitar–horned oryx as extinct in the wild. There has been an unconfirmed sighting of the species in Chad since then. In 1996, there were an estimated 1,250 scimitar–horned oryx in captivity in zoos and parks worldwide and about 2,145 more animals on ranches in Texas.

History and conservation measures

This species was once quite common in the areas surrounding the Sahara Desert. Herds sometimes joined together to form groups that numbered in the thousands. In the past few decades, however, desertification, drought, competition from domestic livestock, and uncontrolled hunting by humans have all combined to eliminate this oryx from much of its original habitat.

Desertification is the gradual transformation of productive land into that with desertlike conditions. Even a desert can become desertified, losing its sparse collection of plants and animals and becoming a barren wasteland. Much of the scimitar–horned oryx's habitat has been desertified by natural and man–made actions. Droughts have plagued the region, and overgrazing by farm animals has depleted what little vegetation has been able to grow.

The greatest threat to the scimitar–horned oryx, however, has been hunting. Wanton (merciless) killing by humans has brought the animal to near extinction in several parts of its range during various times of the twentieth century. By the mid–1970s, almost all of the region's scimitar–horned oryx were confined to a single place: the Ouadi Rime–Ouadi Achim Faunal Reserve in Chad. Established in 1969, the reserve was a suitable, well–protected habitat area. By 1978, the oryx population in the reserve numbered about 5,000. That same year, civil war broke out in the country and protection for the reserve ceased.

A breeding–in–captivity program was initiated in the 1960s for the scimitar–horned oryx. In the early 2000s, reintroduction of the species to the wild is taking place, with the first releases occurring in Tunisia. If these new populations in Tunisia begin to reproduce and sustain themselves, the species will once again exist in the wild.

OTTER, MARINE
Lontra (lutra) felina

PHYLUM: Chordata
CLASS: Mammalia
ORDER: Carnivora
FAMILY: Mustelidae
STATUS: Endangered, IUCN
Endangered, ESA
RANGE: Argentina, Chile, Peru

Otter, marine
Lontra (lutra) felina

Description and biology

Otters are members of the weasel family. The marine otter, sometimes called the sea cat, has a long body, a flat head, small ears, and a broad, whiskered muzzle. Its short legs and webbed feet help make it an agile swimmer. Thick, glossy dark brown hair covers its body. An average marine otter has a head and body length of 22 to 31 inches (59 to 79 centimeters) and a tail length of 12 to 14 inches (30 to 36 inches). It weighs 7 to 31 pounds (3 to 14 kilograms).

Marine otters feed mainly on crustaceans (such as crabs and shrimp) and mollusk (such as snails, clams, and oysters). While swimming on their backs, they often lay their prey on their chests and use rocks to smash open the hard shells. The otter's main predator is the orca (killer whale).

Marine otters prefer to inhabit exposed rocky coastal areas and secluded bays and inlets near estuaries.

The otters are primarily solitary animals, but groups of three or more have been observed in the wild. Male and female marine otters mate at any time during the year, although primarily during the summer. After a gestation (pregnancy) period that lasts between 60 and 120 days, female marine otters usually give birth to a litter of two pups.

Habitat and current distribution

The marine otter ranges along the Pacific coastline of Peru and Chile south to the Strait of Magellan, a narrow channel separating South America from Tierra del Fuego and other islands south of the continent. The otters are found primarily in the southern region of their range. One scientific study estimated that the total marine otter population numbers less than 1,000.

Marine otters prefer to inhabit exposed rocky coastal areas and secluded bays and inlets near estuaries (regions where a river empties into an ocean). While searching for freshwater shrimp, marine otters have been known to swim 2,000 feet (610 meters) up a river from the ocean.

History and conservation measures

Marine otters were once plentiful throughout their entire range. However, because the animals have been long hunted for their fur, they are now endangered or on the verge of extinction in many areas. Water pollution also may be responsible for the destruction of sections of their habitat.

International treaties have banned the sale of marine otter pelts, but no other current conservation measures are underway.

DID YOU KNOW?

The preservation of otters is important for all species, including humans. Otters are found on all continents except Australia, live both in water and on land, and are near the top of the food chain. For this reason, they are an important indicator species (plants or animals that, by their presence or chemical composition, give some distinctive indication of the health or quality of the environment). A drop in the number of otters could indicate that the areas they inhabit (watermeadows, rivers, estuaries, lakes, coastal zones) or the food they eat (fish, crustaceans, mollusks, frogs) may be in poor condition.

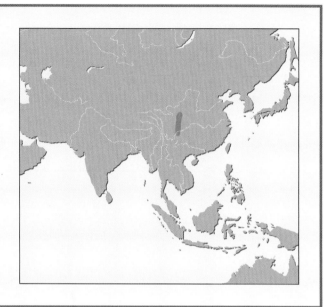

PANDA, GIANT
Ailuropoda melanoleuca

PHYLUM: Chordata
CLASS: Mammalia
ORDER: Carnivora
FAMILY: Ursidae
STATUS: Endangered, IUCN
Endangered, ESA
RANGE: China

Panda, giant
Ailuropoda melanoleuca

Description and biology

Recognized worldwide, the giant panda has become a symbol in the fight to save endangered species from extinction. The animal shares many characteristics with both bears and raccoons. Since recent genetic tests reveal it is more closely related to the bear, scientists classify it as a member of the bear family (Ursidae).

An average giant panda has a head and body length of 4 to 6 feet (1.2 to 1.8 meters) and weighs between 165 and 350 pounds (75 and 160 kilograms). Its tail measures 5 inches (13 centimeters) in length. The animal's thick, woolly coat is primarily white. Its legs, shoulders, ears, and eye patches are black.

Bamboo stalks and roots make up 95 percent of the giant panda's diet. One of its wrist bones is enlarged and elongated, and the animal uses it like a thumb when grasping stalks of bamboo. The giant panda also has strong jaws and teeth to crush bamboo. The remainder of its diet is made up of grass, bulbs, insects, rodents, and fish. The animal spends 10 to 16 hours eating the 20 to 40 pounds (9 to 18 kilograms) of food it needs each day.

Giant pandas are solitary and territorial. They have a home range of 1.5 to 2.5 square miles (4 to 6.5 square kilometers), which they mark with secretions from scent glands. Males and females come together to mate between March and May. After a gestation (pregnancy) period of 125 to 150 days, a female giant panda gives birth to one to two cubs in a sheltered den. The cubs are very fragile at birth, weighing only 3 to 5 ounces (85 to 142 grams). If two cubs are born, usually just one survives. It remains with its mother for up to a year. The average life span of a giant panda in the wild is 15 years.

Habitat and current distribution

Among the rarest mammals in the world, giant pandas are found only in the mountains of central China, in the Sichuan, Shaanxi, and Gansu provinces. Biologists (people who study living organisms) estimate that about 1,000 giant pandas exist in the wild. The animals prefer to inhabit dense bamboo and coniferous (cone bearing) forests at elevations between 5,000 and 10,000 feet (1,525 and 3,050 meters).

History and conservation measures

The giant panda has existed in China for hundreds of thousands of years. It was once common throughout the country, but over the last 2,000 years it has disappeared from Henan, Hubei, Hunan, Guizhou, and Yunnan provinces. In 1869, the French missionary and naturalist Armand David became the first European to describe the giant panda. The species was not well known in the West until a captive specimen was brought to the United States in the 1930s. As a gesture of goodwill, the Chinese government presented U.S. president Richard Nixon with a pair of giant pandas (Ling–Ling and Hsing–Hsing) in 1972. The animals were kept at the National Zoo in Washington, D.C. until their deaths in the 1990s.

Habitat destruction is the primary danger to giant pandas. Since bamboo grows slowly, the pandas need a large range in which to feed. This range is constantly being threatened by China's growing human population—estimated at over 1,000,000,000. To help save the dwindling giant panda

population, the Chinese government has set aside 11 nature preserves where bamboo flourishes.

Another threat to the giant panda is poaching, or illegal killing. The animal is protected by international treaties, and the Chinese government sentences those convicted of poaching a giant panda to life in prison. Nonetheless, the animal is still hunted for its fur, which is sold illegally in Southeast Asian markets at a high price.

More than 100 giant pandas are currently found in Chinese zoos. Several others are housed in North Korean zoos. Only about 15 giant pandas live in zoos outside of these two countries. The animals are often difficult to breed in captivity. The first giant panda birth outside China occurred at the Mexico City Zoo in 1980.

A giant panda eating. These animals spend 10 to 16 hours a day consuming food.

PANDA, RED
Ailurus fulgens

PHYLUM: Chordata
CLASS: Mammalia
ORDER: Carnivora
FAMILY: Procyonidae
STATUS: Endangered, IUCN
RANGE: Bhutan, China, India, Laos, Myanmar, Nepal

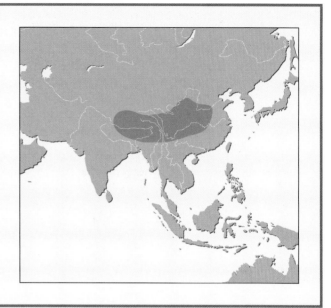

Panda, red
Ailurus fulgens

Description and biology

The red panda, also known as the lesser panda, has rust–colored fur with chocolate brown markings. The Chinese call this striking animal "firefox" because of its flame–colored fur. The red panda has short, pointed ears and a mask similar to a raccoon's. In fact, the red panda is considered a member of the raccoon family, unlike its relative the giant panda, which is a member of the bear family.

An average red panda has a head and body length of 20 to 23.5 inches (51 to 60 centimeters) and weighs between 7.7 and 11 pounds (3.5 and 5 kilograms). Its banded tail measures 12 to 20 inches (30 to 51 centimeters) in length. The animal is most active at dawn and at dusk. Although it spends most of its time in trees, it feeds on the ground. Its diet consists mainly of bamboo leaves, but it also eats grasses, berries, fruits, roots, and other plant matter.

Red pandas are solitary and territorial. A male red panda will often patrol the boundary of his territory, while a female

A red panda perched in a tree. The animal is sometimes called the "firefox" by the Chinese because of its flame–colored fur.

will often remain in the center of hers. The territory of a single male will overlap the territories of several females. Males and females come together to mate in January and February. During the courtship period, males and females will groom each other. After mating is complete, the male leaves and will not care for the female or her young. A female red panda gives birth to 1 to 4 cubs in a secure den (hollow tree, cave, or rock crevice) after a gestation (pregnancy) period of 90 to 145 days.

The newborn pandas are tan in color, blind, and totally dependent on their mother. They nurse for about 5 months, then begin eating bamboo leaves. A month later, they leave to stake out their own territories.

Habitat and current distribution

The red panda is found in the Himalayas and other mountains in northern India, southern China, Nepal, Bhutan, northern Myanmar, and northern Laos. It inhabits mountain spruce and fir forests at elevations between 6,500 and 13,000 feet (1,980 and 3,960 meters). The animal has been studied extensively only in Nepal. Scientists are unsure of the total number of red pandas in existence.

History and conservation measures

The major threat to red pandas is the loss of their habitat. Forests throughout much of the animal's range have been cleared to create farmland to feed a growing human population. In areas where forests have not been completely cleared, many trees have been cut down for use as fuel or building materials. The little "islands" of forest that remain are often not large enough to support the number of red pandas that have been forced to live there. With limited food sources, many of the animals starve to death.

Because of its attractive fur, the red panda has been hunted for its coat. Traps set for other animals in its range, such as the musk deer, also have taken their toll on the red panda. International treaties prohibit the trading of red panda pelts, and the animal is fully protected in China and Nepal.

In China, a number of red pandas also benefit by inhabiting the parks and reserves that have been set up for giant pandas. Displayed in zoos worldwide, red pandas have been bred in captivity with reasonable success. The International Red Panda Management Group is leading an effort to unite breeding programs around the world into a single global program.

PORCUPINE, THIN–SPINED
Chaetomys subspinosus

PHYLUM: Chordata
CLASS: Mammalia
ORDER: Rodentia
FAMILY: Echimyidae
STATUS: Vulnerable, IUCN
Endangered, ESA
RANGE: Brazil

Porcupine, thin-spined
Chaetomys subspinosus

Description and biology

The thin–spined porcupine, also known as the bristle–spined porcupine, gets its common names from the thin, bristly spines that cover its body. The animal is not considered a member of the family of true porcupines, but a member of the family of spiny rats. Unlike true porcupines, the thin–spined porcupine has no spines on its lower back. The spines on the animal's head and shoulders are kinky and short, just 0.6 inch (1.5 centimeters) in length. Those on its upper back, legs, and tail are wavier and longer, up to 2 inches (5 centimeters) in length. The spines are usually tricolored, ranging from pale yellow at the base to dark brown in the middle and back to pale yellow at the tip. The animal's body is brownish gray in color, while its feet and tail are darker.

An average thin–spined porcupine has a head and body length of 15 to 18 inches (38 to 46 centimeters) and a tail length of 10 inches (25 centimeters). All four of the animal's limbs have four digits (resembling human fingers or toes), which end in long, curved claws. These sharp claws help make the thin–spined porcupine an excellent climber, able to scale stone walls.

The thin–spined porcupine is nocturnal (active at night), feeding on fruits and cocoa tree nuts. Biologists (people who study living organisms) have been unable to study the animal well enough to learn its social structure or its reproductive habits.

Habitat and current distribution

The thin–spined porcupine is found only in the eastern and southeastern Brazilian states of Bahia, Sergipe, Espírito Santo, and Rio de Janeiro. It inhabits the edges of Atlantic coastal forests near open areas. The number of thin–spined porcupine existing in the wild is unknown, but the animal is believed to be quite rare.

History and conservation measures

The main threat facing the thin–spined porcupine is the loss of its habitat due to forest clear–cutting (process of cutting down all the trees in a forest area). Because scientists and conservationists (people protecting the natural world) know very little about the habits of the animal, saving its forest ecosystem (animals, plants, and microorganisms with their environment) is the best strategy to preserve the thin–spined porcupine. Other highly endangered species that inhabit the same ecosystem in the Atlantic coastal forests of Brazil, such as the golden lion tamarin, the white–eared marmoset, and the woolly spider monkey, would be saved at the same time.

POSSUM, MOUNTAIN PYGMY
Burramys parvus

PHYLUM: Chordata
CLASS: Mammalia
ORDER: Marsupialia
FAMILY: Burramyidae
STATUS: Endangered, IUCN
Endangered, ESA
RANGE: Australia

Possum, mountain pygmy
Burramys parvus

Description and biology

The mountain pygmy possum is a small marsupial (mammal whose young continue to develop after birth in a pouch on the outside of the mother's body). It has an average head and body length of 4 to 5 inches (10 to 13 centimeters) and weight of just 1 to 2 ounces (28 to 57 grams). Its 5.5–inch (14–centimeter) tail is prehensile, meaning it can hold onto items such as tree limbs by wrapping around them. The animal is covered with brownish gray fur that ends at the base of its tail.

Nocturnal (active during the night), the mountain pygmy possum forages on the ground and in trees for seeds, fruit, leaves, and insects. It is the only marsupial that stores seeds for use during the winter.

Male and female mountain pygmy possums mate in late October and early November. After a gestation (pregnancy) period of only 13 to 16 days, a female mountain pygmy possum

Although preyed on by foxes and cats, the mountain pygmy possums' main threat is destruction of its Australian habitat.

gives birth to a litter of four. The young remain in the mother's pouch for at least three weeks and are nursed for up to nine weeks.

Habitat and current distribution

Mountain pygmy possums inhabit the mountains of eastern Victoria and southeastern New South Wales in Australia. The animals are most often found at elevations between 5,000 and 6,000 feet (1,525 and 1,830 meters), living among the loose stones or rocky debris at the base of a slope or cliff. Biologists (people who study living organisms) believe around 900 of these animals exist in the wild.

History and conservation measures

Before the mid–1960s, the mountain pygmy possum was known only from fossilized remains found in New South

Wales. A live mountain pygmy possum was then found and identified in Victoria. Further animals were later found in New South Wales.

The main threat to the mountain pygmy possum is habitat destruction caused by the development of ski resorts. It is also preyed upon by cats and foxes.

Mountain pygmy possums are protected in the Bogong National Park in Victoria and the Mount Kosciusko National Park in New South Wales.

PRAIRIE DOG, MEXICAN
Cynomys mexicanus

PHYLUM: Chordata
CLASS: Mammalia
ORDER: Rodentia
FAMILY: Sciuridae
STATUS: Endangered, IUCN
Endangered, ESA
RANGE: Mexico

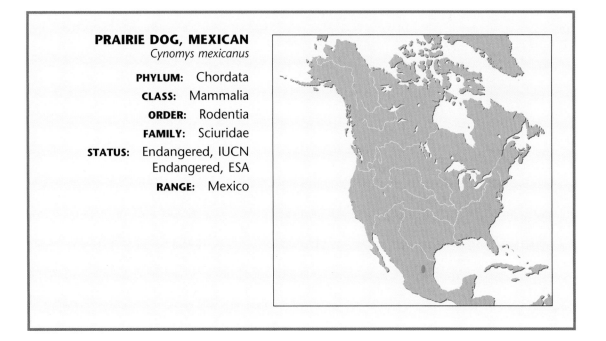

Prairie dog, Mexican

Cynomys mexicanus

Description and biology

The Mexican prairie dog is a large, stout member of the squirrel family, closely related to ground squirrels, chipmunks, and marmots. An average Mexican prairie dog measures 12 to 16 inches (30 to 41 centimeters) in length and weighs 1.5 to 3 pounds (0.7 to 1.4 kilograms). The animal's buff–colored fur is tinted with black, white, red, and yellow. The tip of its short tail is black. Twice a year, its fur is shed and replaced by a new coat (a process called molting).

Like other prairie dogs, the Mexican prairie dog is active above ground during the day. It feeds on grasses and other plants. Badgers, coyotes, weasels, eagles, hawks, and snakes are its main predators.

Mexican prairie dogs live in coteries, or groups, in large burrows they have dug with several entrances. A coterie is made up of one or two adult males, one to four adult females,

and a number of young. Mating between males and females usually takes place between late January and July. After a gestation (pregnancy) period of about 30 days, a female Mexican prairie dog gives birth to a varying number of pups.

Much of the Mexican prairie dogs' former habitat has been destroyed to create farmland to feed a growing human population.

Habitat and current distribution

The Mexican prairie dog is found only in northeastern Mexico in the states of Coahuila and San Luis Potosi. The animal prefers to inhabit open plains, valleys, and plateaus at elevations between 5,200 and 7,200 feet (1,600 and 2,200 meters). Biologists (people who study living organisms) do not know the total number of Mexican prairie dogs currently in existence.

History and conservation measures

The greatest threat to the Mexican prairie dog is habitat loss. Much of its former habitat has been destroyed to create

DID YOU KNOW?

Prairie dogs greet each other with a kiss. All members of a coterie (group) press their mouths together as a way of confirming their kinship within a coterie. Sometimes the kiss is a simple, quick peck. Other times its a long, drawn–out affair in which one prairie dog and then the other rolls on its back in seeming pleasure before going off to feed together.

When a prairie dog rejects a kiss, it is instantly viewed as an outsider. The prairie dog that offered the kiss immediately lifts and spreads its tail in a show of anger. If the second prairie dog does not then return the kiss, a confrontation ensues. Often the crisis ends quickly with the prairie dogs returning to their own territories.

farmland to feed a growing human population. Some colonies of Mexican prairie dogs have been intentionally poisoned by humans who view the animals as pests that destroy crops and grazing land.

Since little is known about the Mexican prairie dog's habits and biology, no specific conservation measures have been devised.

RABBIT, VOLCANO
Romerolagus diazi

PHYLUM: Chordata
CLASS: Mammalia
ORDER: Lagomorpha
FAMILY: Leporidae
STATUS: Endangered, IUCN Endangered, ESA
RANGE: Mexico

Rabbit, volcano
Romerolagus diazi

Description and biology

The volcano rabbit, also known as the Mexican pygmy rabbit, has short, thick dark brown hair. It is one of the few species of short–eared rabbits. Its rounded ears measure just 1.6 inches (4 centimeters) long. The animal also has short hind legs and feet and a very short tail. An average volcano rabbit has a head and body length of 10.5 to 13 inches (26.5 to 33 centimeters) and weighs between 14 and 18 ounces (397 and 510 grams).

Active mainly during the day, the volcano rabbit feeds on the tender young leaves of zacaton or bunchgrass (various wiry grass species that grow in low clumps in Mexico and the south-western United States). Its main predators are long–tailed weasels, bobcats, and rattlesnakes.

A volcano rabbit blending in with its surroundings.

Volcano rabbits construct elaborate burrows in deep sandy soil. Entrances are hidden in the base of grass clumps. For temporary shelter during the day, the animals sometimes use abandoned pocket–gopher burrows or the hollows between rocks and boulders.

Scientists know little about the social structure of volcano rabbits. Groups of two to seven animals have been observed in the wild. Male and female volcano rabbits mate primarily between January and April. After a gestation (pregnancy) period of 38 to 40 days, a female gives birth to a litter of one to five infants.

Habitat and current distribution

The volcano rabbit is found only in central Mexico on the slopes of four volcanoes: Popocatépetl, Iztaccíhautl, El Pelado, and Tláloc. The animal inhabits pine forests on those slopes at elevations between 9,000 and 14,000 feet (2,740 and 4,270 meters). These areas are often dry in the winter and rainy in the summer. Biologists (people who study living organisms) are unsure of the total number of volcano rabbits currently in existence.

History and conservation measures

The volcano rabbit has traditionally been hunted for food and sport. Although laws have been passed outlawing the hunting of the animals, they are seldom enforced.

Forest fires, the conversion of forest land into farmland, the overgrazing of cattle and sheep, and the cutting of trees for timber have all contributed to the destruction of volcano rabbit habitat. Many of the forest fires result when farmers burn bunchgrass areas in hopes of promoting new growth for their livestock (a process known as slash–and–burn agriculture).

Each of the remaining volcano rabbit populations lies within a 45–minute drive of Mexico City. Now the world's largest city, it has a rapidly growing population of 20,000,000 people. As the city and rural settlements around it continue to expand, volcano rabbit habitat continues to decrease. As of 1998, only 16 patches of suitable habitat exist.

Part of the volcano rabbit's present–day range lies within the Izta–Popo and Zoquiapan National Parks. However, habitat destruction continues even with these protected areas.

RAT, GIANT KANGAROO
Dipodomys ingens

PHYLUM: Chordata
CLASS: Mammalia
ORDER: Rodentia
FAMILY: Heteromyidae
STATUS: Critically endangered, IUCN
Endangered, ESA
RANGE: USA (California)

Rat, giant kangaroo
Dipodomys ingens

Description and biology

The kangaroo rat, a desert rodent related to the pocket mouse, is so–named because it uses its long legs and tail to leap like a kangaroo. There are about 20 kangaroo rat species, the largest of which is the giant kangaroo rat. This species can have a head and body length of up to 14 inches (36 centimeters) and weigh up to 6 ounces (170 grams). Its tail can measure up to 8 inches (20 centimeters) long. The animal has a mouselike head, large eyes, and cheek pouches in which it stores food. Its body is covered with long, silky fur that is pale brown above and white underneath. Its tail ends in a tuft of black–and–white hair.

The giant kangaroo rat eats seeds, leaves, stems, and buds of young plants. Like other desert animals, the kangaroo rat seldom drinks water, but obtains the moisture it needs from

Although much smaller, the giant kangaroo rat resembles a kangaroo in the way it uses its long hind legs and tail to leap.

the food it eats. It also conserves the water it takes in by foraging only at night.

Giant kangaroo rats live in underground burrows, where they store food for the winter months. The normally solitary male and female kangaroo rats come together only to mate, which may occur at any time during the year. After a gestation (pregnancy) period of about 30 days, a female giant kangaroo rat gives birth to a litter of two to five young.

Habitat and current distribution

The giant kangaroo rat is now restricted to a grassland area of less than 5 square miles (13 square kilometers) between the Carrizo Plain and the city of Taft in southwestern California.

History and conservation measures

The giant kangaroo rat, like all kangaroo rat species, is threatened by habitat destruction due to a growing human population. Its former habitat has been turned into farmland, oil fields, or residential areas. The animal also faces the risks of pesticide poisoning (from overspraying on nearby farms) and attacks by domestic cats.

Conservationists are trying to obtain land in Kern and San Luis Obispo Counties in southwestern California in order to save suitable habitat for the giant kangaroo rat.

RAT, SILVER RICE
Oryzomys argentatus

PHYLUM: Chordata
CLASS: Mammalia
ORDER: Rodentia
FAMILY: Muridae
STATUS: Endangered, ESA
RANGE: USA (Florida)

Rat, silver rice

Oryzomys argentatus (sometimes mistakenly called Oryzomys palustris natator)

Description and biology

The silver rice rat is a small rodent. It has a head and body length of 10 inches (25 centimeters) and a tail length of 5 inches (13 centimeters). The silver–gray color of the coarse fur on its back gives the animal its name.

The nocturnal (active at night) silver rice rat is a good swimmer. It feeds on seeds, insects, small crabs, and the succulent (sap–filled) parts of plants. Predators of the silver rice rat include foxes, skunks, snakes, and raccoons.

Biologists (people who study living organisms) know very little about the animal's breeding behavior, but they believe a female silver rice rat gives birth to one to five young after a gestation (pregnancy) period of about 25 days.

Habitat and current distribution

Found throughout Florida, the silver rice rat is most endangered in the lower Florida Keys in Monroe County. It

The silver rice rat is in danger of extinction due to the unchecked raccoon population in the rat's habitat. As the number of raccoons increases, so does their need for silver rice rats as prey.

prefers to inhabit freshwater marshes, flooded mangrove swamps, and saltmarsh flats.

History and conservation measures

The silver rice rat faces the threat of habitat destruction as humans continue to develop areas in the Florida Keys. Much of its wetland habitat has been drained to create land suitable for homes and businesses.

Although the silver rice rat is preyed upon by a number of species, its most serious predator is the raccoon, which is native to the Florida Keys. As human development has increased on the islands, so has the amount of garbage. With an increased food source (the garbage), the raccoon population has grown unnaturally high. This has thrown the normal predator–prey relationship between the raccoon and the silver rice rat out of balance, and the number of silver rice rats has declined as a result.

RHINOCEROS, BLACK
Diceros bicornis

PHYLUM: Chordata
CLASS: Mammalia
ORDER: Perissodactyla
FAMILY: Rhinocerotidae
STATUS: Critically endangered,
IUCN
Endangered, ESA
RANGE: Angola, Botswana,
Cameroon, Ethiopia, Kenya,
Malawi, Mozambique, Namibia,
Rwanda, South Africa, Swaziland,
Tanzania, Zambia, Zimbabwe

Rhinoceros, black

Diceros bicornis

Description and biology

The black rhinoceros is one of two species of rhinoceros found in Africa (the other is the white rhinoceros). Despite its name, the animal is actually gray in color. An average black rhinoceros has a head and body length of 9 to 12 feet (2.7 to 3.7 meters), stands 4.5 to 5.25 feet (1.4 to 1.6 meters) tall at its shoulder, and weighs between 2,000 and 4,000 pounds (908 and 1,816 kilograms). The animal's huge size is deceiving, as it can move quite quickly when it decides to charge. It has very poor eyesight—it can see clearly only up to 30 feet (9 meters) away—but acute senses of hearing and smell.

Rhinoceros means "horn nosed." The black rhinoceros has two horns on its snout. The front one is longer and can measure up to 53 inches (135 centimeters). The animal uses its horns (made of keratin fibers, the same substance as in hu-

man fingernails) to dig in the ground for mineral salt, to defend its territory against other rhinos, and to defend itself against predators such as lions and hyenas.

The black rhinoceros protects itself against the intense African heat by sleeping during the day in a patch of brush. It awakens in the cool of the evening to begin feeding. The animal is an herbivore (plant–eater), eating branches, leaves, and bark. Its pointed upper lip is prehensile, meaning the lip can actually grasp branches to help pull and break them.

Black rhinos are mostly solitary animals, and males and females come together only to mate. Mating may take place at any time during the year. Males will often fight over the right to mate with a female, and males and females often fight during their courtship. After a gestation (pregnancy) period of 15 to 18 months, a female black rhinoceros gives birth to a

Although named the black rhinoceros, the animal is often gray in color.

single calf, which weighs about 90 pounds (41 kilograms). The calf nurses for up to two years and remains dependent on its mother for another year. Black rhinos have an average life span of 30 to 35 years.

Habitat and current distribution

The black rhinoceros prefers to inhabit open dry scrublands, savannas, dense thickets, and mountain forests. It is found only in small pockets in eastern and southern Africa. In 1995, the estimated population of the species was an all–time low of 2,410 animals. The number had risen to 2,700 by 1999.

History and conservation measures

Until it stabilized in 1995, the black rhinoceros was disappearing faster than any large animal on the planet. It once ranged widely throughout the savannas of Africa. In 1970, biologists (people who study living organisms) estimated that the black rhinoceros population numbered 65,000. By the late 1990s, that number had dropped by over 95 percent. At that rate black rhinos would be extinct by the early twenty–first century. It has been determined that the large populations of free–ranging rhinos have disappeared for the most part. Because they traveled over vast areas, they could not be adequately protected. The rhinos surviving in the early 2000s live within more concentrated areas in which they can be protected from hunters.

The direct cause for the decline of black rhinos has been the demand for their horns. For centuries, people in Asia have believed that the powder of ground rhino horns can cure fevers, nose bleeds, measles, food poisoning, and other illnesses. Many believe it increases sexual desire and stamina, as well. Rhino horns have also been used to make handles for the traditional "jambia" daggers worn by men in Yemen.

International treaties now outlaw the trade or sale of any rhino products. Nonetheless, poaching continues. A pound of rhino horn powder can sell for as much as $2,000. The animal's skin, blood, and urine are also sold. In the late 1980s, some wildlife agencies in Africa began tranquilizing black rhinos and removing their horns so the animals would not be as attractive to poachers. These attempts have proved fruitless, as over 100 dehorned black rhinos have since been slaughtered by poachers.

In 1994, the U.S. Congress passed the Rhino and Tiger Conservation Act. This measure provides financial assistance for the development of conservation measures for rhinos and tigers.

RHINOCEROS, NORTHERN WHITE

Ceratotherium simum cottoni

PHYLUM: Chordata

CLASS: Mammalia

ORDER: Perissodactyla

FAMILY: Rhinocerotidae

STATUS: Near threatened (listed along with southern white rhinoceros) IUCN Endangered, ESA

RANGE: Congo, Sudan

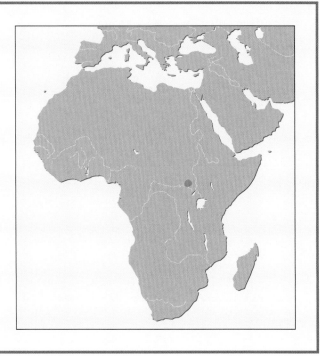

Rhinoceros, northern white

Ceratotherium simum cottoni

Description and biology

The northern white rhinoceros is also called the northern square–lipped rhinoceros. The animal derives its common name from the Afrikaans (language of white South Africans of Dutch descent) word *weit,* meaning "wide." The reference is to the animal's wide snout. However, the word *weit* was mistranslated as "white," and so the animal is now known as the white rhinoceros.

The white rhinoceros is not actually white but light gray in color. Two subspecies of white rhinoceroses exist in Africa: the southern white rhinoceros and the northern white rhinoceros. The southern white rhinoceros is found in South Africa, Swaziland, Namibia, Botswana, Zimbabwe, Mozam-

bique, Zambia, and Kenya. The most common of all rhinos, its population numbers about 7,500.

The northern white rhinoceros has a large, square–shaped mouth that allows it to graze on short grass. The second largest land mammal (only elephants are larger), an average northern white rhinoceros has a head and body length of 12 to 13 feet (3.7 to 4 meters) and stands 5 to 6.5 feet (1.5 to 2 meters) tall at its shoulder. Its tail measures 20 to 28 inches (51 to 71 centimeters) long. The animal may weigh between 5,000 and 8,000 pounds (2,270 and 3,630 kilograms). Despite its large size, the northern white rhinoceros can gallop as fast as 25 miles per hour (40 kilometers per hour).

Northern white rhinoceroses have short legs, broad ears, and two horns on their snout (rhinoceros means "horn–nosed"). White rhinos have the largest horns of any rhinoceros

Although it is light–gray in color, a mistranslation of the Afrikaans word weit *has led to the animal becoming known as the northern white rhinoceros.*

species, measuring 18 to 48 inches (46 to 122 centimeters) in length. They use their horns to fight over territory and females, to defend themselves against predators such as lions and hyenas, and to dig in the ground for mineral salt. The animals have poor vision, but highly developed senses of hearing and smell.

During the heat of the day, northern white rhinoceroses rest in shady spots. To keep cool, they often wallow in mud. When no water is available, they roll in dust to keep cool and to keep insects away. They feed in the evening and in the early morning. Average feeding territory is about 0.75 square miles (2 square kilometers). Females have larger territories than males.

Male and female northern white rhinoceroses come together only to mate. Mating can take place any time of the year, but peaks in February and June. The courtship period may last between 5 and 20 days. After a gestation (pregnancy) period of about 16 months, a female gives birth to a single calf. The mother tends to the calf for two years before chasing it away to live on its own.

Habitat and current distribution

The northern white rhinoceros prefers to inhabit open grasslands and savannas that have water available. Critically endangered, the animal is found only in Congo and southern Sudan in central Africa. Its population is extremely low. Most northern white rhinoceros live in the Garamba National Park in Congo.

History and conservation measures

The northern white rhinoceros is one of the most endangered animals in Africa. In 1980, 821 of the animals existed in the wild. Just six years later, only 17 remained in Congo (then Zaire). Intensive conservation measures were begun and by 1993, the northern white rhinoceros population had increased to 33.

The northern white rhinoceros was driven to the brink of extinction by hunting, specifically for its horns (made of keratin fibers, the same material in human fingernails). For hundreds of years, humans in Asia have used the powder of ground rhino horns in medicines and aphrodisiacs (pronounced af–row–DEEZ–ee–aks; drugs or food that stimulate sexual desire). In the Middle East, daggers with rhino–horn handles are highly valued.

Despite international treaties currently banning the sale of any rhino products, poaching (illegal hunting) of the animals continues.

SEAL, GUADALUPE FUR
Arctocephalus townsendi

PHYLUM: Chordata
CLASS: Mammalia
ORDER: Carnivora
FAMILY: Otariidae
STATUS: Vulnerable, IUCN
Threatened, ESA
RANGE: Mexico, USA (California)

Seal, Guadalupe fur

Arctocephalus townsendi

Description and biology

Fur seals and sea lions differ from true seals in that they have external ear flaps. They are also able to turn their hind flippers forward for walking on land. While they use all four flippers for walking, they use only their long front flippers for swimming.

The Guadalupe fur seal can be distinguished from other fur seals by its long, pointed snout and light–colored whiskers. An average male Guadalupe fur seal may grow up to 6.5 feet (2 meters) in length and weigh up to 310 pounds (141 kilograms). Females are smaller, reaching 4.4 feet (1.3 meters) in length and weighing 110 pounds (50 kilograms).

Guadalupe fur seals have a behavioral trait that makes them unique among seals. When on land, they often retreat onto rocky recesses or into caves. Some scientists believe this

trait developed in the species in the nineteenth century when hunters mercilessly slaughtered the animals. To survive, Guadalupe fur seals withdrew to caves, a behavior that has since been passed down to the current generation.

The Guadalupe fur seal's diet includes squid and fish such as the lantern fish. The animal travels widely at sea and has been found 186 miles (300 kilometers) away from its main home range. Unlike other seals, the Guadalupe fur seal may be found on shore at any time during the year.

Mating between male and female Guadalupe fur seals takes place between May and July. Males compete with each other over the right to mate with females. A dominant male may breed with as many as ten females. After a gestation (pregnancy) period of about 12 months, a female Guadalupe fur seal gives birth in a cave to one or two pups.

Although having similar characteristics as other fur seals, the Guadalupe fur seal can be distinguished by its long, pointed snout and light–colored whiskers.

Habitat and current distribution

Guadalupe fur seals range in the Pacific Ocean from the Farallon Islands off the coast of San Francisco, California, south to Islas Revillagigedo, a group of islands 450 miles (724 kilometers) off the coast of the Mexican state of Colima. The animals are known to breed only on the rocky east coast of Guadalupe Island, located west of the Baja California peninsula. Biologists (people who study living organisms) estimate the total Guadalupe fur seal population to be 6,000.

History and conservation measures

As many as 200,000 Guadalupe fur seals may have existed on Guadalupe Island alone before the nineteenth century. Hunters seeking the animals' fur and blubber (fat that was melted down to make oil) nearly wiped out the species. In fact, the Guadalupe fur seal was considered extinct until 1928, when two males were caught by fishermen. In 1954, a small breeding colony of 14 seals was discovered on Guadalupe Island. Since then, the population of Guadalupe fur seals has slowly increased.

In 1922, the Mexican government declared Guadalupe Island a wildlife sanctuary. In 1978, it declared all islands around Baja California wildlife reserves.

Despite these protective measures, the Guadalupe fur seal remains vulnerable because it has little fear of humans. Although legally protected, the animal may still fall prey to hunters. Noise from cruise ships and other human activities often prevent the Guadalupe fur seal from breeding.

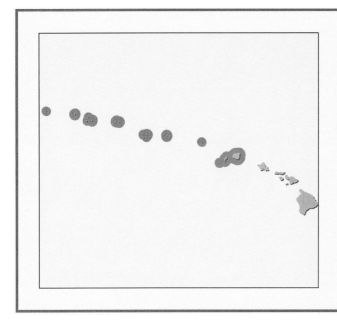

SEAL, HAWAIIAN MONK
Monachus schauinslandi

PHYLUM: Chordata

CLASS: Mammalia

ORDER: Carnivora

FAMILY: Phocidae

STATUS: Endangered, IUCN
Endangered, ESA

RANGE: USA (Hawaii)

Seal, Hawaiian monk

Monachus schauinslandi

Description and biology

The Hawaiian monk seal is a large warm–water seal. It is a member of the family of true seals because it does not have external ear flaps as fur seals and sea lions do. An average Hawaiian monk seal measures 7 to 7.5 feet (2.1 to 2.3 meters) long and weighs 450 to 550 pounds (204 to 250 kilograms). Unlike in most other species, female Hawaiian monk seals are larger than their male counterparts. The color of a monk seal's body varies slightly, from slate gray on top to silver gray underneath.

Hawaiian monk seals eat a variety of aquatic animals, including fish, eels, and octopi. They feed mainly along the shorelines of the islands they inhabit. Sharks often prey upon the seals.

Male Hawaiian monk seals choose a mate by wandering the beaches where females sun themselves. Since there are three times as many males as females, the females are often

A sunning Hawaiian monk seal. In order to survive, the seals must have an undisturbed habitat with as little human contact as possible.

disturbed. When a male and female decide to mate, they do so in the water. After a gestation (pregnancy) period of about 330 days, a female Hawaiian monk seal gives birth on the beach to a single pup. She nurses the pup for five weeks, during which time she fasts (does not eat). At birth, the pups are weak swimmers, and they must practice under their mother's supervision until they are weaned.

Habitat and current distribution

The Hawaiian monk seal inhabits the islands and atolls (ring–shaped reefs surrounding lagoons) of the northwestern Hawaiian Islands. Breeding takes place primarily around Nihoa Island, Necker Island, French Frigate Shoals, Laysan Island, Lisianski Island, Pearl and Hermes Reef, the Midway Islands, and Kure Atoll. An estimated 1,200 Hawaiian monk seals remain in the wild.

Although some Hawaiian monk seals move between is-lands, most remain fairly close to their home beaches.

History and conservation measures

Hawaiian monk seals evolved in an environment totally free of humans. Since they did not know humans, they had no fear of them when contact was made. This made them easy prey for nineteenth–century hunters who sought their fur and blubber (fat that was melted down to make oil). Hunting was so rampant during this period, the species was pushed to the brink of extinction.

The population of Hawaiian monk seals increased slightly, however, in the early twentieth century as the animals sought out undisturbed, remote areas. During World War II (1939–45), humans began occupying more and more of the Hawai-ian Islands, and the seals suffered. Any intrusion into their range has a negative effect on the seals. When disturbed by humans, a pregnant female may abort her fetus. If a nursing female is disturbed, she may be unable to continue nursing and her pup may die.

Increased fishing activity in the Hawaiian monk seal's range leads to conflicts between fishermen and seals. Many fishermen kill the seals, believing the animals steal their catch and damage their fishing nets. Some seals do become entan-gled in fishing nets and drown.

In 1940, a number of the islands and atolls in the Hawai-ian monk seal's range were designated the Hawaiian Islands National Wildlife Refuge. In 1976, this area was further de-clared a Research Natural Area. These protective measures limit the number of human landings on the islands, insuring that Hawaiian monk seals—among the most endangered seals in the world—remain as undisturbed as possible.

SEA LION, STELLER'S
Eumetopias jubatus

PHYLUM: Chordata
CLASS: Mammalia
ORDER: Carnivora
FAMILY: Otariidae
STATUS: Endangered, IUCN
Endangered, ESA (USA: Alaska, Russia); Threatened, ESA (USA: California, Oregon, Washington), Canada
RANGE: Canada, Japan, Russia, USA (Alaska, California, Oregon, Washington)

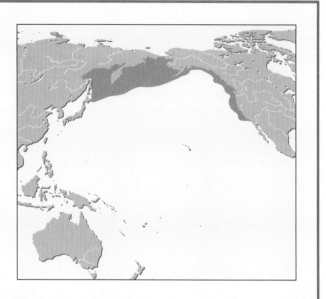

Sea lion, Steller's
Eumetopias jubatus

Description and biology

Sea lions and fur seals are members of the family of eared seals. They differ from true seals in that they have external ear flaps, a flexible neck, and hind flippers that can be turned forward for walking on land.

The Steller's sea lion, also known as the northern sea lion, is one of the largest species of sea lion. Males may grow up to 13 feet (4 meters) in length and weigh as much as 2,200 pounds (1,000 kilograms). Females are much smaller, weighing about half as much. The sea lion's thin coat of short, coarse hair is tawny brown in color.

Steller's sea lions feed primarily on fishes, squids, octopi, and crustaceans (shellfish such as shrimp and crabs). They hunt in relatively shallow waters, but can make 20–minute dives down to depths of about 650 feet (198 meters).

During the spring breeding season, the sea lions gather in large groups called rookeries. The Aleutian Islands, a chain of volcanic islands curving in an arc about 1,200 miles (1,931 kilometers) west off the Alaska Peninsula, are one of the animals' principle gathering places. Males come ashore first and stake out their individual territories, occasionally through fighting. They will try to mate with females that pass through their territory. A dominant male who is able to defend his territory successfully may mate with as many as 30 females over a two–month period.

Females arrive on the islands shortly after the males. They first give birth to pups that had been conceived during the previous breeding season. A few weeks later, they are ready to mate again. The pups remain dependent on their mothers for about a year.

Although they are not sure why the Steller's sea lion population is decreasing, scientists believe that if the decline continues, the animal will become extinct throughout much of its range.

Habitat and current distribution

Steller's sea lions inhabit the coastal waters around rocky islands. They occasionally come on shore to rest and sun themselves on the beaches. Their range extends from the Aleutian Islands west into the Bering Sea and down the Asian coast to northern Japan, and east into the Gulf of Alaska and down the Canadian and American coasts to southern California.

History and conservation measures

Steller's sea lions, along with other sea lions, were hunted extensively in the nineteenth century for their hides and blubber (fat that was melted down to make oil). In the twentieth century, they have been killed by fishermen who have blamed the animals for robbing their catch of fish.

In 1972, the U.S. Congress passed the Marine Mammal Act, which prohibited the hunting of sea lions in U.S. territorial waters. The Steller's sea lion received further protection in 1990 when it was placed on the Endangered Species List. The National Marine Fisheries Service has acted to protect breeding spots from shipping and to reduce the number of accidental deaths of sea lions during commercial fishing operations.

Despite these protective measures, the population of Steller's sea lions continues to decline. Disease, pollution, predators, habitat destruction, and other possible causes have all been investigated. Not one of these has proven conclusive. Scientists remain baffled as to the reason. If the decline continues unchecked, the Steller's sea lion may soon disappear from most of its range.

TAMARIN, GOLDEN LION
Leontopithecus rosalia

PHYLUM: Chordata

CLASS: Mammalia

ORDER: Primates

FAMILY: Callitrichidae

STATUS: Critically endangered, IUCN
Endangered, ESA (*Leontopithecus spp.*)

RANGE: Brazil

Tamarin, golden lion

Leontopithecus rosalia

Description and biology

Tamarins, also known as marmosets, are unique New World (Western Hemisphere) monkeys that have a golden mane and long, silky fur. The most striking of the tamarins is the golden lion tamarin, which has a flaming reddish–gold coat and a luxuriant mane. It has an average head and body length of 8 to 13 inches (20 to 33 centimeters) and weighs between 21 and 28 ounces (595 and 794 grams). Its furry tail measures 12 to 16 inches (30 to 41 centimeters) long.

Golden lion tamarins are tree dwellers. Active during the day, they travel from tree to tree, feeding on fruit, insects, plant matter, and other small animals.

The animals often form family groups ranging from two to eight members. A male–female pair forms the center of the

A golden lion tamarin perched
on a tree branch. As tree
dwellers, tamarins travel from
tree to tree in search of food.

group. After a gestation (pregnancy) period of 126 to 132 days, female golden lion tamarins normally give birth to twins. Most births occur between September and March. Both mother and father share responsibility for raising their young.

Habitat and current distribution

The golden lion tamarin prefers to inhabit tropical forests along the Atlantic coast at altitudes below 1,300 to 1,600 feet

(396 to 488 meters). The animal is usually found 10 to 33 feet (3 to 10 meters) above the ground in trees where dense vines and interlacing branches provide cover.

The animal is limited to the Brazilian state of Rio de Janeiro. In the 1970s, biologists (people who study living organisms) estimated that only about 200 golden lion tamarins existed in the wild. Since then, with much work from conservations (people who protect nature), the population has increased to 1,000 and the animal's natural habitat has expanded.

History and conservation measures

The home of the golden lion tamarin is one of the most densely populated parts of Brazil. The major cause of the animal's decline has been—and continues to be—the clearing of its forest habitat. Trees are cut down to supply the lumber market and to create farmland and grazing land for domestic animals. As a result, only isolated pockets of forest provide suitable habitat for the golden lion tamarin. The animal is still extremely endangered.

The Poco D'Anta Reserve was established in Rio de Janeiro specifically to protect the golden lion tamarin. The area of forest under protection in the early 2000s is about 41,000 acres (16,600 hectares). Since 1984, 147 captive–born golden lion tamarin have been successfully released into the wild. Mostly have gone to the Poco D'Anta Reserve. The National Zoo in Washington, D.C. and the Rio de Janeiro Primate Center have exchanged golden lion tamarins in an effort to prevent members of the same family from mating. This helps keep captive populations of the animal as genetically diverse as possible.

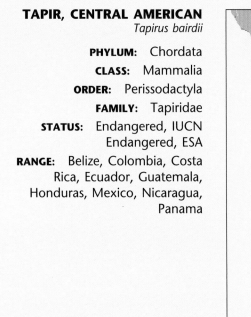

TAPIR, CENTRAL AMERICAN
Tapirus bairdii

PHYLUM: Chordata

CLASS: Mammalia

ORDER: Perissodactyla

FAMILY: Tapiridae

STATUS: Endangered, IUCN
Endangered, ESA

RANGE: Belize, Colombia, Costa
Rica, Ecuador, Guatemala,
Honduras, Mexico, Nicaragua,
Panama

Tapir, Central American

Tapirus bairdii

Description and biology

The Central American or Baird's tapir is a large animal with a medium to dark brown coat. Related to the horse and rhinoceros, it is almost as large as a donkey. An average Central American tapir has a head and body length of 6.5 to 8 feet (2 to 2.4 meters) and weighs between 550 and 660 pounds (250 and 300 kilograms). It stands 36 to 42 inches (91 to 107 centimeters) tall at its shoulder.

The animal has short legs and a stout body that narrows in front, which allows it to move quickly through the forest. A good swimmer, it spends much time in water or in mud. With small, deeply set eyes, the animal has poor vision, but its senses of hearing and smell are acute. Its nose and upper lip extend to form a short trunk, which the animal uses to

shovel food into its mouth. Its diet consists of grass, leaves, and a variety of fruit. Jaguars and mountain lions are the Central American tapir's main predators.

Male and female Central American tapirs mate at any time during the year. After a gestation (pregnancy) period of 390 to 405 days, a female tapir gives birth to a single calf. At birth, the calf is covered with protective colored markings that allow it to blend easily into its forest environment. These markings begin to fade within a few months. The calf may remain dependent on its mother for up to a year.

Habitat and current distribution

The Central American tapir is found from southern Mexico to northern Colombia. It lives in a variety of humid habitats, including marshes, mangrove swamps, and tropical rain

The Central American tapir shovels food into its mouth by extending its nose and upper lip to make a short trunk.

forests. Biologists (people who study living organisms) estimate the total population of the species to be about 5,000 animals.

History and conservation measures

The Central American tapir once ranged as far south as Ecuador. In the past, the animal was hunted for its meat and hide and for sport. Now legally protected, the tapir nevertheless continues to be the target of poachers. Despite this problem, the most serious threat to the Central American tapir today is habitat destruction. Over the past four decades, around 70 percent of Central American forest areas have been lost to deforestation. Vast tracts of land in the tapir's range have been cleared to create farmland to feed the growing human population in the area. Guerilla warfare within the range presents another threat, particularly because it impedes research and conservation measures.

For the most part, the Central American tapir is now confined to reserves in Belize, Guatemala, Honduras, Nicaragua, Costa Rica, and Panama.

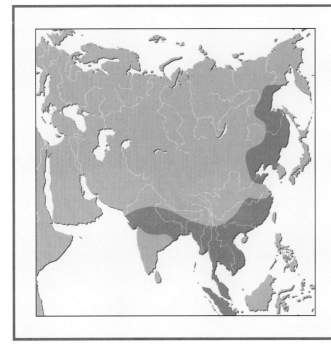

TIGER
Panthera tigris

PHYLUM: Chordata
CLASS: Mammalia
ORDER: Carnivora
FAMILY: Felidae
STATUS: Endangered, IUCN Endangered, ESA
RANGE: Bangladesh, Bhutan, Cambodia, China, India, Indonesia, Laos, Malaysia, Myanmar, Nepal, North Korea, Russia, Thailand, Vietnam

Tiger
Panthera tigris

Description and biology

Tigers are members of the cat family. They are the biggest of the big cats, a group that includes leopards, lions, and jaguars. There are eight subspecies of tiger. Three of these—the Bali, Caspian, and Javan—all became extinct in the twentieth century. The remaining five subspecies are the Bengal (or Indian), Indo–Chinese, Siberian (or Amur), South Chinese, and Sumatran.

The color, size, and general appearance of tigers varies according to the subspecies. On average, a male tiger has a head and body length of 5 to 9 feet (1.5 to 2.7 meters) and a tail length of 2 to 3 feet (0.6 to 0.9 meter). It stands about 3.5 feet (1 meter) tall at its shoulder and weighs between 220 and 660 pounds (100 and 300 kilograms). Since the animal is found in a variety of climates, from the snowy forests of Siberia to the jungles of Indonesia, the length of its coat

A Bengal tiger walking along a beach. Of the eight original subspecies of tiger only five remain. The Bengal tiger is one of these remaining subspecies.

varies. In general, its coat is orange–yellow in color, with numerous black stripes. Its underparts are white. The striping pattern varies not only among subspecies but with each individual tiger.

Tigers are mainly nocturnal (active at night). They are able climbers, good swimmers, and fast runners. Tigers can leap up to 32 feet (10 meters) and swim up to 18 miles (29 kilometers). They are carnivores (meat –eaters), preying on deer, antelope, wild pigs, cattle, and other mammals. Their senses of hearing, sight, and smell are all keen. Tigers stalk or ambush their prey, pouncing on it from the rear or the side. The prey is usually killed by a bite to the neck or spine. Despite their abilities, tigers are successful hunters only about 10 percent of the time. Because of this, most tigers travel between 10 and 20 miles (16 and 32 kilometers) a night in search of food. Tigers that attack and eat humans are generally too old or sick to hunt wild animals.

Tigers are solitary animals with home ranges that vary between 4 and 1,500 square miles (10 and 3,885 square kilometers). They are not entirely loners, as they will band together to hunt and to share their kill. Males and females come together to mate at any time during the year, though primarily between November and April. After a gestation (pregnancy) period of just over 100 days, a female gives birth to a litter of two to four cubs. The cubs are blind and helpless for the first two weeks. They nurse for six to eight weeks, then begin accompanying their mother on hunting trips. After almost two years, they leave their mother's territory to establish their own.

Habitat and current distribution

Tigers occupy a wide variety of habitats, including rain forests, evergreen forests, mangrove swamps, marshlands, grasslands, and savannas.

There are currently as few as 5,000 tigers left in the wild. The Bengal tiger has the largest population of any tiger subspecies. Found in India, Bangladesh, Myanmar, Nepal, and Bhutan, it has an estimated population of about 3,750. The Indo–Chinese tiger is found in Laos, Malaysia, Thailand, Myanmar, and Vietnam. The South Chinese tiger, now almost extinct in the wild, is found only in southern China. The Siberian tiger, the largest of all subspecies, is found in North Korea, northern China, and the Amur–Ussuri region of Siberia in Russia. The Sumatran tiger, the smallest of all living tiger subspecies, is found on the island of Sumatra, Indonesia.

History and conservation measures

The protection of tigers has been an international concern since the 1970s. At the beginning of the twentieth century, an estimated 100,000 tigers roamed the Asian forests and grasslands. That population has since decreased by about 95 percent. The Bali tiger, the smallest of the eight subspecies, became extinct in 1937. The Caspian tiger, once found as far west as Turkey, disappeared in the 1970s. The Javan tiger was last seen in 1983.

Historically, the tiger has been hunted as a trophy and for its beautiful coat. For centuries, many Asian cultures have used other tiger parts (bones, eyes, teeth, nails) in medicines, believing they cure diseases such as rheumatism and dysentery. Some people even believe that a soup made from the genitals of a male tiger can increase sexual ability. International treaties now protect tigers, but because of these ancient beliefs, the animals are still hunted and traded. Conservationists believe that two or three tigers are killed each day in China and Taiwan.

The primary threat to the tiger's current survival is habitat destruction. As forests throughout Asia are cleared for timber or to create farmland, tigers are forced into smaller and smaller areas. These tiny islands of forest do not hold enough prey for the animals, and they are forced to feed on livestock and even humans. Increased contact with humans has only resulted in more tiger deaths.

In 1972, the Indian government launched Project Tiger, a program that established 23 tiger reserves. Even though these reserves are patrolled by guards, poaching or illegal hunting still takes place.

Great efforts made by conservationists (people protecting the natural world) in concert with the Russian government and local residents seem to have stabilized the Siberian tiger population in eastern Russia in the early 2000s. Increased scientific understanding of habitat requirements is leading many biologists to believe that the tiger population in the wild can be increased.

VICUÑA
Vicugna vicugna

PHYLUM: Chordata

CLASS: Mammalia

ORDER: Artiodactyla

FAMILY: Camelidae

STATUS: Lower risk: conservation dependent, IUCN Endangered, ESA

RANGE: Argentina, Bolivia, Chile, Peru

Vicuña

Vicugna vicugna

Description and biology

The smallest member of the camel family, the vicuña is closely related to the llama and the alpaca. The color of the vicuña's soft and silky coat is light brown above and off–white below. A patch of longer hair covers the animal's throat and chest, keeping it warm when it rests on the ground. The vicuña has a small head in comparison with its body, and its eyes and ears are small and prominent. Its neck is long.

An average vicuña measures 4 to 6 feet (1.2 to 1.8 meters) in length and weighs 88 to 110 pounds (40 to 50 kilograms). It stands 30 to 40 inches (76 to 102 centimeters) tall at its shoulder. It feeds primarily on grasses, mosses, and other vegetation. Pumas and Andean foxes are its main predators.

Vicuña are social animals. They form family groups consisting of a dominant male and a number of adult females with their young. The male defends a feeding and sleeping territory averaging 17 to 74 acres (7 to 30 hectares). Those males unable to defend a territory (and thus breed with females) live a solitary life or join other males to form bachelor groups.

Male and female vicuña mate in March or April. A female gives birth to one infant after a gestation (pregnancy) period of 330 to 350 days. The young vicuña nurses for up to ten months and becomes independent after about a year.

Vicuñas are highly communicative, signaling one another with body postures, ear and tail placement, and numerous other small movements. Their vocalizations include an alarm call—a high pitched whinny—that alerts the herd to danger. They also emit a soft humming sound to signal bonding or greeting and a range of guttural sounds that communicate anger and fear. "Orgling" is their most unique noise. This male-only, melodic mating sound attracts females.

The vicuña is known for its wool—often said to be among the finest in the world. One thing that makes the wool of the vicuña so popular is its warmth. Vicuña wool is softer, lighter and warmer than any other wool. The vicuña will only produce about one pound of wool in a year (as opposed to the alpaca, which can produce fifteen pounds in a similar time period). This, of course, adds to the rarity of the wool.

Habitat and current distribution

The vicuña is found in the central portion of the Andes Mountains in the South American countries of Argentina, Bolivia, Chile, and Peru. Biologists (people who study living organisms) estimate the current population to be over 100,000.

The vicuña prefers to inhabit semiarid (semidry) grasslands and plateaus at elevations of 9,850 to 15,100 feet (3,000 to 4,600 meters). Groups spend the day in one feeding territory, then move at night to a territory at a higher elevation to sleep.

History and conservation measures

Because of its lustrous wool the vicuña has been sought since the days of the Inca, native Quechuan people of Peru who established an empire in South America in the fifteenth

A female vicuña and her young. It takes about a year for young vicuñas to become independent and leave their mothers.

century. The Inca pursued the animal not to kill it, but to shear its wool, which was then made into certain types of ritual clothing. When Spanish explorers (conquistadors) conquered the Inca in the sixteenth century, they began to hunt the vicuña without care.

Before they became the target of hunters, as many as several million vicuña may have existed. By the time of the conquistadors, the animals' population had been reduced to less than 500,000. By 1965, only 6,500 vicuña survived.

Although international treaties now ban the taking of the vicuña, illegal hunting is still a problem in parts of the animal's range, particularly in Peru and Bolivia. However, the majority of vicuña currently live on protected reserves.

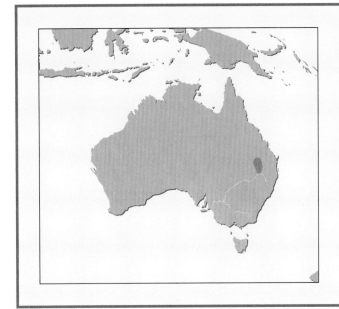

WALLABY, BRINDLED NAIL–TAILED
Onychogalea fraenata

PHYLUM: Chordata
CLASS: Mammalia
ORDER: Marsupialia
FAMILY: Macropodidae
STATUS: Endangered, IUCN Endangered, ESA
RANGE: Australia

Wallaby, brindled nail-tailed

Onychogalea fraenata

Description and biology

A member of the kangaroo family, the brindled nail–tailed wallaby gets its name from its silver–gray coat with dark flecks ("brindled") and from the horny spur on the end of its tail ("nail–tailed"). An average brindled nail–tailed wallaby has a head and body length of 17.5 to 23.5 inches (44.5 to 59.7 centimeters) and weighs about 11 pounds (5 kilograms). Its tail is almost as long as its body, measuring 13.5 to 19.5 inches (34.3 to 49.5 centimeters).

This wallaby is a solitary animal that rests in a shallow depression under a shrub, tree, or log during the day. At night, it feeds on a variety of grasses and herbs. Dingoes, wild Australian dogs, are the animal's main predator.

Wallabies are marsupials, or mammals whose young continue to develop after birth in a pouch on the outside of the

Although considered extinct by 1930, a small population of brindled nail–tailed wallabies was found during the 1970s and is now protected on a reserve.

mother's body. Other than this fact, biologists (people who study living organisms) know very little about the breeding habits of this particular species of wallaby.

Habitat and current distribution

The only population of brindled nail–tailed wallabies is near the town of Dingo in the northeastern Australian state of Queensland. In the early 1980s, biologists estimated that their population numbered 800.

During the day, brindled nail–tailed wallabies prefer to inhabit forest areas dominated by trees or shrubs. At night, they feed in open woodland or grassland areas.

History and conservation measures

The brindled nail–tailed wallaby was once common throughout eastern and southeastern Australia. In the early

1800s, farmers and ranchers moved into the animal's range, bringing with them domestic livestock. The brindled nail–tailed wallaby was then forced to compete for food with these grazing animals, especially sheep. The farmers and ranchers soon considered the wallaby a pest and began paying to have the animal killed. By 1930, it was considered extinct.

In 1973, a small population of brindled nail–tailed wallabies was discovered near the town of Dingo. Later that decade, the Taunton Scientific Reserve was established to protect this new population. The majority of surviving brindled nail–tailed wallabies now exist there.

WHALE, BLUE
Balaenoptera musculus

PHYLUM: Chordata

CLASS: Mammalia

ORDER: Cetacea

FAMILY: Balaenopteridae

STATUS: Endangered, IUCN
Endangered, ESA

RANGE: Oceanic

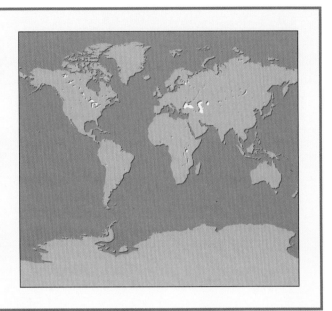

Whale, blue

Balaenoptera musculus

Description and biology

Scientists consider the blue whale to be the largest animal that has ever lived on Earth. An average adult measures 79 to 88 feet (24 to 27 meters) long and weighs between 130 and 150 tons (118 and 136 metric tons). In the past, some blue whales reached a length of 100 feet (30 meters). Now, the animals seldom grow that large because of extensive whaling (the hunting of whales). The blue whale has a wide, U–shaped head and a dorsal (on its back) fin. Its body is slate blue in color. Sometimes, microorganisms accumulate on the whale's body, giving it a faintly yellow sheen. This is why it is also called the sulfur–bottomed whale.

The blue whale feeds mainly on krill, which are small, shrimplike shellfish. Like all whales in its family, the blue whale uses the fringed baleen (whalebone) plates that line its mouth to strain krill from seawater. The animal has 80 to 100 furrows (called ventral grooves) lining its narrow neck. When

it sucks in seawater, the grooves allow its throat to expand like a pouch. As it expels the large volume of water from its mouth, its baleen plates trap the krill.

Blue whales mate at the end of winter. After a gestation (pregnancy) period of 300 to 330 days, a female blue whale gives birth to one calf, which measures 20 to 23 feet (6 to 7 meters) long. The calf nurses for up to seven months.

Habitat and current distribution

Blue whales are found in all of the major oceans. Most blue whales prefer cold waters and open seas. In summer, they inhabit arctic and Antarctic waters, feeding on krill in the water of melting ice packs. In winter, they migrate to warmer waters near the equator, where they will mate. Some blue whales, however, do not appear to migrate, residing year–round in

The fin of a blue whale. Scientists consider the whale to be the largest animal to ever live on the Earth.

tropical coastal areas. Such whales have been observed off the coast of Peru and in the northern Indian Ocean.

Scientists estimate that less than 2,000 blue whales currently exist in the world's oceans.

History and conservation measures

When large–scale whaling began in the seventeenth century, blue whales were considered too difficult to hunt because of their size, speed, and strength. This view changed in the mid–nineteenth century with the development of the exploding–head harpoon and the factory ship (which could completely process whales caught at sea). Blue whales were now a prime prey, and their numbers decreased drastically, especially in the twentieth century. Between 1920 and 1970, an estimated 280,000 blue whales were slaughtered.

In 1964, the International Whaling Commission (IWC; body that regulates most of the world's whaling activity) banned the hunting of blue whales. However, various nations defy the rulings of the IWC. The blue whale and other whales continue to be hunted.

The blue whale also faces the loss of its main food source, krill. Scientists have discovered that the krill population has decreased by almost 90 percent since 1980. Krill feed on algae that grow underneath sea ice. As temperatures have risen in Antarctica in the last 20 years, melting a sizable portion of sea ice, the algae population has diminished. In a domino effect, this loss could affect the entire Antarctic food chain. Some scientists believe this situation is the result of global warming—the rise in Earth's temperature that is attributed to the buildup of carbon dioxide and other pollutants in the atmosphere.

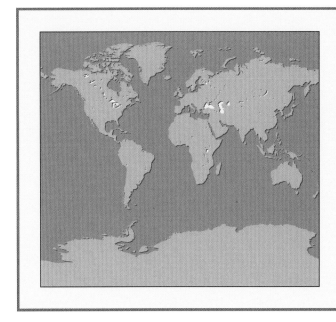

WHALE, HUMPBACK
Megaptera novaeangliae

PHYLUM: Chordata
CLASS: Mammalia
ORDER: Cetacea
FAMILY: Balaenopteridae
STATUS: Vulnerable, IUCN
Endangered, ESA
RANGE: Oceanic

Whale, humpback
Megaptera novaeangliae

Description and biology

The humpback whale is most known for its acrobatic leaps and for its distinctive pattern of sounds, called songs. An average humpback whale has a head and body length of 42 to 52 feet (13 to 16 meters) and weighs between 30 and 60 tons (27 and 54 metric tons). Its winglike pectoral (chest or side) fins measure 13 to 16 feet (4 to 5 meters) long. While the whale's upper body is dark gray, its underparts are lighter. White patterns mark the pectoral fins. Despite the animal's large size, it is able to breach (leap out of the water) and perform spectacular spins.

The diet of humpback whales includes herring, pink salmon, Arctic cod, certain mollusks, krill (small, shrimplike shellfish), and other small fishes. Those humpback whales inhabiting Antarctic waters feed primarily on krill. The whales have brush-like plates of baleen (whalebone) lining the roofs of their mouths. Their narrow throats are lined with furrows (called

A humpback whale comes to the surface for air. Although there is a ban on hunting the whales, illegal hunting still continues.

ventral grooves). To feed, the whales suck in large amounts of water, and the furrows allow their throats to expand like a pouch. The animals then expel the water through their baleen plates, straining out any food.

Large schools of humpback whales form when they migrate between cold and warm waters. Humpback whales inhabiting the waters of the Northern Hemisphere mate between October and March; those in the Southern Hemisphere mate between April and September. A female humpback whale gives birth to a single calf after a gestation (pregnancy) period of about one year. The calf nurses for about one year afterward.

Although scientists are not sure why, male humpback whales emit their haunting song during the mating season. All males in the same group "sing" the same song, composed of moans, cries, grunts, snores, and chirps. Scientists began recording humpback whale songs in the early 1950s. They have found that the songs change each year and no two songs have ever been the same.

Habitat and current distribution

Humpback whales are found in all oceans on Earth from the Arctic to the Antarctic. They feed in colder waters during spring, summer, and autumn. In winter, they migrate to warmer waters near the equator, swimming in deep water along coastlines. Scientists estimate that 25,000 humpback whales currently exist.

History and conservation measures

About 150,000 humpback whales probably existed world-wide when large–scale whaling (whale hunting) began in the seventeenth century. Whales have been hunted for their oil, which is extracted from their blubber and other body parts. Whale oil was originally used in oil lamps. Today, it is used in soap–making, as a dressing for leather, and as a lubricant. Over the centuries, many carvings and items of jewelry— called scrimshaw—have been made from baleen.

With improved hunting techniques in the nineteenth century (including the development of the exploding–head harpoon), the number of humpback whales quickly declined. By the early twentieth century, the population of whales in the North Atlantic had been depleted. Whalers then began hunting those whales inhabiting the Pacific Ocean and the waters of the Southern Hemisphere.

The International Whaling Commission (IWC; body that regulates most of the world's whaling activity) banned the hunting of humpback whales in 1963. However, some nations disregard the decrees of the IWC and the hunting of protected whales continues. Because humpback whales travel close to shore, they are also threatened by shoreline pollution, boat traffic, and fishing nets.

WOLF, GRAY
Canis lupus

PHYLUM: Chordata
CLASS: Mammalia
ORDER: Carnivora
FAMILY: Canidae
STATUS: Endangered, ESA (Arizona, part of Colorado, New Mexico, Oklahoma, Texas, part of Utah); Threatened, ESA (California, part of Colorado, Connecticut, Iowa, Idaho, Illinois, Indiana, Kansas, Massachusetts, Maine, Michigan, Minnesota, Missouri, Montana, North Dakota, Nebraska, New Hampshire, New Jersey, Nevada, New York, Ohio, Oregon, Pennsylvania, Rhode Island, South Dakota, part of Utah, Vermont, Washington, Wisconsin, Wyoming)
RANGE: Canada, USA

Wolf, gray
Canis lupus

Description and biology

The North American gray wolf, also known as the timber wolf, is the largest member of the canidae (dog) family. An average adult measures 5 to 6 feet (1.5 to 1.8 meters) from nose to tail, and stands 26 to 32 inches (66 to 81 centimeters) at its shoulder. It can weigh between 70 and 110 pounds (32 and 50 kilograms). Females are slightly smaller than males. The wolf's coat is usually tan or a grizzled gray and black. Some wolves are all black or all white.

The gray wolf is well–adapted for hunting. It has long legs and keen senses of hearing and smell. The wolf is a carnivore, or meat–eater. It feeds on a variety of mammals from large hoofed animals such as elk and deer to smaller animals such as beavers and rabbits. It will also eat small rodents like mice. Wolves generally kill animals that are young, old, diseased, or deformed—those that are easy to capture. However, if the opportunity arises, the wolf will kill a healthy adult animal.

Wolves live in packs or family groups typically composed of a set of parents, their offspring, and other nonbreeding adults. The social structure within a pack is complex. The dominant male and female are both called alphas, but they may not mate with each other. The alpha female, who has the dominant role in the pack, will sometimes mate with a superior male (or superior males) in the pack. The hierarchy (pronounced HIGH–a–rar–key) or ranking of dominant and subordinate animals within a pack help it function as a unit.

The packs generally hunt within a specific territory. Territories may be as large as 50 square miles (130 square kilometers) or even extend to 1,000 square miles (2,590 square kilometers), depending on available food. Wolves communicate with fellow pack–mates and other wolf packs through facial and body postures, scent markings (urine and feces), and vocalizations, which include barks, whimpers, growls, and howls.

Gray wolves begin mating when they are two to three years old. A female digs a den or uses an existing shelter or structure in which to rear her pups for the first six weeks of their lives. In early spring, she gives birth to an average litter of six pups. The pups depend completely on their mother's milk for the first month, then they are gradually weaned off the mother's milk. By seven to eight months of age, when they are almost fully grown, the young wolves begin hunting with the adults. Often after one or two years of age, a young wolf will leave and try to form its own pack.

Habitat and current distribution

In North America, the gray wolf is found in wilderness forests and tundra areas of northern Canada and the United States (gray wolves are also found in small pockets in Europe, Asia, and the Middle East). A subspecies of the gray wolf, the Mexican gray wolf, once inhabited Mexico and the southwestern United States.

In the United States, the gray wolf is found primarily in Alaska (listed as neither endangered nor threatened) and

Minnesota (listed as threatened). Where it is found in other parts of the United States—Idaho, Michigan, Montana, Wisconsin, Wyoming, and possibly Washington—it was, until 2003, listed as endangered, but is currently listed as threatened.

Approximately 50,000 wolves remain in Canada and 7,500 to 10,500 in the United States (5,000 to 8,000 of which are in Alaska). Some 150,000 remain elsewhere in the world.

History and conservation measures

Gray wolves once lived everywhere north of about 20° latitude, a parallel that runs through Mexico City and southern India. They occupied an array of climates and ecosystems (ecological communities consisting of living things and their environment), from dry deserts to deciduous (tree or plants that shed) forests to frozen tundra. On the North American continent, they ranged from coast to coast and from Canada to Mexico.

As settlers moved west across America in the nineteenth century, they killed off most of the populations of bison, deer, elk, and moose—animals that were important prey for wolves. With little natural prey left, wolves then turned to sheep and cattle. To protect livestock, ranchers and government agencies began a decades–long campaign to eliminate the animals. Wolves were trapped, shot, and hunted with dogs. Animal carcasses (dead bodies) salted with strychnine (pronounced STRICK–nine; a poison) were left out for wolves to eat. Unfortunately, this practice killed eagles, ravens, foxes, bears, and other animals that also fed on the poisoned carcasses. By the late 1920s, no wolves were left in Yellowstone National Park.

At present, gray wolves occupy just 6 percent of their former range in the contiguous United States (connected 48 states). In 1995 and 1996, the U.S. government relocated about 65 gray wolves from Canada to Yellowstone National Park and central Idaho. The wolves adjusted quickly. Within two years, they had reshaped the Yellowstone ecosystem, improving the overall balance of species in the park. The wolves killed many of the park's coyotes, which allowed the rodent population to increase. This, in turn, allowed animals that feed on rodents

A howling gray wolf. Conservation efforts to protect this animal have been so successful that the gray wolf may be taken off the Endangered Species List over some its range.

to increase in number. Other animals, such as grizzly bears, benefitted by feeding on the remains of elk killed by wolves.

From the beginning, however, ranchers and farm groups have opposed wolf reintroduction efforts, asserting that wolves are a threat to livestock in the area. To ease the concerns of ranchers, the U.S. government downgraded the wolves' status in Yellowstone and Idaho from "endangered" to "threatened." This change gave ranchers the legal right to shoot wolves attacking their livestock.

This compromise was still not enough for some livestock groups. They sued to stop the reintroduction efforts. Certain environmental groups, including the Audubon Society, also filed a suit against the government to stop the reintroduction. They wanted to keep full "endangered" status for the two or three wolves already living in central Idaho.

In December 1997, a federal judge ruled that the government had violated parts of the Endangered Species Act when it reintroduced wolves to Yellowstone. The judge did stay (delay) his decision, allowing federal agencies and other environmental groups time to file an appeal. A federal appeals court reversed the decision, and the gray wolves remained at Yellowstone. If the judge's decision is upheld, all of the gray wolves in Yellowstone (a population of about 160) would have had to be killed.

In a very controversial move in 2003, the U.S. Fish and Wildlife Service announced that gray wolves had been reclassified from endangered to threatened in midwestern, northeastern, and southeastern states, leaving them in endangered status only in the Southwest. The federal agency said it had done this because it had fulfilled its job. It estimates there are 664 wolves in 44 packs in western Montana, Idaho, and in and around Yellowstone National Park. The goal of having more than 30 breeding pairs in those states had been met for three years in a row, which was the target set when wolves were given federal protection. The gray wolf population in the western Great Lakes has also reached its recovery goal; there are more than 2,445 wolves in Minnesota, 323 in Wisconsin, and 278 in Michigan. Conservationists criticized the Fish and Wildlife Service for removing wolves from endangered status in those states in the Northeast and Southeast that have no population of wolves. Without the protection received with endangered status, there is little possibility that wolves could ever be reintroduced into the northeast or elsewhere. The northeastern conservationists in particular protested that reclassification of states where the gray wolf does not currently exist means that the species will be limited to the isolated areas it now inhabits and will never fully recover to roam its former ranges.

WOLF, RED
Canis rufus

PHYLUM: Chordata
CLASS: Mammalia
ORDER: Carnivora
FAMILY: Canidae
STATUS: Critically endangered,
IUCN
Endangered, ESA
RANGE: USA (Florida, North
Carolina, South Carolina;
reintroduced in North Carolina
and Tennessee)

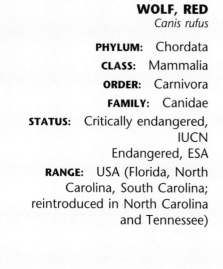

Wolf, red
Canis rufus

Description and biology

Although called the red wolf, the animal has a coat that varies in color from cinnamon–brown to nearly black. Smaller than its relative the gray wolf, the red wolf is about the size of a large dog. It has an average head and body length of 37 to 47 inches (94 to 119 centimeters) and a tail length of about 10 inches (25 centimeters). It weighs between 45 and 65 pounds (20 and 30 kilograms). The animal's most distinguishing features are its long ears and legs.

The red wolf feeds on swamp rabbits, raccoons, birds, white–tailed deer, and other small mammals. It is also known to eat chickens and, sometimes, calves and piglets. A male and female pair hunts on a territory averaging 30 to 40 square miles (78 to 104 square kilometers).

The wolves have a complex social order made up of family groups called packs. Individual males and females form a

mating pair that is long–lasting. During the mating season (January to April), the pair establishes a den, usually in hollow logs, ditch banks, or under rock outcrops. Here they raise their young year after year. A female red wolf gives birth to a litter of two to eight pups after a gestation (pregnancy) period of 61 to 63 days. The pups, who are born with their eyes closed, are completely dependent on their mother for the first two months. They remain with their parents for about two to three years.

Habitat and current distribution

In 1980, the red wolf was declared biologically extinct in the wild. All the animals currently in existence were raised in captivity. In 1987, a small population of captive–bred red wolves was reintroduced into the wild in North Carolina. Another small group was reintroduced into the Great Smoky Mountains National Park in Tennessee in 1992.

The animals prefer to inhabit swamps, wetlands, bushlands, and forests.

History and conservation measures

The red wolf once ranged from central Texas east to the Atlantic coast and from the Gulf of Mexico north to southern Pennsylvania. In the early twentieth century, it began disappearing from much of that range. By the middle of the century, only scattered populations of the animal survived. Its decline was brought about by human settlers moving into its habitat. Forests were cleared for their timber or to create farmland, and the settlers killed the red wolf out of fear and ignorance.

As forests were cut down in eastern Texas and Oklahoma, the separate ranges of the red wolf and the coyote began to meet. The red wolves, whose numbers were very low, started to interbreed with the coyotes. As a result, the number of genetically pure red wolves in the wild became even smaller.

In 1973, the U.S. Fish and Wildlife Service (USFWS) established a captive breeding program in hopes of reintroducing the red wolf into the wild. It was the first recovery plan developed by the USFWS for an endangered species. Over a six–year period, over 400 animals believed to be red wolves were captured in the wild. Only 17 of those were found to be true red wolves, and only 14 of these were able to breed successfully in captivity.

In 1987, four pairs of captive–bred red wolves were reintroduced to the wild on the 120,000–acre Alligator River National Wildlife Refuge in northeastern North Carolina. Although disease and conflicts with humans took its toll on this small population, wild births and additional releases of captive–bred animals have kept it going. Today, there are more than 50 red wolves in this refuge.

Beginning in 1989, the USFWS established island sites where captive–bred wolves can have their first experience in the wild without having much human contact. Cape Romain National Wildlife Refuge on Bull Island, South Carolina; Gulf Islands National Seashore on Horn Island, Mississippi; and St. Vincent National Wildlife Refuge on St. Vincent, Florida are the three pre–reintroduction sites. The red wolves are allowed to breed and roam freely on these islands. After a while, they are captured and taken to the Alligator River refuge or the Great Smoky Mountain National Park.

Red wolves are bred in 31 facilities across the United States. There are between 250 and 300 red wolves currently in existence, two–thirds of which are in captivity. In May 2002, two wolf pups born in captivity were placed in the den of a wild wolf female who was already raising two pups of her own. She raised the new pups without hesitation and they prospered in the wilderness, creating hope that this kind of fostering will allow greater reintroduction to the wilderness for red wolves.

WOMBAT, NORTHERN HAIRY–NOSED
Lasiorhinus krefftii

PHYLUM: Chordata
CLASS: Mammalia
ORDER: Marsupialia
FAMILY: Vombatidae
STATUS: Critically endangered, IUCN
Endangered, ESA
RANGE: Australia

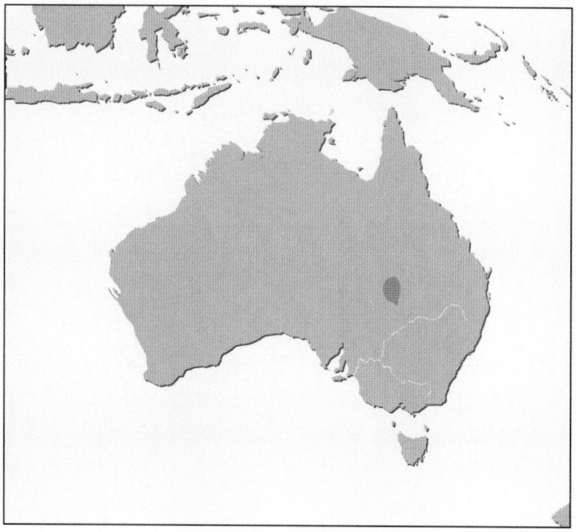

Wombat, northern hairy-nosed

Lasiorhinus krefftii

Description and biology

The northern hairy–nosed wombat is also variously known as the Queensland hairy–nosed wombat or Barnard's hairy–nosed wombat. The animal does, indeed, have a hairy nose, or muzzle. Its body is covered with a soft, silky brown coat. It has a large head, small eyes, pointed ears, and powerful legs with strong claws. The animal's poor eyesight is offset by its keen senses of hearing and smell. An average northern hairy–nosed wombat has a stocky body measuring 3.25 feet (1 meter) in length and weighing between 42 and 70 pounds (19 and 32 kilograms).

The animal uses its strong foreclaws to excavate a series of connected burrows called a warren. Each burrow may be 100 feet (30.5 meters) long, and each warren may have several entrances. The animal's home range surrounding its war-

ren may extend over 14.8 acres (6 hectares). The northern hairy–nosed wombat feeds at night on grass, especially bunch speargrass.

The northern hairy–nosed wombat belongs to an order of mammals known as marsupials, whose young continue to develop after birth in a pouch on the outside of the mother's body. After a female northern hairy–nosed wombat gives birth to a single infant in summer (November to March), she carries her infant in her pouch for about six months. The young wombat nurses for almost nine months.

Habitat and current distribution

The northern hairy–nosed wombat prefers to inhabit open, semiarid (semidry) woodlands or grasslands. It generally digs its burrows in sandy soils that are supported by tree roots.

A northern hairy–nosed wombat. The wombat is considered rare since its current population only numbers 65.

The only known surviving population of northern hairy–nosed wombats is found in the Epping Forest National Park in the northeastern Australian state of Queensland. Biologists (people who study living organisms) estimate that their population numbers 65.

History and conservation measures

The northern hairy–nosed wombat was probably already quite rare when Europeans began settling in Australia in the late eighteenth century. By 1909, it was considered extinct. In 1937, however, a small group of the animals was discovered west of the city of Clermont in east–central Queensland.

The area inhabited by these remaining wombats was declared a national park in the 1970s. At first, the animals were not fully protected, as cattle in the park grazed on the wombat's food source. Although steps have been taken since then to eliminate cattle from the park, the number of surviving northern hairy–nosed wombats continues to be very low.

YAK, WILD
Bos grunniens mutus

PHYLUM: Chordata
CLASS: Mammalia
ORDER: Artiodactyla
FAMILY: Bovidae
STATUS: Vulnerable, IUCN Endangered, ESA
RANGE: China, India, Nepal

Yak, wild
Bos grunniens mutus

Description and biology

The wild yak is a rare and mysterious animal. Its huge body is covered with coarse, shaggy, dark brown hair that hangs almost to the ground. Its muzzle is white. The animal has a large, drooping head, humped shoulders, and short legs. The average male wild yak has a head and body length of 10.75 feet (3.3 meters) and stands 5.5 to 6.5 feet (1.7 to 2 meters) tall at its shoulder. It weighs between 1,800 and 2,200 pounds (820 and 1,000 kilograms). Its upward curved horns are dark and may grow up to 3 feet (0.9 meter) long. Females are substantially smaller.

Wild yaks feed on mosses and lichens (organisms composed of a fungus and an alga) while inhabiting areas at high elevations. At lower elevations, they feed on mosses, herbs, and grasses. Because vegetation is often scarce in their habitat, the animals often cover great distances looking for food. A known predator is the Tibetan wolf.

Because enforcement of the laws protecting the wild yak is difficult, the few hundred existing animals remain in serious danger of extinction.

Males and females form separate herds. During mating season, which begins in September, the herds come together and the males compete with each other over the right to mate with available females. After a gestation (pregnancy) period of 258 days, a female wild yak gives birth to a single calf. The calf then nurses for up to a year.

Habitat and current distribution

Although there are millions of domesticated yaks in the world today, wildlife biologists (scientists who study living organisms) estimate that there are less than 10,000 wild yaks today. They inhabit isolated patches on the Tibetan Plateau at elevations between 13,500 and 20,000 feet (4,115 and 6,096 meters).

History and conservation measures

The wild yak's range once extended into northern Siberia. Biologists believe the animal's population was still quite large at the beginning of the twentieth century. Since that time, excessive hunting has reduced the number of wild yaks to a dangerously low level. Humans have always valued the animal's meat, hide, and coat. Even though the wild yak is protected by international treaties, hunting continues. The Chinese government has been guilty of allowing foreign hunters to kill the animals for sport.

Because of the wild yak's remote mountain habitat, the enforcement of existing laws and the development of conservation plans is almost impossible. As a result, the surviving animals remain in grave danger.

ZEBRA, GREVY'S
Equus grevyi

PHYLUM: Chordata
CLASS: Mammalia
ORDER: Perissodactyla
FAMILY: Equidae
STATUS: Endangered, IUCN
Threatened, ESA
RANGE: Ethiopia, Kenya

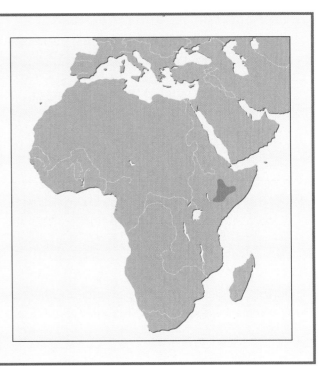

Zebra, Grevy's

Equus grevyi

Description and biology

A member of the horse family, the Grevy's zebra is similar in appearance to a mule. It has an average head and body length of 8 to 10 feet (2.4 to 3 meters) and a shoulder height of 4.5 to 5 feet (1.4 to 1.5 meters). It weighs between 800 and 950 pounds (360 and 430 kilograms). The animal has a large head, rounded ears, a tufted tail, and a short, stiff mane. It feeds primarily on grass. Lions, hyenas, and crocodiles are the Grevy's zebra's main predators.

A beautiful pattern of narrow black and white vertical stripes covers most of the Grevy's zebra's head and body. A dark stripe runs down the top of its back. Its belly is white. Scientists once thought that the stripes on zebras served to camouflage or protect the animals from predators. Some re-

searchers now believe the stripes help the animals recognize other members of their group and, thus, form social bonds.

Grevy's zebras are unique among zebras in that they do not form permanent groups. Nursing females and their foals (young), other females, and solitary males sometimes gather in temporary herds. Some males establish territories ranging between 1 and 4 square miles (2.6 and 10.4 square kilometers) and will compete with other males over the right to mate with females in their territory. Mating takes place any time of the year, but peaks in mid–summer and mid–fall. After a gestation (pregnancy) period of 390 days, a female Grevy's zebra gives birth to a single foal. The newborn foal is brown and black in color, and its mane extends down its back to its tail. After four months, it develops adult coloring. The foal may remain with its mother for up to three years.

Some scientists now believe that Grevy's zebra's black–and–white stripes help it to distinguish other members of its group.

Habitat and current distribution

Grevy's zebras inhabit the semiarid (semidry) scrublands and grasslands in southern Ethiopia and Kenya. Although unsure of the total number of Grevy's zebras currently in existence, scientists believe that number is declining.

History and conservation measures

Between the late 1970s and late 1980s, the Grevy's zebra population decreased by 70 percent. Once populous in Somalia, the animal is now extinct there. Hunting for its beautiful skin was the main reason for its decline in early years. The animal is now legally protected, and poaching (illegal hunting) is not considered a major problem.

The principal current threat to the Grevy's zebra is the loss of its habitat. Increasing numbers of domestic livestock now graze on the animal's food source. Much of the water that flowed through its semiarid habitat in Kenya has been diverted to irrigate nearby developing farmland.

Where to Learn More

Books

Ackerman, Diane. *The Rarest of the Rare: Vanishing Animals, Timeless Worlds.* New York: Random House, 1995. Naturalist and poet Ackerman travels from the Amazon rain forests to a remote Japanese island in search of endangered creatures and their habitats, revealing the factors that are contributing to their endangerment and describing preservation efforts.

Baskin, Yvonne. *The Work of Nature: How the Diversity of Life Sustains Us.* Washington, DC: Island Press, 1997. Science writer Baskin examines the practical consequences of declining biodiversity on ecosystem health and functioning, highlighting examples from around the world.

Chadwick, Douglas W., and Joel Sartore. *The Company We Keep: America's Endangered Species.* Washington, DC: National Geographic Society, 1996. Wildlife biologist Chadwick chronicles past and current conservation efforts, profiling dozens of birds and animals on the top ten endangered list. The book, for readers aged ten and above, also includes rich photographs by photojournalist Sartore, range maps, habitat descriptions, population counts, and current status for all endangered North American species.

Cohen, Daniel. *The Modern Ark: Saving Endangered Species.* New York: Putnam, 1995. Aimed at young adult readers, this work explains the problems faced by endangered species and the solutions—such as the Species Survival Plan—to help protect their futures.

Dobson, David. *Can We Save Them? Endangered Species of North America.* Watertown, MA: Charlesbridge, 1997. For students aged seven to ten, Dobson's work introduces readers to twelve species of endangered animals and plants in North America and suggests ways to restore each one's natural environment.

Earle, Sylvia. *Sea Change: A Message of the Oceans.* New York: Putnam, 1995. Marine biologist and leading deep-sea explorer Earle writes about her three decades of undersea exploration and makes an urgent plea for the preservation of the world's fragile and rapidly deteriorating ocean ecosystems.

Endangered Wildlife of the World. New York: Marshall Cavendish, 1993. Developed for young adults, this 11-volume reference set presents 1,400 alphabetical entries focusing on the plight of endangered species, with a special emphasis placed on the species of North America.

Galan, Mark. *There's Still Time: The Success of the Endangered Species Act.* Washington, DC: National Geographic Society, 1997. For young readers, this photo-essay work features plants and animals that have been brought back from the brink of extinction, primarily because of the Endangered Species Act.

Harris, Michael. *Lament for an Ocean: The Collapse of the Atlantic Cod Fishery: A True Crime Story.* Toronto, Ontario: McClelland and Stewart, 1998. A gripping journalistic exposé about the overfishing that caused the collapse of the Atlantic Cod fishery in Canada, despite the clear warnings of marine scientists.

Hoff, Mary King, and Mary M. Rodgers. *Our Endangered Planet: Life on Land.* Minneapolis, MN: Lerner, 1992. For young adult readers, Hoff's work describes the delicate ecological balance among all living things on land, the damage done by humanity in contributing to the extinction of various species, and ways of preventing further harm.

Hoyt, John Arthur. *Animals in Peril: How "Sustainable Use" Is Wiping Out the World's Wildlife.* New York: Avery Publishing Group, 1995. Hoyt, executive officer of the U.S. Humane Society, contends that conservation agencies are destroying many animal species by cooperating with local governments in a conservation policy that actually promotes slaughter, suffering, and extinction.

Liittschwager, David, and Susan Middleton, in association with the Environmental Defense Organization. *Remains of a Rainbow: Rare Plants and Animals of Hawaii.* National Tropical Botanical Garden and Nature Conservancy of Hawaii, contributers. Washington, D.C.: National Geographic, 2001. A collection of photographs of the endangered species of Hawaii, capturing the delicate balance of Hawaii's lush and rapidly deteriorating ecosystems.

Mackay, Richard. *The Penguin Atlas of Endangered Species.* New York: Penguin, 2002. A resource suitable for young adults and older, this atlas provides vital information on ecosystems, identifying wildlife, the importance of biodiversity, the transplanting of plants and animals across continents, and more. Also included in its 128 pages are case studies illustrating the major threats to biodiversity and the measures being taken to conserve the species.

Mann, Charles, and Mark Plummer. *Noah's Choice: The Future of Endangered Species.* New York: Knopf, 1995. Mann and Plummer examine the controversy over the Endangered

Species Act and call for a new set of principles to serve as a guideline for choosing which endangered species to save.

Matthiessen, Peter. *Wildlife in America*. Rev. ed. New York: Penguin Books, 1995. Acclaimed naturalist-writer Matthiessen first published this classic work on the history of the rare, threatened, and extinct animals of North America in 1959.

McClung, Robert. *Last of the Wild: Vanished and Vanishing Giants of the Animal World*. Hamden, CT: Linnet Books, 1997. For readers aged 12 and above, McClung's work profiles threatened animals around the world and discusses why they are in danger and what is being done to save them.

McClung, Robert. *Lost Wild America: The Story of Our Extinct and Vanishing Wildlife*. Hamden, CT: Shoe String Press, 1993. McClung traces the history of wildlife conservation and environmental politics in America to 1992, and describes various extinct or endangered species.

Meacham, Cory J. *How the Tiger Lost Its Stripes: An Exploration into the Endangerment of a Species*. New York: Harcourt Brace, 1997. Journalist Meacham offers a probing analysis of the endangerment of the world's pure species of tigers and the role of zoos, scientists, and politics in stopping it.

Middleton, Susan, and David Liittschwager. *Witness: Endangered Species of North America*. San Francisco, CA: Chronicle Books, 1994. Through a series of 200 color and duotone portraits, photographers Middleton and Liittschwager capture 100 species of North American animals and plants on the brink of extinction.

Patent, Dorothy Hinshaw. *Back to the Wild*. San Diego, CA: Gulliver Books, 1997. For readers aged ten and above, Patent's work describes efforts to save endangered animals from extinction by breeding them in captivity, teaching them survival skills, and then releasing them into the wild.

Pollock, Stephen Thomas. *The Atlas of Endangered Animals*. New York: Facts on File, 1993. For younger readers, Pollock's work uses maps, pictures, symbols, and text to focus on areas of the world in which human activity is threatening to destroy already endangered animal species.

Quammen, David. *The Song of the Dodo: Island Biogeography in an Age of Extinctions*. New York: Scribner, 1996. In a work for adult readers, Quammen interweaves personal observation, scientific theory, and history to examine the mysteries of evolution and extinction as they have been illuminated by the study of islands.

Schaller, George. *The Last Panda*. Chicago, IL: University of Chicago Press, 1993. Noted biologist Schaller presents an account of the four years he spent in China's Sichuan Province working to protect both panda habitat and the few pandas that remained.

Threatened Birds of the World: The Official Source for Birds on the IUCN Red List. Alison Stattersfield and David R. Capper, eds. Barcelona, Spain: Birdlife International/Lynx Editions, 2000. A comprehensive encyclopedia of endangered, threatened, or vulnerable bird species worldwide, this 852-page reference is illustrated with charts, illustrations, and photographs. Each of the 1,186 threatened birds listed in this comprehensive source receives a half-page, illustrated entry, including a range map, photos or illustrations, a discussion of why the bird is listed as threatened, and information on identification, range and population, ecology, threats, conservation, and action plans.

Tudge, Colin. *Last Animals at the Zoo: How Mass Extinctions Can Be Stopped.* Washington, DC: Island Press, 1992. Zoologist Tudge details the grim conditions many animals must overcome in their natural habitats and the bleak prospects for recovery by those already on the brink of extinction.

Weidensaul, Samuel. *The Ghost with Trembling Wings: Science, Wishful Thinking, and the Search for Lost Species.* New York: North Point Press, 2003. In a series of suspenseful stories set all over the world, the author chronicles the reappearance of some supposedly extinct animals, such as the ivory-billed woodpecker and the coelacanth. In some cases, the reappearances have actually occurred, but in others it has been wishful thinking, and many of the searches have been fruitless. The book discusses both the science and the ethics of such wishful thinking.

Wilson, Edward Osborne. *The Future of Life.* New York: Knopf, 2002. A Pulitzer-prize winning naturalist's overview of the dire problems facing the natural world today, including fascinating stories of struggling species and an imagined conversation with Henry David Thoreau at Walden Pond. Wilson makes and impassioned plea for the future, providing global strategies to save the planet.

Periodicals

Endangered Species Bulletin
Division of Endangered Species
U.S. Fish and Wildlife Service, Washington, DC 20240

Endangered Species UPDATE
School of Natural Resources and Environment
The University of Michigan, Ann Arbor, MI 48109-1115

Sierra Magazine (bimonthly)
Sierra Club
85 Second Street
San Francisco, CA 94105-3441

Web Sites

Birdlife International
http://www.birdlife.net/

Convention on International Trade in Endangered Species
http://www.wcmc.org.uk:80/CITES/english/index.html

EcoNet: Habitats and Species
http://www.igc.apc.org/igc/issues/habitats

EE-Link: Endangered Species, University of Michigan
http://www.nceet.snre.umich.edu/EndSpp/Endangered.html

Endangered! Exploring a World at Risk: The American Museum of Natural History
http://www.amnh.org/nationalcenter/Endangered

Endangered Species Act (brief history), University of Oregon
http://gladstone.uoregon.edu/~cait/

Endangered Species Home Page, U.S. Fish and Wildlife Service
http://www.fws.gov/~r9endspp.endspp.html

Endangered Species Protection Program, U.S. Environmental Protection Agency
http://www.epa.gov/espp

Endangered Species Study Web: General Resources
http://www.studyweb.com/animals/endang/endanger.htm

Endangered Species Update, University of Michigan
http://www.umich.edu/~esupdate/

EnviroLink: Largest online environmental information resource
http://www.envirolink.org/

Environmental Education (EE) Link: Endangered Species
http://eelink.net/EndSpp/specieshighlights-mainpage.html

Environmental Organization Web Directory: Wildlife and endangered species focus
http://www.webdirectory.com/Wildlife/General_Endangered_Species

Green Nature
http://greennature.com

IUCN Red List of Threatened Animals
http://www.wcmc.org.uk/data/database/rl_anml_combo.html

IUCN Red List of Threatened Plants
http://www.wcmc.org.uk/species/plants/plant_redlist.html

SeaWorld Education Department: Endangered Species
http://www.seaworld.org/infobooks/Endangered/home.html

Society for the Protection of Endangered Species (group of endangered species-related weblinks)
http://pubweb.ucdavis.edu/Documents/GWS/Envissues/EndSpes/speshome.htm

Terra's Endangered Species Tour (includes range maps)
http://www.olcommerce.com/terra/endanger.html

Organizations Focusing on Endangered and Threatened Species (selected list)

African Wildlife Foundation
1717 Massachusetts Ave., NW
Washington, DC 20036
(202) 265-8393; Fax: (202) 265-2361
Internet: http://www.awf.org
Organization that works to craft and deliver creative solutions for the long-term well-being of Africa's remarkable species and habitats.

American Cetacean Society
P.O. Box 1319
San Pedro, CA 90733-0391
(310) 548-6279; Fax: (310) 548-6950
Internet: http://www.acsonline.org
Nonprofit organization that works in the areas of conservation, education, and research to protect marine mammals, especially whales, dolphins, and porpoises, and the oceans in which they live.

Animal Welfare Institute
P.O. Box 3650
Washington, DC 20007
(202) 337-2332; Fax: (202) 338-9478
Organization active in the protection of endangered species, among other issues, related to animal welfare.

Center for Biological Diversity
P.O. Box 710
Tucson AZ 85702-0710
(520) 623-5252; Fax: (520) 623-9797
Internet: http://www.center@biologicaldiversity.org
A nonprofit regional conservation organization with over 7,500 members, dedicated to protecting biological diversity through science, policy, education, and environmental law. The Center has been a premier endangered species advocate. It has obtained, often by filing lawsuits in the federal courts, ESA protection for 280 species and the designation of over 38 million acres of critical habitat, helping to protect U.S. coasts, oceans, deserts, forests, rivers and grasslands for threatened species.

Center for Marine Conservation, Inc.
1725 DeSales St., NW, Suite 500
Washington, DC 20036
(202) 429-5609; Fax: (202) 872-0619

Nonprofit organization dedicated to protecting marine wildlife and their habitats and to conserving coastal and ocean resources.

Center for Plant Conservation, Inc.
P.O. Box 299
St. Louis, MO 63166
(314) 577-9450; Fax: (314) 577-9465
Internet: http://www.mobot.org/CPC/
National network of 25 botanical gardens and arboreta dedicated to the conservation and study of rare and endangered U.S. plants.

The Conservation Agency
6 Swinburne Street
Jamestown, RI 02835
(401) 423-2652; Fax: (401) 423-2652
Organization that conducts research and gathers data specifically aimed to preserve rare, endangered, and little-known species.

Defenders of Wildlife
1101 14th St., NW, Suite 1400
Washington, DC 20005
(202) 682-9400; Fax: (202) 682-1331
Internet: http://www.defenders.org/
Nonprofit organization that works to protect and restore native species, habitats, ecosystems, and overall biological diversity.

Earthjustice Legal Defense Fund
426 17th Street, 5th Floor
Oakland, CA 94612-2820
(510) 550-6725; Fax: (510) 550-6749
Internet: http://www.eajusca@earthjustice.org
Founded in 1971 as Sierra Club Legal Defense Fund, Earthjustice is a nonprofit law firm dedicated to protecting nature by working through the courts. Earthjustice has played a leading role in shaping the development of environmental law in the courtrooms and also in Washington, D.C. where it is influential in shaping policies and legislation. The organization also runs environmental law clinics at Stanford University and the University of Denver, educating students in public interest environmental law.

Endangered Species Coalition
666 Pennsylvania Ave., SE
Washington, DC 20003
(202) 547-9009
Coalition of more than 200 organizations that seeks to broaden and mobilize public support for protecting endangered species.

Environmental Investigation Agency (EIA)
P.O. Box 53343
Washington D.C. 20009
(202) 483-6621; Fax: (202) 986-8626
Internet: http://www.EIAgency@email.msn.com
An international campaigning organization formed in 1984, committed to investigating and exposing environmental crime by using advanced investigative techniques. EIA often works undercover to expose international crimes such as illegal trade in wildlife and illegal logging. The organization has brought about changes in international and national laws and policies.

International Union for Conservation of Nature and Natural Resources (IUCN-The World Conservation Union)
U.S. Office: 1400 16th St., NW
Washington, DC 20036
(202) 797-5454; Fax: (202) 797-5461
Internet: http://www.iucn.org
An international independent body that promotes scientifically based action for the conservation of nature and for sustainable development. The Species Survival Commission (SSC) of the IUCN publishes biennial Red List books, which describe threatened species of mammals, birds, reptiles, amphibians, fish, invertebrates, and plants.

International Wildlife Coalition
70 East Falmouth Highway
East Falmouth, MA 02536
(508) 548-8328; Fax: (508) 548-8542
Internet: http://www.webcom.com/-iwcwww
Nonprofit organization dedicated to preserving wildlife and their habitats. IWC's Whale Adoption Project preserves marine mammals.

International Wildlife Education and Conservation
1140 Westwood Blvd., Suite 205
Los Angeles, CA 90024
(310) 208-3631; Fax: (310) 208-2779
Internet: http://www.iwec.org/iwec.htm
Nonprofit organization that seeks to ensure the future of endangered animals and to promote animal welfare through public education and conservation of habitats.

Marine Environmental Research Institute
772 West End Ave.
New York, NY 10025
(212) 864-6285; Fax (212) 864-1470
Nonprofit organization dedicated to protecting the health and biodiversity of the marine environment, addressing such problems as global marine pollution, endangered species, and habitat destruction.

National Audubon Society
700 Broadway
New York, NY 10002
(212) 979-3000
Internet: http://www.audubon.org
A national network of community-based nature centers dedicated to the conservation and restoration of natural resources with emphasis on wildlife, habitats, soil, water, and forests, particularly emphasizing advocacy on behalf of areas sustaining important bird populations.

National Wildlife Federation
Laurel Ridge Conservation Education Center
8925 Leesburg Pike
Vienna, VA 22184-0001
(703) 790-4000; Fax: (703) 442-7332
Internet: http://www.nwf.org
Nonprofit organization that seeks to educate, inspire, and assist individuals and organizations of diverse cultures to conserve wildlife and other natural resources.

Nature Conservancy
1815 North Lynn St.
Arlington, VA 22209
(703) 841-5300; Fax: (703) 841-1283
Internet: http://www.tnc.org
International nonprofit organization committed to preserving biological diversity by protecting natural lands and the life they harbor.

Pacific Center for International Studies
33 University Sq., Suite 184
Madison, WI 53715
(608) 256-6312; Fax: (608) 257-0417
An international think tank specializing in the assessment of international treaty regimes, including the Convention on International Trade in Endangered Species (CITES) and the International Convention for the Regulation of Whaling (ICRW).

Save the Manatee Club
500 North Maitland Ave.
Maitland, FL 32751
(407) 539-0990; Fax: (407) 539-0871
Internet: http://www.objectlinks.com/manatee
National nonprofit organization that seeks to preserve the endangered West Indian manatee through public education, research funding, rescue, rehabilitation, and advocacy.

Wildlife Preservation Trust International, Inc.
400 West Girard Ave.
Philadelphia, PA 19104
(215) 222-3636; Fax: (215) 222-2191

Organization that supports the preservation of endangered species through hands-on field work, research, education, and training.

World Conservation Monitoring Centre
219 Huntington Rd.
Cambridge, England CB3 ODL
(01223) 277314; Fax: (01223) 277136
Internet: http://www.wcmc.org.uk
Organization that supports conservation and sustainable development through the provision of information services on issues relating to nature conservation.

World Society for the Protection of Animals
29 Perkins St.
P.O. Box 190
Boston, MA 02130
(617) 522-7000; Fax: (617) 522-7077
International organization committed to the alleviation of animal suffering and to the conservation of endangered animals.

World Wildlife Fund
1250 24th St., NW
Washington, DC 20037
(202) 293-4800; Fax: (202) 293-9211
Internet: http://www.wwf.org
The largest private U.S. organization working worldwide to protect wildlife and wildlands—especially in the tropical forests of Latin America, Asia, and Africa.

Photo Credits

Photographs appearing in Endangered Species, 2nd Edition, were received from the following sources. Every effort has been made to secure permission; if omissions have been made, please contact us.

Abbott's booby (Papasula abbotti), illustration by Patricia Ferrer. Reproduced by permission.—Addax with lowered head, photograph by Mark Boulton. Photo Researchers, Inc. Reproduced by permission.—African elephant, photograph by Mark Boulton. Photo Researchers, Inc. Reproduced by permission.—African wild dogs, photograph by Nigel J. Dennis. Photo Researchers, Inc. Reproduced by permission.—Agave Living Rock cactus (Ariocarpus agavoides), photograph. © Rick and Nora Bowers / Visuals Unlimited. Reproduced by permission.—American burying beetle, photograph. Photo Researchers, Inc. Reproduced by permission.—American crocodile, photograph by R. Cramm. Photo Researchers, Inc. Reproduced by permission.—Anas bernieri (duck), photograph. BIOS/Peter Arnold, Inc. Reproduced by permission.—Andean flamingo, photograph by Dr. M.P. Kahl. Photo Researchers, Inc. Reproduced by permission.—Atlantic cod, photograph by Tom McHugh. Photo Researchers, Inc. Reproduced by permission.—Audouin's Gull, photograph by Jose Luis G. Grande. Photo Researchers, Inc. Reproduced by permission.—Australian ant with caterpillar prey, photograph. Planet Earth Pictures Limited. Reproduced by permission.—Aye aye, photograph by Mike Dulaney. Cincinnati Zoo. Reproduced by permission.—Bactrian camel, photograph by Renee Lynn. Photo Researchers, Inc. Reproduced by permission.—Baiji dolphin's (Lipotes vexillifer), photograph. © Thomas Jefferson/ Seapics.com. Reproduced by permission.—Bald eagle, photograph by Tim & Pat Leeson. Photo Researchers, Inc. Reproduced by permission.—Baltic sturgeon, photograph by Tom McHugh. Photo Researchers, Inc. Reproduced by permission.—Bay checkerspot butterfly, photograph by Richard A. Arnold. Reproduced by permission.—Bengal tiger walking along beach, photograph by Jeff Lepore. Photo Researchers, Inc. Reproduced by permission.—Black caiman, photograph.

Cincinnati Zoo. Reproduced by permission.—Black rhinoceros, photograph by M. Philip Kahl, Jr. Photo Researchers, Inc. Reproduced by permission.—Black-capped vireo feeding babies, photograph by S. & S. Rucker. Vireo. Reproduced by permission.—Black-cheeked lovebirds, photograph by E. R. Degginger. Photo Researchers, Inc. Reproduced by permission.—Blue whale, photograph by Pieter Folkens. Planet Earth Pictures, Limited. Reproduced by permission.—Braun's rockcress, photograph. U.S. Fish and Wildlife Service. Reproduced by permission.—Bridled nailtail wallaby, photograph by Mitch Reardon. Photo Researchers, Inc. Reproduced by permission.—Bristle fern (Trichomanes radicons), photograph by E.D. Degginger. Bruce Coleman, Inc. Reproduced by permission.—Brown hyena, photograph by Tom McHugh. Photo Researchers, Inc. Reproduced by permission.—Buffy-eared marmoset (Callithrix aurita), photograph. Claus Meyer/Minden Pictures. Reproduced by permission.—Bull trout, photograph by Wade Fredenberg, U. S. Fish and Wildlife Service. Reproduced by permission.—California condor, photograph by Kenneth W. Fink. Photo Researchers, Inc. Reproduced by permission.—California Freshwater Shrimp, photograph. © 1994 Middleton/Littschwager. Reproduced by permission.—California red-legged frog (Rana aurora draytonii), photograph by Bruce Watkins. Animals Animals/Earth Scenes. Reproduced by permission.—Captive imperial Amazon parrot (Amasona imperialis-caribbean), photograph. © Frank W. Lane; Frank Lane Picture Agency/Corbis. Reproduced by permission.—Cape vultures, photograph by Nigel Dennis. Photo Researchers, Inc. Reproduced by permission.—Cave crayfish, photograph by Smith, Ken, Arkansas Natural Heritage Commission. Reproduced by permission.—Central American River Turtle, photograph by Tom McHugh. Photo Researchers, Inc. Reproduced by permission.—Central American tapir, photograph by Thor Janson. Photo Researchers, Inc. Reproduced by permission.—Chapman's rhododendron in bloom, photograph by David & Hayes Norris. Photo Researchers, Inc. Reproduced by permission.—Chatam Island Forget-Me-Not, in bloom, photograph by Brian Enting. Photo Researchers, Inc. Reproduced by permission.—Chatham Island black robin (Petroica traversi), illustration by Emily Damstra. Reproduced by permission.—Cheer pheasant, photograph by Tom McHugh. Photo Researchers, Inc. Reproduced by permission.—Cheetah, photograph by S.R. Maglione. Photo Researchers,

Inc. Reproduced by permission.—Chimpanzee, photograph by Nigel J. Dennis. Photo Researchers, Inc. Reproduced by permission.—Chinchilla, photograph by Stephen Dalton. Photo Researchers, Inc. Reproduced by permission.—Chinese alligator, photograph by Ken King. Planet Earth Pictures, Limited. Reproduced by permission.—Chinese Egret, photograph by M. Strange. Vireo. Reproduced by permission.—Chinese giant salamander, photograph. Cincinnati Zoo. Reproduced by permission.—Ciconia boyciana, photograph. BIOS/Peter Arnold, Inc. Reproduced by permission.—Coelacanth, photograph. Planet Earth Pictures, Limited. Reproduced by permission.— Cook Strait Tuatara, photograph by Tom McHugh. Photo Researchers, Inc. Reproduced by permission.—Crested honeycreeper, photograph by Jack Jeffrey. Photo Resource Hawaii. Reproduced by permission.—Culebra Island Giant, photograph by C. Kenneth Dodd, Jr., USGS. Reproduced by permission.—Dalmation pelican, photograph by Edmund Appel. Photo Researchers, Inc. Reproduced by permission.— Dama gazelle nursing baby, photograph by Joseph Van Wormer. Photo Researchers, Inc. Reproduced by permission.— Danube salmon, photograph by Hans Reinhard. Photo Researchers, Inc. Reproduced by permission.—Delhi sands flower-loving fly, photograph by Greg Ballmer. Reproduced by permission.—Desert pupfish, photograph by Tom McHugh. Photo Researchers, Inc. Reproduced by permission.—Desert tortoise, photograph by Tim Davis. Photo Researchers, Inc. Reproduced by permission.—Dugong, photograph. © Tom McHugh/Photo Researchers, Inc. Reproduced by permission.— Elephant, Asian, photograph by Ben Simon. Stock Market/Corbis. Reproduced with permission.—European Bison or Wisent (Bison bonasus), photograph by Peter Weimann. Animals Animals/Earth Scenes. Reproduced by permission.—European mink (Mustela lutreola), photograph. BIOS/Peter Arnold, Inc. Reproduced by permission.—Fanshell, inside and outside, photograph by S. David Jenike. Cincinnati Zoo. Reproduced by permission.—Fat Pocketbook pearly mussel, photograph by A.E. Spreitzer. Reproduced by permission.—Fiji Island iguana, photograph by Joseph L. Collins. Photo Researchers, Inc. Reproduced by permission.—Florida torreya, photograph by Gary Retherford. Photo Researchers, Inc. Reproduced by permission.—Fountain darter, photograph by Roger W. Barbour. Reproduced by permission.—Galapagos Hawk, photograph by Jeanne White. Photo Researchers, Inc. Reproduced by permission.—Galapagos land iguana, photograph by Margaret Welby. Planet Earth Pictures, Limited. Reproduced by permission.—Galapagos Tortoise, photograph by Francois Gohier. Photo Researchers, Inc. Reproduced by permission.—Gavial sliding on sand, photograph by Jeffrey W. Lang. Photo Researchers, Inc. Reproduced by permission.—Giant anteater, photograph by Robert J. Huffman. Field Mark Publications. Reproduced by permission.—Giant armadillo, photograph by Paul Crum. Photo Researchers, Inc. Reproduced by permission.—Giant catfish, photograph by Roland Seitre. © Roland Seitre/Peter Arnold, Inc. Reproduced by permission.—Giant Kangaroo Rat, photograph by Susan Middleton. © 1998 Susan Middleton. Reproduced by permission.—Giant panda, photograph by Tom & Pat Leeson. Photo Researchers, Inc. Reproduced by permission.—Golden bandicoot, photograph by Jiri Lochman. Planet Earth Pictures Limited. Reproduced by permission.—Golden Lion Tamarins, photograph. Cincinnati Zoo. Reproduced by permission.—Golden parakeet, photograph by Lynx Edicions. Vireo. Reproduced by permission.—Goldenrod, photograph by John MacGregor. Reproduced by permission.—Goliath frog with gold watch near head, photograph by Paul A. Zahl. Photo Researchers, Inc. Reproduced by permission.—Gorilla, posed, photograph by Jerry L. Ferrara. Photo Researchers, Inc. Reproduced by permission.—Gray fruit bat clinging to rock, photograph by Merlin D. Tuttle. Photo Researchers, Inc. Reproduced by permission.—Gray wolf howling, photograph by Myer Bornstein. Planet Earth Pictures Limited. Reproduced by permission.—Great Phillipine Eagle, photograph by Alain Evrard. Photo Researchers, Inc. Reproduced by permission.—Green pitcher plant, photograph. Photo Researchers, Inc. Reproduced by permission.—Green sea turtle, floating in water, photograph by Dr. Paula A. Zahl. Photo Researchers, Inc. Reproduced by permission.—Grevy zebra, photograph by Leonard Lee Rue III. Photo Researchers, Inc. Reproduced by permission.—Grizzly bear, photograph by Jeff Lepore. Photo Researchers, Inc. Reproduced by permission.—Guadalupe fur seal, photograph by C. Allan Morgan. Reproduced by permission.—Harvestman, photograph. U. S. Fish and Wildlife Service. Reproduced by permission.—Hawaiian crow, photograph by R. & N. Bowers. Vireo. Reproduced by permission.—Hawaiian goose, photograph by Roger Wilmshurst. Photo Researchers, Inc. Reproduced by permission. —Hawaiian hawk, photograph by Tom McHugh. Reproduced by permission.—Hawaiian monk seal, photograph. U. S. Fish and Wildlife Service. Reproduced by permission.—Hines emerald dragonfly, photograph. Reproduced by permission.—Honeycreeper, photograph by H. Douglas Pratt. Reproduced by permission.—Hoolock gibbon, southeast Asia, photograph by Tom McHugh. Photo Researchers, Inc. Reproduced by permission.—Houston toad, photograph by Joseph T. Collins. Photo Researchers, Inc. Reproduced by permission.—Humpback whale, photograph by Francois Gohier. Photo Researchers, Inc. Reproduced by permission.—Huon tree kangaroo, photograph. © Art Wolfe/Photo Researchers, Inc. Reproduced by permission.—Iberian lynxes at a zoo in southern Spain, photograph. © Reuters New-Media Inc./Corbis. Reproduced by permission.—Indian python, photograph by Mandal Ranjit. Photo Researchers, Inc. Reproduced by permission.—Iowa pleistocene snails, photograph. U. S. Fish and Wildlife Service. Reproduced by permission.—Island fox (Urocyon littoralis santarosae), photograph. © Kennan Ward/Corbis. Reproduced by permission.—Ivory-billed woodpecker, photograph by Ken Lucas. Planet Earth Pictures, Limited. Reproduced by permission.—Jaguar, photograph by Renee Lynn. Photo Researchers, Inc. Reproduced by permission.—James River Spinymussel, photograph. A.E. Spreitzer. Reproduced by permission.—Kakapo, photograph. Photo Researchers, Inc. Reproduced by permission.—Kentucky cave shrimp, photograph. U. S. Fish and Wildlife Service. Reproduced by permission.—Kirtland's warbler, photograph by Bill Dyer. Photo Researchers, Inc. Reproduced by permission.—Koala, photograph by Robert J. Huffman. Field Mark Publications. Reproduced by permission.—Komodo Dragon, photograph. Cincinnati Zoo. Reproduced by permission.—Laysan finch in grassy area, photograph by Karl W. Kenyon. Photo Researchers, Inc. Reproduced by permission.—Laysan Teal duck (Anas layanensis) at the Houston Zoo, photograph by Mickey Gibson. Animals Animals/Earth Scenes. Reproduced by permission.—Lear's Macaws, photograph by Kenneth W. Fink. Photo Researchers, Inc. Reproduced by permission.—Leatherback sea turtle, photograph by C. Allan Morgan. Reproduced by permission.—Leopard, photograph by Gregory G. Dimijian. Photo Researchers, Inc. Reproduced by permission.—Leopard lizard, photograph by Rod Planck. Photo Researchers, Inc. Reproduced by permission.—Little wing pearly mussel, photograph by A. E. Spreitzer. All Rights Reserved.

Reproduced by permission.—Lord Howe Wood Rail, photograph by Vincent Serventy. Planet Earth Pictures, Limited. Reproduced by permission.—Madison Cave Isopod, photograph. © 1994 Middleton/Littschwager. Reproduced by permission.—Manatee (Trichechus manatus), photograph. © Douglas Faulkner/Corbis. Reproduced by permission.—Mandrill, photograph by Gregory G. Dimijian. Photo Researchers, Inc. Reproduced by permission.—Manus Island green snail (Papustyla pulchenrima), photograph. © L. Newman & A. Flowers. Reproduced by permission.—Marbled murrelet, photograph by R. L. Pitman. Vireo. Reproduced by permission.—Marine otter (Lutra felina), photograph. © Roland Seitre/Peter Arnold, Inc. Reproduced by permission.—Markhor, photograph. Cincinnati Zoo. Reproduced by permission.—Mauna Loa, photograph by Derral Herbst. Reproduced by permission.—Mauritius kestral, photograph by Nick Garbutt. Planet Earth Pictures, Limited. Reproduced by permission.—Meadow viper (Vipera ursinii rakosiensis), photograph. © Zoltan Takacs. Reproduced by permission.—Mexican prairie dog (Cynomys mexicanus), photograph by Patricio Robles Gil. Reproduced by permission.—Mongoose lemur, photograph by Tom McHugh. Photo Researchers, Inc. Reproduced by permission.—Monito gecko, photograph by C. Kenneth Dodd, Jr., USGS. Reproduced by permission.—Mountain pygmy possum, photograph by Tom McHugh. Photo Researchers, Inc. Reproduced by permission.—Musk deer, photograph by M. K. Ranjitsinh. Photo Researchers, Inc. Reproduced by permission.—Nashville crayfish, photograph. U. S. Fish and Wildlife Service. Reproduced by permission.—Nevin's barberry, photograph by Steve Junak. Reproduced by permission.—Northern white rhinoceros, photograph by Kenneth W. Fink. Photo Researchers, Inc. Reproduced by permission.—Northern bald ibis, photograph. Cincinnati Zoo. Reproduced by permission.—Northern spotted owl, photograph by Tom & Pat Leeson. Photo Researchers, Inc. Reproduced by permission.—Numbat, photograph. Photo Researchers, Inc. Reproduced by permission.—Numenius borealis, photograph. © J. Pierre Sylvestre/BIOS/Peter Arnold, Inc. Reproduced by permission.—Orangutan, photograph by Tim Davis. Photo Researchers, Inc. Reproduced by permission.—Orinoco crocodile, photograph by Tom McHugh. Photo Researchers, Inc. Reproduced by permission.—Ornithoptera alexandrae butterfly, photograph. © Francois Gilson/BIOS/Peter Arnold, Inc. Reproduced by permission.—Pallid sturgeon, photograph. U. S. Fish and Wildlife Service. Reproduced by permission.—Peregrine falcon with wings outstretched, photograph by Tim Davis. Photo Researchers, Inc. Reproduced by permission.—Piping plover, photograph by Bill Dyer. Photo Researchers, Inc. Reproduced by permission.—Plowshare tortoise with baby, photograph by Nick Garbutt. Planet Earth Pictures, Limited. Reproduced by permission.—Prairie white fringed orchid, photograph by Jim W. Grace. Photo Researchers, Inc. Reproduced by permission.—Pristis perotteti, photograph. BIOS/Peter Arnold, Inc. Reproduced by permission.—Przewalski's horse, San Diego Zoo, photograph by J. Gordon Miller. Reproduced by permission.—Puerto Rican boa (Epicrates inornata), photograph by John Mitchell. Photo Researchers, Inc. Reproduced by permission.—Puerto Rican boa, photograph. U. S. Fish and Wildlife Service. Reproduced by permission.—Puna grebe (Podiceps taczanowskii), photograph. Peter Arnold, Inc. Reproduced by permission.—Purple-winged dove (Claravis godefrida), photograph. © Luis C. Marigo/Peter Arnold, Inc. Reproduced by permission.—Pygmy hippopotamus, photograph. Cincinnati Zoo. Reproduced by permission.—Pygmy hog, photograph by Tom McHugh. Photo Researchers, Inc. Reproduced by permission.—Pygmy sculpin, photograph by Noel Burkhead. Reproduced by permission.—Pygmy-owl, photograph by Mike Wrigley, U.S. Fish and Wildlife Service. Reproduced by permission.—Queen conch on star coral, photograph by Charles V. Angelo. Photo Researchers, Inc. Reproduced by permission.—Red panda, photograph by Toni Angermayer. Photo Researchers, Inc. Reproduced by permission.—Red wolf, photograph by Tom & Pat Leeson. Photo Researchers, Inc. Reproduced by permission.—Red-cockaded woodpecker, photograph by David & Hayes Norris. Photo Researchers, Inc. Reproduced by permission.—Relict trillium, photograph by Jeff Lepore. Photo Researchers, Inc. Reproduced by permission.—Reslendent Quetzal, photograph by Gregory G. Dimijian. Photo Researchers, Inc. Reproduced by permission.—Ring pink mussel, photograph by A. E. Spreitzer. All Rights Reserved. Reproduced by permission.—Robbin's cinquefoil, photograph. U. S. Fish and Wildlife Service. Reproduced by permission.—Rothchild's starling, photograph. Cincinnati Zoo. Reproduced by permission.—Salt water crocodile, photograph by Tom McHugh. Photo Researchers, Inc. Reproduced by permission.—San Francisco Garter snake (Thamnophis sirtalis tetrataenis), photograph by Paul Freed. Animals Animals/Earth Scenes. Reproduced by permission.—Santa Cruz salamander, photograph. Cincinnati Zoo. Reproduced by permission.—Scimitar-horned oryx, photograph by Tom McHugh. Photo Researchers, Inc. Reproduced by permission.—Seychelles Magpie Robin, photograph by Pete Oxford. Planet Earth Pictures, Limited. Reproduced by permission.—Short-tailed albatross, photograph by Gilbert S. Grant. Photo Researchers, Inc. Reproduced by permission.—Shortnose Sucker, photograph by Joseph Tomelleri. Cimarron Trading Co. Reproduced by permission.—Siberian cranes, photograph. Planet Earth Pictures, Limited. Reproduced by permission.—Sichuan hill-partridge (Arborophila rufipectus), illustration by Bruce Worden. Reproduced by permission.—Silver rice rat (Oryzomys argentatus), photograph by Numi C. Mitchell. The Conservation Agency. Reproduced by permission.—Skinheads, photograph. Corbis. Reproduced by permission.—Small whorled pogonia flower, photograph. © Hal Horwitz/Corbis. Reproduced by permission.—Snow leopards, photograph. Cincinnati Zoo. Reproduced by permission.—Somali wild ass (Equus africanus), photograph. © Steve Kaufman/Corbis. Reproduced by permission.—Spiral aloes, photograph by Robert Story. Planet Earth Pictures Limited. Reproduced by permission.—Squirrel Monkey with baby on back, photograph. Planet Earth Pictures, Ltd. Reproduced by permission.—Steller sea lion (Eumetopias jubatus), photograph by Yva/Eastcott Momatiuk, John (Eastcott/Momatiuk). Animals Animals/Earth Scenes. Reproduced by permission.—Stirrup shell, photograph by A. E. Spreitzer. All Rights Reserved. Reproduced by permission.—Sun bear, photograph by Tom McHugh. Photo Researchers, Inc. Reproduced by permission.—Swamp deer, photograph by Tom McHugh. Photo Researchers, Inc. Reproduced by permission.—Texas blind cave salamander, photograph by Charles E. Mohr. Photo Researchers, Inc. Reproduced by permission.—Texas Wildrice, photograph by Paul M. Montgomery. All Rights Reserved. Reproduced by permission.—Tooth cave spider, photograph. U. S. Fish and Wildlife Service. Reproduced by permission.—Vancouver Island Marmot, photograph by Fletcher and Baylis. © Fletcher & Baylis/Photo Researchers, Inc. Reproduced by permission.—Venus flytrap, photograph by J.H. Robinson. Photo Researchers, Inc. Reproduced by permission.—Vicunas, mother and baby, photograph. Photo Researchers, Inc. Reproduced by permission.—Volcano Rabbit, photograph. Planet Earth Pictures Limited. Reproduced by permission.—West Indian Mahogany Tree (Swietenia mahogany), photograph by Patti Murray. Animals Animals/Earth Scenes. Reproduced by pemission.—Western big-eared bat (Plecotus townsendii) hibernating in a West Virginia cave, photograph. © J. L. Lepore. Reproduced by permission.—White-breasted thrasher, photograph by Doug Wechsler. Vireo. Reproduced by permission.—Whooping crane, photograph by Tim Davis. Photo Researchers, Inc. Reproduced by permission.—Wild buffalo (Bubalus bubalus), photograph by Khalid Ghani. Animals Animals/Earth Scenes. Reproduced by permission.—Wild yak, photograph by Tom McHugh. Photo Researchers, Inc. Reproduced by permission.—Wombats (Lasiohinus krefftii), photograph. © John Cancalosi/Peter Arnold, Inc. Reproduced by permission.—Wooly spider monkeys, photograph by Andrew L. Young. Photo Researchers, Inc. Reproduced by permission.—Wyoming black-footed ferret in den, photograph by Alan D. Carey. Photo Researchers, Inc. Reproduced by permission.—Wyoming toad, photograph by E. Maruska. Cincinnati Zoo. Reproduced by permission.—Yellow-eyed penguin, photograph by George Holton. Photo Researchers, Inc. Reproduced by permission.—Yellow-shouldered blackbird, photograph by Bruce A. Sorrie. U.S. Fish and Wildlife Service. Reproduced by permission.

Index

Italic *type indicates volume numbers;* **boldface** *type indicates main entries and their page numbers; (ill.) indicates illustrations.*